Collected Works of Sebastian Kappen
Volume IV

Liberation Theology and Marxism
and Related Essays

Collected Works of Sebastian Kappen
Volume IV

Liberation Theology and Marxism and Related Essays

Compiled and Edited by

Sebastian Vattamattam

2021

Collected Works of Sebastian Kappen, Volume IV: Liberation Theology and Marxism and Related Essays, Ed. Sebastian Vattamattam — Published by the Indian Society for Promoting Christian Knowledge (ISPCK), Post Box 1585, Kashmere Gate, Delhi-110006.

Online order: http://ispck.org.in/book.php

Also available on amazon.in

ISBN: 978-93-90569-09-0

Cover image: C F John

Laser typeset by

ISPCK, Post Box 1585, 1654, Madarsa Road, Kashmere Gate, Delhi-110006 • *Tel:* 23866323

e-mail: ashish@ispck.org.in • ella@ispck.org.in
website: www.ispck.org.in

Sebastian Kappen (1924 - 1993)

Sebastian Kappen, an Indian Jesuit theologian, doctored in 1961 from the Gregorian University, Rome, with a thesis on "Praxis and Religious Alienation according to the Economic and Philosophical Manuscripts of Karl Marx." His subsequent studies had been geared to the requirements of transformative social action in India. This led him to an investigation into the liberative and humanizing potential of the original teachings of the historical Jesus as well as of Indian religious traditions, particularly the tradition of dissent represented by the Buddha and the medieval *Bhakti* Movement. He wrote and lectured extensively on the cultural restructuring of Indian society.

In 1977 appeared Kappen's major work in English, *Jesus and Freedom*. It was followed by *Marxian Atheism* (1983), *Jesus and Cultural Revolution - an Asian Perspective* (1983), *Liberation Theology and Marxism* (1986), and *The Future of Socialism and Socialism of the Future* (1992). His posthumous publications are *Tradition Modernity Counterculture* (1994), *Hindutva and Indian Religious Traditions* (2000), *Divine Challenge and Human Response* (2001), *Jesus and Society* (2002), *Jesus and Culture* (2002), *Towards a Holistic Cultural Paradigm* (2003), *Marx Beyond Marxism* (2012), *Ingathering* (2013), *What the Thunder Says* (2013). His books in Malayalam are *From Faith to Revolution* (1972), *A Sexual Morality for Tomorrow* (1973), *Ecology and Culture* (1988), *An Introduction to the Philosophy of Marx* (1989), *Prophecy and Counterculture* (1992), *In Search of the Non-Christian Jesus* (1999), *Liberation of Jesus from the Churches* (2012), and *Death of God and the Birth of the Human - tr. of Marxian Atheism* (2015)

Sebastian Kappen had been visiting professor to the Pontifical Seminary (Pune), Vidyajyoti (Delhi), The Catholic University of Louvain (Belgium) and Maryknoll Seminary (New York). Mother Earth called him back on 30 November 1993.

Contents

Introduction

The first part of this Volume 4 is Fr. Kappen's book, *Liberation Theology and Marxism*. In this book, Kappen calls the theology he proposes 'a Theology of Integral Freedom.' He makes a radical critique of the traditions in which the Christians and the Marxists in India are stagnating and challenges them to return to their sources and recapture their creative power for the reconstruction of Indian society and culture. The first chapter in this part is the revised version of an article that appeared in The Illustrated Weekly of India in 1985. In 1986, the Vatican released two documents attacking Liberation Theologians for their 'flirtation with Marxism.' The fourth chapter, "Church, Liberation Theology and Marxism" is a sharp repudiation of the Vatican dictates. The last chapter is part of an interview published in Sunday Herald, Bangalore, in 1983.

In the second part, Chapter 11 is a paper presented at a seminar organized to felicitate the great Theologian Dr. M. M. Thomas on the occasion of his sixtieth birth anniversary in 1976. Chapter 18 is an essay contained in the book *Bread and Breath*, published in honour of another great theologian and Fr. Kappen's close associate, Dr. Samuel Rayan S. J., on the occasion of his Seventieth Birth Anniversary. Chapter 19 is a paper presented at the ninth annual seminar of the Indian Theological Association at Poonamallee, Madras, in 1985. The remaining chapters are taken from the series Anawim, the journal Jeevadhara, and Fr. Kappen's books *Jesus and Society, Jesus and Culture,* and *Ingathering*.

Let me express my gratitude to Mercy Kappen, and artist C F John, both closely related to Fr. Kappen, for their consistent support and encouragement in completing this volume. The cover image of this book is John's artistic creation.

Sebastian Vattamattam

PART - I

LIBERATION THEOLOGY AND MARXISM

Preface

Of late, there has been much interest shown on the part of Christians and non-Christians alike in what has come to be known as Liberation Theology, as may be seen from articles appearing in the secular press. But all too often, in discussions on the topic, it is taken for granted that the Latin Americans have set the pattern of theological reflection for the rest of the world, particularly for the so-called developing countries. This assumption needs to be called in question. Confronted as he is with the challenges arising from religious and cultural pluralism, the Asian theologian who is committed to radical social transformation has no other option but to strike out a new path in his discourse about the Divine. The present volume represents a tentative attempt in that direction.

It consists of papers originally written for publication in Reviews or presentations at conferences in India and abroad. In any such collection, a certain amount of overlapping is unavoidable. I have tried to reduce it to the minimum by abridging or even deleting passages. If nevertheless, some themes recur, they are each time handled from a different perspective so that the various contributions go to complete one another.

Chapter one gives an overall view of the main concerns of Liberation Theology. The two chapters that follow discuss the method of theological reflection relevant to the Asian context. Since, however, the method can never be dissociated from content; the reader will find in them the essential message of Liberation Theology as well. The liberation of humans involves at the same time the liberation of the Divine from the prison-house of dogma, and of the Church from its inbred, ingrown sectarianism. This forms the burden of chapters four and five. Chapter six is a critical appraisal of the two recent Vatican documents on the new Theology, with special reference to the attack on Liberation Theologians' alleged flirtation with Marxism. It thus links up with the ensuing chapters which focus on the points of convergence and divergence between Marxism and Christianity and on the possibility and the need for dialogue and collaboration between the two.

The new conception of the Divine, underlying these essays, calls for a break with the theological language we are used to. Terms like God, sin, grace, salvation, and heaven are loaded with connotations long since become obsolete. Similarly, the on-going collapse of patriarchy and the emergence of Women's Liberation Movements require that we eschew the customary sexist language. Convinced though I am of the need for a linguistic revolution, for practical reasons, I have, on the whole, conformed to the traditional mode of discourse.

Though I have not been able to slough off my academic style, I have always written for the benefit of socially committed persons and groups. It is, therefore, a matter of great satisfaction to me that Ajit Muricken of Asha Kendra, a centre involved in educating and organizing the poor in Maharashtra, undertook to publish the book. My sincere thanks to Enas S. J., who prepared the cover design, and to Philip Mathew for proofreading.

S. Kappen,

TC 9/277, Jawaharnagar,

Trivandrum

1

Why Liberation Theology?

Time was when all thinking in the Catholic Church was monolithic. The Pope spoke, and the rest, from bishops to laypersons, said Amen. The result was a perfect union of minds and wills. As for theological reflection, it followed the line of incestuous circularity, confined as it was within the four walls of seminaries. Then came the Second Vatican Council, which opened the Church's doors to the wider world of other religions and ideologies. With that, the monolith crumbled. Different voices began to be heard among Christians about God, man, and the universe. Gradually, pluralism in theology came to be accepted. And now, with the emergence of Liberation Theology, pluralism has given way to polarization. So much so that the official Church now sees in the new theology a threat to its very survival, as may be seen from the "Instruction" issued by the Sacred Congregation for the Doctrine of the Faith on "Certain Aspects of Liberation Theology."

Indian Christianity did not remain impervious to the new development. In the Seventies, many Christians took to educating and organizing the tribals and the poorer classes, rural and urban. In this, they drew inspiration from the Bible, the teachings of the Second Vatican Council, and the so-called Social Encyclicals which recognize the struggle for justice as a valid expression of faith. But, once in the field of action, they experienced the contradiction between their new commitment and the kind of theology they had inherited. At a meeting of activists held in Bangalore in the mid-Seventies, many voiced the need for a more relevant interpretation of the message of Jesus. Thus was launched the publication a series of tracts called Anawim for circulation among socially committed Christians all over India. In 1977 appeared *Jesus and Freedom* by the present writer, which provoked the ire of the concerned Vatican Secretariat, which tried in vain to have it revised in line with orthodoxy. In the new theological venture, significant contributions came from scholars like Samuel Rayan and George Soares Prabhu in the form of articles in periodicals and papers presented at seminars. All this generated a wave of rethinking in the Catholic Church. Similar developments also took place in the other Christian churches. A pioneer in this field was Dr. M. M. Thomas who, though himself, not a Liberation Theologian, had already paved the way for a more relevant theology in his many writings on the Christian presence in secular India.

The upsurge of radicalism found concrete expression in groups of like-minded priests, nuns, and laypersons, particularly in Kerala. Such groups have since become rallying points for a Christian praxis markedly divergent from the traditional one. That they are a force to reckon with is clear from the fact that they are being made the object of repressive action on the part of the official churches. The faithful are warned from pulpits against the pernicious contagion of Liberation Theology; troublesome priests and nuns are summarily transferred to remote areas or otherwise silenced; pressure is being brought by Bishops on Superiors of Religious Congregations to have the radicals held in check or removed from their dioceses. Editors of periodicals sympathetic to the new thinking are replaced by those who toe the official line.

What is all this row about? — is the query one hears from uninformed Christians and non-Christians alike. Is Christianity disintegrating? is Communism infiltrating it in order the better to explode it from within? Or, is it that the CIA in Marxist-Christian clothing is at its game of preempting Soviet expansion in the Third World? Or again, could it be that conversionism is raising its head again, this time under the guise of liberating the oppressed?

To those who entertain such suspicions and fears, the plain truth might come as an anticlimax: what Liberation Theologians are saying and doing today is just what that unknown prophet from Nazareth said and did two thousand years ago. I said 'unknown', for today he lies buried beneath accumulated layers of interpretations, laws, procedures, credit bills, bank accounts, and the paraphernalia of a State apparatus.

The Prophet and His Dream

The focal point of Jesus' life was the hope that God would soon come and usher in a new age of human fullness; when the poor will take possession of the earth; when their hunger and thirst for justice will be satisfied; when humans everywhere will become brothers and sisters to one another; when prisons will be pulled down to let the inmates free, and the sorrowing will have every tear wiped away from their eyes. But, for that hope to become reality, men and women had to cooperate, reorienting their lives in tune with the future envisioned. Hence Jesus' journeyings up and down Palestine calling upon his hearers to repent and believe in the 'good news' that the absolute future of mankind was irrupting in the *here-and-now* of their own history.

Utopias threaten none so long as they do not become the deed. With the Galilean prophet, word did become deed. Committed to the project of a future of wholeness and freedom, he had to take a stand in regard to the realities of the present. Hence his option for "those who labour and are burdened", meaning the working class. Hence, too, his denunciation of the rich who sought to serve God and Money at the same time; of the Roman rulers who lorded it over their subjects and made them feel the weight of their authority; of the high priests who turned God's temple into a market place and a den of thieves; and of the lawyers and the Pharisees who made up heavy packs and piled them on men's shoulders and went about converting fellow humans but only to make them twice as fit for hell as were themselves, who paid tithes of mint and dill and cummin while overlooking the weightier demands of justice, mercy, and good faith.

By not mincing words, Jesus knew he was inviting trouble. His relatives thought him mad; his enemies dubbed him a glutton and a drunkard and a friend of social outcasts and accused him of driving out demons with the help of the prince of demons. On occasion, such psychic violence turned physical. The people of his hometown took him to the top of a hill, meaning to hurl him over the precipice. Herod and the Jewish authorities sought to get him out of their way. In the end, he was captured, taken outside the city and done to death.

Prophecy Betrayed

What Liberation Theologians from Latin America to India are doing is nothing but recapturing the liberating message of the murdered prophet. Why then does the official Church view it with hostility? Because it has come a long way from its own prophetic moorings.

The process started early enough, whose beginnings can be discerned in the New Testament itself. For instance, on many issues, Matthew would tone down the radicalism of Jesus. The original words of Jesus, "Blessed are the poor" (Lk 6:20), are reinterpreted by the author of the first Gospel to read, "Blessed are the poor in spirit" (Mt 5:3). Whereas Jesus told the rich young man, "go, sell what you have, and give to the poor" (Mk 10:21), Matthew would make the demand conditional: "If you would be perfect, go, sell..." (Mt 19:21) Similarly, he renders innocuous Jesus' stringent criticism of the Law by putting into his mouth the saying, "Whoever then relaxes one of the least of these commandments and teaches men so, shall be called least in the kingdom of heaven" (Mt 5:19). Paul would do the same in his epistle to the Romans. In contrast to Jesus who condemned all rulers who lorded it over their subjects and made them feel the weight of their authority (Mk 10:42-44), he exhorts the Christian community to be subject to the governing authorities as there is no authority except from God (Rm13:1). What is more, as though to compensate for the non-realization of the hoped-for kingdom of God, Jesus himself would be identified with God and the Church with the Kingdom. Jesus, thus transformed, would become the object of cult, paving the way for the subsequent development of Christianity into a cult-centred religion.

The self-estrangement of the prophetic movement started by Jesus must be seen against the background of its expansion from the Palestinian to the Hellenistic world. Accommodation to Graeco-Roman culture made the new religion attractive to intellectuals and the upper classes, who eventually dominated what was originally a movement of the disprivileged and the marginalized. The decisive rupture with its prophetic past occurred when, in the fourth century, Christianity was adopted as State religion by Emperor Constantine, thus opening an era of the unholy alliance between the Cross and the imperial sword.

However, from the beginning, there were dissenting men and women, such as Montanus in the second century who denounced the growing institutionalization of the Church; Jerome who bemoaned the confusion of Church and State as a fall from the purity of the Gospel; the sects of the Waldenses, the Anabaptists, and the Hussites who called upon their contemporaries to return to the days of early Christian communism when the property was held in common, and distribution made to each according to his need; Thomas Muenzer who took up the cause of the oppressed peasants, while the Catholic Church sided with the landed aristocracy and Luther with the emerging bourgeoisie. Mention must also be made of the monastic movement which arose as a protest against the wealth and the worldliness of the Church. This shows that hidden beneath the imposing superstructure of rituals and institutions, there has always been the explosive power of the Gospel ready to burst into flame under favourable conditions. And Liberation Theology is just that — the prophetic message of Jesus come alive.

But why today?

The Role of Marxism

In the contemporary world, no liberative faith can become relevant practice unless it is conjoined to an adequate social theory, that is, a theory that seeks not only to interpret but also to change the world. In earlier societies based on personal or group dependence, the structures of domination were transparent. Not so under capitalism whose internal dynamics are hidden from common observation. It is here the tools of social analysis provided by Marx can be of immense help. But Marxism is not only a sociology and a theory of revolution but also a global vision of history and a philosophy of hope. There is some truth in the words of Sartre,

> "Marxism, as the formal framework of all contemporary philosophical thought, cannot be superseded."

But this in no way dispenses Marxists from leaving behind the reductionist tendencies in Marx and the imprint his thought received from 19th century capitalism.

Be that as it may, Liberation Theology could not have arisen had it not been for the fruitful confrontation between the Gospel and the philosophy of Marx. This has been recognized by no less a person than Gustavo Gutierrez, the father of Latin American Liberation Theology. In India, too, all those who are making any meaningful contribution to a more relevant theology are persons who have in one way or another been influenced by Marxism while the majority stagnates in the backwaters of tradition-bound thinking. This is because Marxism can help the theologian criticize his own premises and distinguish between the historically conditioned and the perennially valid in his religious tradition.

Here allow me to recall by way of illustration my own experience. Way back in 1959, when I decided to write my doctoral thesis on the Early Writings of Marx, it was with the specific intention of equipping myself to fight, on my return to India, the then Communist regime in Kerala. Little did I realize then that the venture would involve me in nothing less than a mental revolution. Grappling with the original texts of Marx brought me down from the rarefied world of Aristotelian concepts to the stark realities of the world we live in. It taught me to think from below, from the heart of the fragmented, demented world around. In the process, the realization dawned on me that not a few of the beliefs and practices prevalent in the Church are but products of history and have no basis in the teachings of Jesus. Marx thus enabled me to encounter the historical Jesus. Paradoxical as it might seem, it was also Marx who opened my eyes to the limitations of his own theory and to the need to correct and enrich it with insights from other schools of thinking.

The Latin American Response

For a Theology of Liberation to emerge, it is not enough that the Gospel encounters Marxism. It must also answer the felt needs of a people. And the need for a rethinking of Christian faith and practice was most intensely felt in Latin America. Here is a country rich in natural resources, made the richer with the blood of the natives massacred by the conquerors from Spain and Portugal. These divided the land between themselves on the principle of might-is-right. Today Latin America's wealth is in the hands of an oligarchy composed of big landlords, the army, and the bureaucracy. In the Sixties, the ruling classes invited American Transnational Companies to come in and invest in key sectors of the economy. The national economy was restructured to suit the international division of labour and subserve the imperialist interests of the U.S.A. The system of dependent capitalism that came into being excluded the masses from all social wealth, condemning millions to unemployment and starvation. In most countries, the oligarchy, abetted by the CIA and the Transnational Companies, set up repressive regimes based on the perverse ideology of 'national security'. The common people were denied all political rights; political Parties and trade-unions were suppressed; and 'death commandos' let loose on the Opposition. Religion itself was sought to be brought under the control of the State to serve as a weapon against international Communism. The irony of it all is that in Latin America both the oppressors and the oppressed, the elites and the masses, belong to the Christian fold.

It was to meet this impossible situation of organized inhumanity that the poorer Christians formed themselves into 'Base Communities' and initiated a process of collective reflection on the biblical message, this time from the point of view of their own situation of misery. This led them to a rediscovery of the living God of history who called them to dignity and freedom; who called the Hebrews to shake off the yoke of slavery in Egypt and set out on the long march to the Promised Land. From the 'Base Communities' and their pastors, poised for a new exodus, there arose new Moseses, prophets, and Theologians of Liberation. The new theology effected "an epistemological rupture" with the old. Whereas the latter started from reflection on the dogmas and by way of their application came down to the realities of practical life, the former took off from below, that is, from the practice of liberation, and in its light proceeded to grasp the meaning of the Bible. This methodological reversal has had far-reaching consequences. The new wine burst the old wineskins of dogma and tradition, causing jitters in Christian circles used to a God broken in and made to serve their interests. The Theology of Liberation pointed an accusing finger at those Church leaders who maintained close links with international capitalism and oppressive regimes. All this has had repercussions extending beyond Latin America to Asia and Africa and even to the countries of the First World.

Prospects for an Indian Theology of Liberation

As far as India is concerned, Liberation Theology is likely to be in a low key in the years ahead, and this due to the specific conditions obtaining here. The Parties of Revolution have been tamed and absorbed into the bourgeois politics of power and expediency to a point where they scarcely differ from the Parties of Order. Gandhism is today a spent force being no more than a convenient ritual. The prospects of fresh revolutionary energies springing up from the subterranean consciousness of the masses are not bright either. The power of the Establishment to neutralize dissent knows no bounds. With such great success does it employ the technology of misinformation that the structures of oppression assume legitimacy in the eyes of the oppressed themselves. Worse, the fissiparous tendencies inherent in caste and religion hinder the formation of a collective agent of transformative action. This means there is little in the contemporary situation from which the Theologian of Liberation can draw inspiration. He can only fall back on the resources of his own faith and on the conviction that the basic problems facing our people cannot be solved without a radical restructuring of the social system.

Seen from another angle, the Indian context is particularly suited to the birth of a Liberation Theology that will be more radical in its sweep and more universal in its validity than similar theologies elsewhere. For, unlike his counterparts in Latin America, the theologian here has to carry on his search for a more relevant theology in the context of a religiously pluralist society where Christians form but a minority. These can effectively act on society only in so far as they join hands with like-minded Hindus, Muslims, and Marxists, forming wider communities. This, in fact, is what is happening wherever Christians have come forward to organize the poor. If so, the matrix and the testing ground of an Indian Theology of Liberation cannot be the praxis of closed Christian communities but that of open, pluralistic communities.

As faith becomes radicalized and bodies forth in action, it would increasingly pose a threat to the current social praxis of the churches. Admittedly, these have come a long way from the days when their social involvement was confined to charitable works and education. They have since awakened to the need for structural changes in society and the legitimacy of Christian participation in people's struggles. But theory is one thing, practice another. It has been the experience of Christian activists for the last two decades that action for justice inevitably brings them into conflict with the official churches. This is understandable, for, in the end, all radical action goes counter to the socio-economic interests of the churches themselves. Over the years, Indian Christianity has built up an imposing network of institutions and projects (under

Catholic auspices alone over 10,000 institutions in 1977 and 6,700 projects between 1968 and 1973) requiring colossal financial investments. These secular enterprises involve the Churches in a three-fold dependence: on foreign donors, on the State, which alone can guarantee the inflow of foreign money and provide the needed legal infrastructure, and on the institutions of capitalism which the same enterprises patronize as buyers, sellers or investors. In addition, they create relations of dependence in the local community: dependence of the laity on the clergy, of non-Christians on Christians. This is not to belittle the great contribution Christianity has made in the field of education and social service, much less to doubt the sincerity and dedication of the personnel involved. What causes concern is the fact that the structural links the churches have with the powers that are generate an operative theory of general conformism, which is often at variance with official teaching itself. It is the hold this operative theory has on Church leaders that, more, than anything else, explains their hostile reaction to Liberation Theology.

Will the nascent Theology of Liberation gather ever greater momentum and fulfill the promises it holds? The answer would depend, above all, on the intellectual integrity and prophetic courage of the theologian himself. He must vindicate his fundamental right to err and to ask unasked questions and tread unbeaten paths. He must at the same time be on his guard against the jet-age temptation of going in search of the one lost white sheep abroad while leaving the ninety-nine brown ones at home to shift for themselves. Nor may he delude himself into thinking that he can fashion a Theology of Liberation from within the insured existence of academic institutions. He must rather pitch his tent in the midst of ordinary people and share their joys and sorrows and struggles. What is true of the theologian applies to theology as well. It cannot hang in the air nor be a foreign body on the Indian soil. It must insert itself in our cultural tradition, particularly in the tradition of dissent from the days of the Buddha to our own times.

(Revised version of an article that appeared in The Illustrated Weekly of India, Bombay, June 9-15, 1985.)

2

Orientations for a Theology of Integral Freedom

The aim of this paper is neither to summarize nor evaluate Asian Christian theology, past or present, but to suggest, tentatively, the direction theologizing should take in the future. Any such venture already presupposes a conception of theology. In the present case, the conception presupposed is itself the result of a protracted process of grappling with the problem of God and humans in the Asian context, especially in the context of religious pluralism, Marxism, and the prevailing socio-political situation. Therefore, an elucidation of what I mean by theology will itself provide the framework for deriving guidelines for the future. It will also provide the frame of reference for a critique of past and present theologies. Admittedly, my views are largely shaped by the Indian experience. Whether and how far they apply to other Asian countries is up to theologians from those countries to decide.

The fundamental notion that constitutes both the point of departure and the point of arrival of this paper is that theology is a critical reflection on our primordial encounter with God. Let me explain what this means.

God-Encounter: The Matrix of Theology

It is on purpose that I have used the word encounter in preference to experience. Experience is liable to be understood in a purely subjective sense, as though God were a mere projection of the human mind. Encounter, on the other hand, involves a coming face to face with an 'other', in this case, with the ultimate 'Other', the ground and goal of human beings and history. This 'Other' is neither personal nor impersonal but transpersonal. In any genuine God-encounter, the absolute Other is experienced as the inmost within of the subject who encounters, be it individual or community. Encounter, in this sense, is not a function of any of the human faculties such as sensation, intelligence, or will. It takes place at the inmost being of the person; where feeling, knowing, willing, and loving have their common root. It is there that we are invaded and inhabited by the Absolute, where the transcendent becomes immanent, where the in-breaking of the Divine becomes an in-dwelling and an in-spiriting as well. To meet God in this manner is to be taken hold of by him, to be uprooted and swept off one's feet in such a manner that one is no more one's own master; it is, at the same time, to experience the relativization of everything else, whether it be job, security, fame, wealth, or even life itself. Such relativization is, in fact, the only guarantee that one has encountered the Absolute.

But where does our primordial encounter with God take place? It cannot be on the level of religious symbols, whether word-symbols (myths, legends, creeds, scriptures), act-symbols (cult, prayer, religious dance, ceremonies), thing-symbols (temples, altar, consecrated food, sacred utensils, sacred places), or person-symbols (priests, religious teachers, consecrated virgins). These are, at best, forms in which an original God-encounter expresses itself and, as such, are derivative in character. No form is adequate to the content; no symbol is capable of expressing the richness of the original experience, which is ineffable and unfathomable. Furthermore, forms and symbols which emerge subsequently can even distort what they are meant to convey and thus become alienated and alienating, especially when they become institutionalized. Finally, even the original God-encounter, which these symbols are meant to represent and to communicate, is itself historically conditioned and need not necessarily be relevant to the contemporary person.

It follows, then, that the primary locus of God-encounter is to be sought not within but outside and beyond religion in its institutionalized forms. This does not mean that symbols traditionally handed down are necessarily incapable of mediating religious experience. Whether they effect such mediation or not will have to be judged in each case on its merits. What I want to stress is that the primary focus of theological reflection should be our meeting with God in the contemporary historical situation, in the realities of practical life, individual and social, whose texture is made up of all that we do and of all that happens to us — dating and mating, sowing and reaping, producing and consuming, buying and selling, planning and organizing. This is the world of praxis, meaning the historical process whereby we transform ourselves in transforming our environment of things, persons, and structures (economic, social, political, and cultural). Praxis comprises not merely action but also passion: passion as openness to the mystery of life, and passion as striving for values, ideals, and goals. It is the world of praxis that mediates the presence and the in-breaking of the Divine. For us, Asian theologians, this means that it is in the action and passion of our people, in their condition of bondage to systems of exploitation and domination, in their struggles to fashion a more just and humane society that we have to meet the living God.

How does this God confront us today? He comes to us, to every one of goodwill, in the form of an unconditional challenge to shake off our shackles and fashion a new home for the human family, a new society in which the free development of everyone will be assured. In truth, this is a primordial way in which the Divine appears to human, beings. For what is God but the absolute negation of all evil and the absolute affirmation of all that is good, true, and beautiful? Not in the sense that we form a notion of God by negating all limitations and imperfections, but in the sense that God is himself the act of negating, just as light is the act of dispelling darkness. To encounter God, therefore, is to become both a wielder of the sword and a herald of peace. Through the one who has encountered God, the divine NO to misery, injustice, and exploitation and the divine YES to whatever furthers the fullness of human beings reverberate in history and radiate to the ends of the earth. In other words, our response itself mediates the presence of God in the world. To have responded to God in this manner is the essential precondition for any valid theological reflection. But theologians should by no means confine themselves to their own personal God-encounter. They should bring within their purview also the God-encounter of others around them, to whichever caste, religion, or community they may belong. If God is the Absolute NO to evil, it is obvious that theologians will find God not so much in the Establishment — religious or secular — as in those social forces and trends which strive to break the fetters which it imposes on people. For, the Establishment generally tends to imprison the human spirit in predetermined moulds and prevents people from responding to the ever-new invitations of God.

Theological reflection is genuine only when it forms a moment in the total human response to the challenge of God embedded in history. It is but one phase of a movement that originates from and returns to, the world of praxis. But in any living process, any one moment includes all the others. So, too, theologizing should encompass not only the God encountered but also the one who encounters God and the encounter itself; it should direct itself both to the divine challenge and the human response. Keeping this in mind, let us elucidate further the concrete task of theological reflection.

Let me state first what theology is not. It is not an attempt to flee from the concrete world of praxis to the world of sterile abstractions. It is rather a process of greater and greater immersion in reality, in the reality of God's challenge enfleshed in history. An analogy might prove useful here. Looking down from an airplane as it flies at a high altitude, one sees the landscape below but without being able to discern the various objects. But as the plane glides to a landing, objects begin to appear more and more distinctly, revealing their proper contours and colours. So it is with theological reflection. Reflection leads one to perceive clearly what was already perceived confusedly in the primordial God-encounter. Hence it is more like contemplation than discursive reasoning. And yet, it is not mere contemplation; it is also a process of becoming what one contemplates and thereby attaining to a richer and fuller mode of being. For the same reason, it can in no way be termed an 'inscape' into the inwardness of one's self where one is alone with oneself. Such a self in isolation is but a fiction of the mind. For, our deepest being is a *being-with*: with things, with other people, and with the Absolute Other. Centered upon ourselves, we are also centered upon our kind and God. In our inmost being, we are openness to the mystery of existence, a hearer of words, a hearer of the Word. Theological reflection must, therefore, take place in a spirit of communion with all that is and of compassion for all who belong to the human family.

The Structure of Theological Reflection

The main thrust of reflection must be directed to rendering explicit (= thematizing) the dimensions of meaning implicitly contained in the original God-encounter. The dimensions of meaning to be thematized are many. Here I can do no more than indicate a few important ones.

To begin with, there is the existential dimension. The experience of being taken hold of by the Absolute is what throws light on the deeper problems of existence such as our *being-unto-death*, the ambivalence of freedom, the bondage to sin, and guilt, and, finally, the loss of hope. For the Divine that invades us is also power — a power that enables us to conquer the forces of death and decay, to cast off all that smothers freedom and to overcome the inner breach between what we are and what we ought to be. However, since the texture of our personal existence is conditioned by the objective structures of society, the manner in which the existential meaning of our God-encounter is perceived and responded to will show many variations depending on the prevailing social system. That is why the answers which traditional religions like Buddhism and Hinduism give to existential problems, however profound and valid they may be in themselves, cannot be taken as the last word on the matter. They need to be radically rethought and reformulated in the context of contemporary social situation. This applies equally to the other dimensions of meaning to be discussed below.

A second dimension that needs to be thematized is the social. The divine challenge, the human response, and the new reality that response always creates, all these have a social significance. The divine challenge is mediated through a social situation, say, of exploitation or domination. Take, for instance, the oppression of landless labourers in a particular place. All who are sensitive to human values will see in it an unconditional, divine challenge to organize the affected labourers against the forces of oppression. The collective resistance that results is equally revelative of God, in so far as it makes the divine NO to evil operate in the here-and-now of history. Finally, if as a result of organized struggle there is greater equality and justice in that area, that, too, has a theological meaning. For, the splendour of God is reflected on human faces; the Divine reveals itself as the depth-dimension of the love that binds the many into one.

Our encounter with God has also a cosmic dimension. For our *being-with-others* is always mediated by things, whether given or produced by labour. Conversely, our relation to things is mediated by our fellow human beings. Hence the material world is something like the extension in time and space of our social existence. But in all societies dominated by the institution of private property - and Asian societies are no exception to this - nature and the products of labour act as principles of division and instruments of exploitation and domination. From being expressions of creativity, products tend to smother every authentic manifestation of the human. If so, for Asians, the divine challenge assumes the form of a call to socialize property so that both nature and the products of labour become vehicles of human togetherness. Furthermore, in order that the world may radiate and manifest the glory of human beings and God, it is equally necessary that the production of the useful is at the same time the creation of the beautiful. For the beautiful is that point of convergence where human transcendence unto (reaching out to) the Divine and God's immanence (indwelling) in the world meet and fuse into one single incandescence. That is why the theology of the future will have also to be an aesthetics.

Only then shall we recapture something of that reverence which the ancient seers of Asia felt for the earth and its fruits, for labour and its products. Only then shall nature cease to be something to be violated and ravished by the lust for profit and power. This means that the goal of Asian development will have to be qualitatively different from the Western brand of gadget civilization.

Finally, the theologian must also focus on the historical dimension of God-encounter. History is not merely the stage on which the drama of our meeting with our Maker is enacted. It is essentially constituted by the divine challenge and the human response. What is history but the transcendence of God becomes the self-transcendence of human beings through project and praxis? It is the unconditional call of the Divine which enables us to break loose from the ever-rotating wheel of cyclic time and march forward to the horizon of human-divine fullness, despite reverses and regressions. The goal of history, the realization of *theandric* (= divine-human) fullness, too, transcends all concrete historical achievements. That is why it can be expressed more adequately through myth and symbols than through concepts. As examples, one may cite the myth of the kingdom of God in Christianity and that of the classless society in Marxism. The Divine reveals itself not only in the challenge to create history and in the goal of historical development but also in the *unto-deathness* of praxis that aims at translating the ultimate project into reality. History is made only by those who are prepared to risk death so that others may have life, life in full measure, and overflowing.

The dimensions of meaning inherent in our primordial God-encounter, are essentially intertwined, one implying and flowing into the other. This underlying unity is only implicit in the original experience and must in its turn be thematized. It is the failure to do so that explains the fragmentation of Western theology into the dogmatic, the mystical, the spiritual, and so on. The Asian mind with its native genius for the unity of all is better equipped to avoid this pitfall.

The structured unity of meanings we arrive at should not be set up as an eternal and immutable dogma valid for all times. All dogmas point to the pathetic attempt of man to reify the living God by housing Him in fixed conceptual moulds. Their emergence is understandable in the ages gone by when people lived in a relatively stable universe in which the consciousness of historical time was all but rudimentary due to the low development of productive forces. But today God is encountered not so much as one who is but as one who comes. And his *coming* coincides with human *becoming*, which is history. That is why every knowledge of God must be subjected to critical revision in the light of subsequent historical experience.

Theologizing as Prophesy

If theological reflection is but a moment in the total human response to the divine challenge as revealed in history, it is obvious that it cannot stop at the stage of thematization. Theologians cannot remain neutral before the call of God as though they were mere onlookers. They are personally involved in what they are contemplating; they stand challenged by the same call from the Beyond which they are trying to fathom. To refuse to respond to it is to deny the living God. One cannot deny God and at the same time claim to theologize. On the other hand, to respond to God is to proclaim the challenge one has accepted of working for total human freedom. And what is this but to prophesy? Hence every theologian is also a prophet, one who challenges others to march forward to their ultimate destiny.

But the prophet is impelled not only to proclaim the new age of freedom but also to make it present in the world, here and now. Thus, through prophecy, theology becomes world-transforming praxis; knowledge becomes a power that renews the face of the earth. But theology can become power only if it is appropriated by the oppressed masses in whose interest it is to change the world. The Asian theology of the future - or any genuine theology for that matter - will, therefore, have to be one that expresses the mute longings of the downtrodden and the unwanted of the earth. So, too, the theologians of tomorrow will have to be people who have made a historic option in favour of the disprivileged and the disinherited. Only then will theology slough off its esoteric character, its elitist jargon, and its exclusivist, sectarian features. Herein is to be sought also the criterion for the validity of theology. Only that theological reflection is true which grips the masses and thereby becomes a power that changes the world. All theologies of impotence, therefore, stand self-condemned and must be discarded once and for all. Under this category fall all traditional theologies, whether Christian, Hindu, or Muslim. Where, on the contrary, theology becomes power, the resulting praxis will prepare the ground for ever more profound encounters with God. For, to eradicate injustice and oppression is to clear an open space where the Divine can appear before human beings; it is to prepare the way of the Lord.

The Critical Function of Theology

We encounter God not in a vacuum but as men and women inserted in specific social relations and structures of power, and as bearers of a particular culture. We go to meet the living God with minds and hearts shaped by ideas, values, beliefs, attitudes, assumptions, myths, and symbols handed down to us from past generations. All these factors determine the way we are attuned to the total mystery of human existence and therefore, also to God. The specific attuning we have received, the conditioning we have inherited may be good or bad. Good, if it renders us perceptive to the various dimensions of meaning in our God-encounter; bad if it obscures or falsifies them. Criticism aims to identify the latter so that by eliminating them we may dispose ourselves the better for an adequate grasp of what the living God demands of us today. In this sense, criticism is preparation for theological reflection. Seen from another angle, it is also a constituent element of theological reflection. For, we seldom, if ever, meet the naked God. God appears before us clad in the garb we ourselves have put on Him. It is the role of criticism to remove the veils hiding his face, just as it should help remove the blinkers from our own eyes.

Here I shall dwell on three important biases which may blur, distort, or frustrate our encounter with God and our attempts at theologizing. They have to do, respectively, with money, power, and what I would call the anti-God.

The Renunciation of Money

Money is more than a mere means of hoarding. As the universal equivalent of all commodities, it confers control over production, circulation, and consumption. In the money are expressed all the evils of an economy based on private property, competition, and exploitation. Money presupposes as well as creates the division of society into the propertied and the propertyless, into employers and workers, into consumers and producers. As the reification of all social relations, it expresses the alienation of people from other people as well. More than anything else, it distorts our perception of reality, not excluding the reality of our primordial experience of God.

Where theologians — or any believer for that matter — either belong or owe allegiance to the moneyed classes, they are likely to use God as a means to legitimize their own class interests or as an accomplice in exploiting the poor. In the process, theology is degraded to the level of an ideology, and the Divine to the level of a commodity. Money, the universal equivalent, can from now on be exchanged also for things divine. The rich can buy the favour of God by making donations to religious institutions or by having religious services held for their spiritual benefit. They can even buy theological expertise and use it to serve economic interests. Thus we see the amusing phenomenon of the glitter of gold passing for the brilliance of theological reflection, and of theologians parading as ideologues of Mammon. If money can be exchanged for divine favours, no less can the latter be exchanged for the former. Those who claim the right to mediate the favour (grace) of God can convert it into money.

In consequence, the higher the position one occupies in the religious hierarchy, the greater is his command over money - over production, circulation, and consumption. Similarly, those who have 'accumulated' the knowledge of God can now indulge in the accumulation of capital or at least in hoarding. As a result, money is divinized and the Divine monetized. The believer develops a religious attitude to money and a monetary attitude to God. But all exchange is based on equivalence. If so, God and money must have a common essence which is nothing but abstract human labour. It follows then that the God who is exchanged for money is not the living God but a product of the human brain.

This is not just a possible but a real danger to Asian theology if the situation of the Indian churches can be taken as typical of the whole of Asia. The individual theologian may not be a monied person or indulge in conspicuous consumption, but he theologizes within the framework of churches which own immense property and whose economic interests coincide with those of the privileged classes. Besides, the system of values operative in church institutions and organizations is, more often than not, capitalist, consisting of private interest, competition, individualism, and consumerism. No wonder that the theologies currently taught in seminaries largely tend to legitimate the status quo. They legitimate not only exploitation within the country but also economic imperialism, for the obvious reason that the financial nerve centre of the Asian churches lies in the capitalist countries of the West.

To develop a theology that is faithful to the living God, Asian theologians have, therefore, no other alternative but to dissociate themselves from the practice, if not also from the theory of the churches. They have to make a historic option in favour of the poor and the oppressed; in other words, they have to declass themselves. Like the rich young man of the Gospel, they too, are called upon to sell what they have and give it to the poor.

Renunciation of Power

Power is understood here as the possibility some have to impose their options — ends and means — on others. As such, it is in principle opposed to God. For God is encountered as an unconditional demand to march forward to the reign of total freedom. Those, therefore, who exercise power or are in league with the wielders of power, will either fail to encounter the living God or use God to sanction the existing structures of domination. This need not necessarily be a conscious process involving bad faith. It can coexist with good intentions. A classic instance of this may be found in Paul's advice to Christians:

> "Let every person be subject to the governing authorities. For there is no authority except from God, and those that exist have been instituted by God" (Rm 13:1).

This God too, is of human making and, therefore, can be exchanged for power, which is no less a human product. In consequence, religious authority is vested with secular power and secular power with religious authority. God thus becomes king-ified, and kings deified. In either case, human beings are reduced to slaves.

Here, too, we are not describing a possible deviation that may affect religious practice and thinking. It describes more or less the actual course taken by religions; especially Christianity. It is well-known that in medieval times there were magistrates who enjoyed episcopal powers, and bishops vested with magistrate's powers. Coming to our own times, the Indian churches have been using God to legitimize whatever regime happened to be in power. Very much to the point is the support given by the official churches to the dictatorial rule of Indira Gandhi. True, bishops are no longer in a position to exercise direct political power, except in the case of the bishop of Rome. This, however, is more than compensated for by the possibilities of exercising power within the Christian Establishment itself. The structure of power embodied in church institutions is largely feudal, characterized by personal dependence and patronage. In the case of the Catholic Church, it is also centralized and monarchical. The possibilities of domination are further enhanced by the inflow of foreign money. Such being the case, it is understandable that God is pressed into service to reinforce and consecrate ecclesial power structures. That is why the emergence of a theology of the living God will be possible in Asia only when theologians dare to renounce all power and, like Jesus, identify themselves and the powerless and the downtrodden.

Renouncing the Anti-God

The process we have described whereby people use God to legitimize their own interests already explains the birth of the Anti-God. But there are other factors, too, which more directly contribute to his emergence, of which the chief are cult, dogma, and law.

A cult may be authentic or inauthentic. A cult is authentic when it is part of a person's response to the demand of God as revealed in history. It will then inevitably lead to creative, liberating praxis. Cult, in this sense, belongs essentially to the domain of prophetic-symbolic action, and never leaves the terrain of human self-transcendence in history. It becomes inauthentic, alienated and alienating, when it is detached from the dialectic of divine challenge and human response, and is set up as something autonomous. Where this happens, cult is transposed from historical time to cyclic time in which nothing new ever happens. A false cult is the result of our attempt to have a God whom we can manipulate and dispose of as we please. The God of such cult is a silent, passive God who is bound to make himself available where and when people choose. In this sense, cult may be seen as a way of reifying the Divine, which has for its counterpart the divinization of things (of the alter, the consecrated bread, etc.). Made in the image of alienated human beings, this God is neutral to the rich and the poor and dispenses favours equally to the exploiter and the exploited. He is very much alive in the Asian churches and his rule is reinforced by ever new and spurious cults imported from the West. He has his array of theologians, too, vowed to defend and extend his kingdom.

The Anti-God also breeds and is bred by dogma. Dogma, too, de-historicizes and fixes God into eternal and immutable concepts. The reification that cult accomplishes at the level of symbolic action, dogma accomplishes through conceptualization. It, too, is the result of our striving to be the measure of our own Maker. The same tendency is noticeable in the development of religious laws. If dogma is the law of human thinking about God, law is the dogma concerning human action in response to God. Through law, what human beings perceived as the will of God in earlier ages is absolutized as valid for all ages. Thus it, too, de-historicizes the demands of God. Both deflect our attention from the challenge of the living God in the *here-and-now* of history. Both curtail human freedom: the first, freedom of thought; the second, freedom of action. Of the two, law is the greater source of unfreedom, because what passes for the law of God is often the sum of norms formulated by the privileged classes for the furtherance of their own interests. Besides, the religious laws operative in most Asian churches smack of ecclesiastical imperialism, imported as they have been from the West and imposed on us as normative for our thinking and acting. Fortunately, both dogma and the law are on the way out and the voice of the living God is beginning to be heard at least in certain Christian circles.

As far as Asian Christianity is concerned, the Anti-God is a domiciled foreigner. However, it should not be forgotten that he has his counterpart in indigenous religious traditions, with whom he stands in a certain relationship of cultural symbiosis. Though there is much that is beautiful and profound in the Hindu Scriptures, what these, on the whole, project is a Class-God. For, the Vedas, the Upanishads, the Epics, and the Puranas were either written or rewritten by the dominant castes to maintain their supremacy. No wonder, they contain innumerable myths, legends, and discourses that provide ideological legitimation for the exploitation of the lower castes and the untouchables. A case in point is the famous *Purusha-sukta* (Creation Hymn) of the *Rigveda*, which describes the divine origin of caste. Furthermore, one can find, in the religious lore, texts sanctioning every conceivable form of inhumanity including rape, violence, war, and treachery. Such being the case, no theologian, whether Christian or Hindu, who is responsive to human values, can unreservedly identify himself with the religious traditions of the past.

Jesus the Theologian

The Christian theologizes between memory and hope - between the memory of Jesus and hope in the Kingdom to come. If in our reflections, we have focused on the God of hope, it is out of reverence for the memory of Jesus. His entire life and teaching go to prove the validity of the approach to theology we have been advocating so far. To substantiate this, nothing less than a critical survey of the Synoptic Gospels as a whole is needed. Since that is not possible here, I shall confine myself to a few general observations.

Jesus lived from one unique experience: his own primordial encounter with God. To judge by the Gospel narratives, that encounter took place on the banks of Jordan when, significantly, he identified himself with the common run of humankind by choosing to be baptized for the remission of sins. From then on he was a man possessed, taken hold of by the Spirit (power) of God, by that Spirit which was to lead him to the desert, to the villages and towns of Palestine, to confrontation with the powers that were, and finally to death on the cross. Every word he uttered, every deed of his, was in response to the challenge of the living God he encountered.

The God of Jesus is to be encountered in the domain not of cult but of history. God is one who comes to usher in a new age, in which there will not be any division of society into the rich and the poor (Mt 5:3), in which the dispossessed will regain possession of the earth (Ibid., 5:5), in which human hunger for justice will be satisfied (Ibid., 5:6), in which class conflict will be replaced by brotherhood and the sword by peace (Ibid., 5:9). Equally, it is in history that human beings go to meet God. The good Samaritan met Him in responding to a human in need (Lk 10:29-37); Zacchaeus in redressing the injustice he had done to others (Ibid., 19:1-10); the rich young man was told that he should sell what he had and give it to the poor if he wished to have a share in the life of the new age to come (Mk 10:17-22). Jesus' teaching on this point reflects his own experience of God. It was in the heart of the world that he met his God - at weddings, at festal meals, by the lakeside where fisherfolk cast and hauled their nets, by the wayside wells where women came to fetch water, at gatherings of people, in the company of outcasts, in the fellowship of his disciples, in the togetherness of friendship, and in the innocence of children, and, above all, in contesting the forces of oppression.

Jesus was no theologian in the sense of one who wrote treatises on God. But there is no doubt that he did reflect on his own encounter with God and sought to grasp its implication for himself and for all people. His parables, discourses, and sayings gave expression to the various layers of meaning, existential, cosmic, social, economic, and political - embedded in his own God-encounter. I have elsewhere tried to bring out some of these dimensions of meaning (*Jesus and freedom*). Here I shall only comment on Jesus' manner of religious discourse. He did not speak in the abstract, cut, and dry concepts. Neither did he employ an esoteric language as do most theologians today; instead he spoke in images, symbols, pictures, and parables. This is not to be attributed solely to the historical conditioning of a more 'primitive' age. It shows rather that his thinking vibrated in unison with the life of his people. Besides, he was too involved in the unspeakable mystery of the God he encountered to be able to speak of Him in the manner in which a scientist would speak of test-tube babies. He would not dissect God with the surgical knife of cold reason. For him, knowing was also loving, speaking was also prophesying. It is in a similar fashion that the Buddha spoke, that the ancient seers of India spoke, of the ultimate meaning of life. Asian theology will come to its own only when it will make a complete break with the rationalism of Western theology and evolve a new manner of discourse about God, drawn from the life of God's people. We have to develop a new theological language that would express the fusion of thinking and loving, seeing and prophesying, vision, and commitment.

For Jesus, reflecting and speaking were but aspects of his total response to the Father. And that response he himself summed up as one of preaching the good news to the poor, proclaiming release for prisoners, giving sight to the blind, setting free the oppressed, and restoring land to the landless (Lk 4:18-19). With him, word became power, reflection became prophecy resonant with the divine force that re-creates the world. No wonder that, at his words, the blind saw, the deaf heard, the dead rose, and the paralytic took up his bed and walked away. The same force was at work in his fierce denunciation of the scribes and the Pharisees, whom he called a brood of vipers and whited sepulchers (Mt 23:33), and in his defiant labeling of Herod a fox (Lk 13:32). If such words of force have long since been muted in the churches, it is because theologizing has been divorced from an encounter with God, and faith from practice. Where reflection starts not from one's own meeting with God but from the interpretations, raised to the nth degree, of the God-encounter other people are supposed to have had, it will naturally end up in sterile speculations which change neither the world nor the thinker. The springtime of Asian Christian theology will burst forth only when we refuse to theologize by proxy, to be mere relaying stations for ideas fabricated elsewhere, and muster enough courage to face the naked God and respond to his challenge to create a social order of justice and freedom.

Like the prophets of old, Jesus too instituted severe criticism of wealth, power, and the Anti-God, a criticism which was a consequence of his own encounter with God. He rejected the service of Mammon as incompatible with faith in God and required of his followers that they sell what they have and give it to the poor (Mk 10:21; Mt 6:42). Thereby he also repudiated the prevalent notion that wealth was a sign of divine favour, a notion manifestly born of an attempt to use God to legitimate the exploitation of the poor. No less severe was his criticism of power and of those who "made their subjects feel the weight of their authority" (Mk 10:42). He envisaged a society in which power will give way to service. For him, the spirit of God was a subverter of all power, one who pulled down the mighty from their thrones, overthrew all oppressors, and demolished prisons (Lk 4:18). True to this conviction, he identified himself with the powerless: the simple, the uneducated, the little ones, and the socially despised.

An equally fundamental concern of his was the liquidation of the Anti-God. He would have nothing to do with a cult that does not change the world. For him, worship that coexisted with unlove was an empty gesture (Mt 5:23-24; Mk 12:32-33). Furthermore, he repudiated the distinction between the pure and the impure, between the sacred and the profane, a distinction which is the very basis of all religions (Mk 7:15). Of course, he prayed; but his prayer was directly geared to meeting the immediate challenges that faced him in the critical phases of his life. It was rooted in history, not transposed to the realm of cyclic time. Nor was what came to be called the Eucharist originally a cultic act. It had its basis in the meals he had with the outcasts of society, with the publicans and the sinners, meals which anticipated the new humanity of the future, the festal gathering of the end-time, when "many will come from the east and west and sit at the table with Abraham, Isaac, and Jacob in the kingdom of heaven" (Mt 8:11). It may, therefore, more appropriately be called a prophetic action. Only subsequently was it interpreted in cultic terms. Similarly, even a cursory reading of the Gospels will show that Jesus was opposed to reifying God into dogmas and laws. He had no hesitation in radically reinterpreting the Law and the prophets. He even went to the extent of abrogating parts of the written law (Mt 5:25-48). More significantly, he subordinated the law to the wellbeing of human beings and thereby rendered it relative and provisional (Mk 2:27). In short, his teaching is an emphatic repudiation of every manner of reifying God.

It follows that we have to return to the Jesus of the Gospels and make our own his vision of God and humankind. However, Jesus is more than a mere example to be followed in our quest after God. He is also one in whom we encounter God. And this is just what marks us out from other believers. These, too, meet God in the realities of life, just, as we do. But, unlike them, we have met God also in the words and deeds of Jesus. However, these two modes of encountering the Divine — in Jesus and in the world of today — do not run on parallel lines. They condition and illumine each other forming a unity in tension.

Therefore, for the disciples of Jesus, to theologize is to try to understand the Gospel in the light of our encounter with God today and, conversely to understand our encounter with God in contemporary history in the light of the Gospel.

A prophetic theology that does justice to God's self-revelation both in Jesus and in the world of today is more likely to emerge in Asia than in the West. In countries where Christians are the majority, it is easy for them to nurse the illusion that the church is the centre of the universe. And where the church is made the centre, hope in the kingdom of God is rendered peripheral. In Asia, on the contrary, any exclusive claim Christians may entertain will fall to the ground when they see that they are no better in respect of concern for human values than the followers of other faiths. This makes it easier for them to recapture Jesus' vision of the kingdom of God which includes all irrespective of caste or creed who seeks the well-being of their neighbours. However, even in Asia, it is vain to hope that the Christian Establishment will give the lead in fashioning a theology centered upon the Kingdom since it is still very much under the sway of the Anti-God. A relevant theology is more likely to emerge from those groups of dissenting Christians who, in loyalty to Jesus, have inserted themselves in the life of the people and are partners in their struggle for justice. It is heartening to note that more and more of such groups are being formed in India. They can forget all denominational differences and meet on the common basis of discipleship under Jesus and of commitment to the new humanity he envisioned. They, in truth, anticipate the Jesus-community of the future which will transcend all human barriers. Understandably, such groups have no difficulty in joining hands with peoples of other religions or even with Marxists. The Christ of dogma divides; Jesus of the Gospel unites

3

For a Contextual Theology
of Liberation

There is as yet no distinctive school of thought among Indian Christians that may be called Theology of Liberation. What one finds instead are gropings towards a new interpretation of the Gospel prompted by the Second Vatican Council and the exigencies of organized action for social justice.[1] Nor has any attempt been made to define the specificity of the Indian approach to Liberation Theology. The present paper, therefore, is bound to be more prescriptive than descriptive. That is, it seeks to explore the lines theologizing must take if it is to be fully contextual and truly responsive to the challenge of transformative action on society.

A Civilizational Crisis

Profound changes are taking place in the Indian sub-continent affecting its social institutions, culture, and, world-view. With the advance of science, technology, and modern education, the world above of the sun, the moon, and the stars has shed its aura of divinity and has collapsed into the human world below. The same fate has befallen the earth, the trees, the rivers, and the waters of the sea. From being deities of fertility, these have become mere raw materials for human labour thereby also part of human history. Much in the same manner, social and cultural institutions have lost the status they have hitherto enjoyed of divinely willed, immutable realities. They are being recognized for what they are: man's handiwork which he can remake or unmake at will. This new awareness has created the necessary mental climate for popular struggles against oppressive social structures. Such struggles at once presuppose and generate the consciousness in the masses that they are the creators of their own future. Involved here is the transition from cyclic to historical time.[2] Temporality begins to follow the rhythm not of cosmic processes but of human decisions. This mutation in self-awareness and world-awareness is a universal phenomenon affecting people all over the world. What is specific to India is the telescoping of historical processes, which elsewhere took centuries to reach maturity, so that the future becomes present before the present has receded into the past, resulting in an anguishing conflict between the old and the new.

The absorption of natural history into human history and the transition from cyclic to human historical time carry with it a revolution in the way humans conceive the Divine. They can no longer look for it in a mysterious world above or around. They must seek it in history, in temporality to which they themselves give name and form.[3]

But where in history do we encounter the Divine? The Divine comes to us both as gift and challenge. As gift, in the experience of beauty, love, friendship, and togetherness. Though confined within the bounds of the *here-and-now,* such experiences open a window into that which is beyond the beyond. The Divine confronts us as challenge when, through historical situations, it demands that we break loose all fetters and march forward to the unknown, hoping against hope. Both theophanies are mediated by history and call for an appropriate answer. The gift requires that we safeguard and preserve it for the future; the challenge must issue in transformative action that re-creates ourselves and the world. The two responses complete and enrich each other. He who has not experienced the absoluteness of beauty, love, and community will seldom revolt against conditions of ugliness, oppression, and the fragmentation of the human. Similarly, whoever ignores the challenge of creating the future is likely to miss the annunciation of the Divine in the present. The twofold response of humans we call theandric practice (practice of man = *aner*, in response to God = *Theos*). In it are blended contemplation and action, celebration and creation, safeguarding and subverting, memory and hope, self-transformation, and world-transformation. It is in theandric practice and what it brings into being that the gift-call of the Divine becomes flesh. If so, Revelation is, in a sense, mankind's historical task. Humans have much to create the truth about the Divine as they have to discover it. Lest I introduce too complex a perspective, in what follows I shall focus on the transformative character of theandric practice.

The Cry of the Poor and the Marginalized

To further define the call of the Divine at this critical juncture in our history, it is necessary to examine the social system as a whole and the conflicting forces at work in it. Since a detailed social analysis is not possible here, I shall confine myself to pointing out the main problems facing the country.

What we have in India is a form of dependent capitalism characterized by a vast concentration of the means of production (agricultural and industrial) in a few hands. Though it has contributed to the development of the productive forces, capitalism has created wide disparities in income and opportunity, which have only increased since Independence. While the top ten percent of the population live in relative affluence, 47 percent are doomed to live below subsistence level. Here is how an economist sums up the results of capitalist development thus far:

> "Nine-tenth of India's population is left behind in economic backwaters. Mass poverty is on the rise; the net availability of the most basic human necessities per capita such as food grains and clothing is scarce; rural indebtedness has multiplied; unemployment and underemployment have reached the level of 20.8 million person-years."[4]

To this must be added the proliferation of slums, the marginalization of tribals and the outcastes, the destruction of traditional handicrafts, and the ecological ravages wrought by profit-oriented production.

On the political front, the affluent classes - the landlords, the rich capitalist peasants, and the middle and big bourgeoisie - can use democratic institutions for their own purposes. They manipulate elections, create powerful lobbies in the Assemblies and the Parliament, corrupt the bureaucracy, and control local self-government bodies. What is more, political power has become highly centralized; reducing peoples' participation to the minimum and denying States and ethnic groups their legitimate autonomy.

Deeper than the economic and the political is the cultural crisis, which has its matrix in the conflict between tradition and bourgeois modernity transplanted here from outside. At one extreme of the cultural spectrum is the traditional casteist culture coupled with an obsolete religiosity; at the other, bourgeois modernity in its pure form patronized by a section of the westernized urban elite. In between is a hybrid culture that combines the worst elements of tradition with the capitalist values of private interest, competition, aggressiveness, and consumerism. It is this monstrous un-culture that holds sway over the vast majority of the Indian people. It has vitiated the well-springs of societal life and has ushered in an era of moral decadence and universal corruption. Under its spell, every social reality begets its evil, grotesque shadow. White money has its counterpart in black money, genuine goods in adulterated ones, true ownership in fake ownership, bourgeois democracy in mafia politics, the written law in the unwritten law of might and manipulation, genuine religion in the worship of spurious god-men and god-women.

The challenge that faces the Indian people is clear; to restructure the economy in such wise that production for profit is replaced by production for social needs; to give power back to the people so that they can mould their own lives; to create a counterculture consonant with the dignity of the human and with the positive values of tradition. This last task must receive the highest priority in the Indian context where no genuine socio-political revolution is possible without a preceding cultural revolution. But who will bring about these changes? Gandhism is a spent force today and has all but degenerated into a mere cult. The Parties of the Left have been absorbed into the politics of power and to the bastardized culture in vogue.[6] It is to fill this political vacuum that, in the last decade, grassroots groups sprang up all over India. Once in the field, the Christian activists among them experienced the contradiction between commitment to the unconditional call of the Divine enfleshed in the historical situation and the kind of theology they had inherited. Liberation Theology in India is an attempt to solve that contradiction.

A Foundational Theology of Liberation

The self-revelation of the Divine, concretized in the contemporary historical situation, is addressed to all irrespective of religious affiliation. Hence the possibility of, and the need for, a foundational theology of liberation that cuts across the barriers of religions and ideologies. Understood thus, theology is committed, critical reflection on the historical self-manifestation of the Divine as gift-call and on the human response to it. Let me explain the terms. The theme of theology is not God. For God is a loaded word implying a personal supreme being. As such, it is a product of earlier theology. Hence the term, the Divine, is preferred as it can better express what is neither personal nor impersonal but transpersonal. Nor is the theme of theology the Divine as it is in itself but as it reveals itself to men and women in history and bodies forth in theandric practice. Seen from this angle, all genuine theology is liberative, since the divine gift-call and the human practice it provokes issue in freedom from every alienation and freedom for love, communion, and creativity.

On this ongoing theandric practice, the theologian is called upon to reflect. Reflection involves a conceptual element. This is not so much the theologian's strength as his weakness. For, his theme can more adequately be expressed in the multi-dimensional language of symbols (poetry, drama, music, painting, sculpture, dance, etc.) than in the uni-dimensional language of concepts. Hence in the future, theology will have to recapture the poetic-symbolic language of the parables of Jesus and of the dialogues of the Buddha and the Upanishadic seers.

Reflection must fulfill a critical function. For, human beings do not come on the scene with empty minds but burdened with symbols, myths, conceptions, and biases deriving either from their own religious background or from other beliefs and ideologies encountered in day-to-day life. Such presupposition is generally ambivalent. They may either illumine or throw a veil over, reality. Hence the need for criticism aimed at verifying whether the divine gift-call and the human response to it have been correctly interpreted or have been misconstrued due to wrong preconceptions.

Besides being critical, reflection must also be committed. The theologian cannot remain neutral in respect of that which he is reflecting on. For, doing theology is itself part of the human response to the divine gift-call mediated through history. It is a form of subversive-creative action and is more akin to prophesy than to science. For the same reason, the theologian cannot escape the destiny of the cross.

The theology of liberation whose bare outlines I have just delineated is foundational and universal. Foundational, because the revelation of the Divine in the *here-and-now* of individual-collective existence and the theandric practice it provokes have immediacy which revelation in the past does not have. As such, it is the ultimate criterion by which all earlier theologies have to be judged. Universal, because its theme is accessible to the followers of all religions and even of secular ideologies like Marxism. It is based on this underlying unity that religious and theological pluralism has to be understood.

Indian-Christian Theology of Liberation

The reflection, thus far, enables us to define Christian Theology of Liberation as a critical, committed reflection on the Gospel, in the light of theandric practice and on theandric practice in the light of the Gospel. Before elucidating what this means concretely, let me make two preliminary observations.

It is generally believed that the Indian Christian is a being apart, having little in common with Hindus. Such awareness is jealously instilled in him by the churches from early childhood. But, anthropologically, he is first an Indian and then only a Christian. He is a child of the soil as much as any Hindu. The deeper recesses of his being reverberate with the collective unconscious of the Indian people. To cite but one instance, though fanatically fond he may be of Christian liturgical music, what strikes the deepest chord in him is often the *gayatri* (hymn to the Sun sung at dawn) pealing forth from the nearby temple. More, from early childhood, he is exposed to the symbols, myths, rituals, and conceptions proper to other religions. This makes the average Indian Christian a cross-cultural, cross-religious being. The same holds true of the average Hindu or the Muslim, though to a much smaller degree. These too have in varying ways and degrees assimilated ideas, values, and symbols from the Christian tradition. This symbiotic relation between many religions is the living context in which the Indian Christian carries on theological reflection.

My second observation concerns the theologian's relation to the theandric practice he reflects on. In countries like Latin America, where Christians form the majority, the theologian and the human community on whose practice he reflects both belong to the Christian fold. That is why Gustavo Gutierez could define Liberation Theology as "Critical reflection on Christian praxis in the light of the Word." This makes little sense in India where the agent of theandric practice has necessarily to be a broader community comprising men and women of different religions and persuasions. It is as one inserted in such ecumenical communities that the Indian Christian does theology. This is not a matter of expediency but is rooted in a shared commitment to the humanization of society. The stirrings of a new theology can be found only among theologians and such Christian groups who have broken loose, at least mentally if not also physically, from the ghettos of church institutions and have cast anchor in the secular world.

From Theandric Practice to the Gospel

The first task of any Liberation Theology in India is to critically reflect on the Gospel in the light of our contemporary theandric practice. But the Gospels are read by the average Christian with the spectacles provided by tradition. Hence tradition too needs to be critically examined. Theandric practice will help us distinguish between such elements in tradition as are perennially valid and others that have become obsolete, and to criticize away the interpretative accretions that have either covered up or distorted the true meaning of Jesus' life and message. I shall now indicate a few important areas where a rethinking is necessary and is already taking place in India, though but timidly and gropingly.

1. The intuition that the Divine reveals itself in the challenges and experiences of secular life explodes the notion of a God who spoke his last word two thousand years ago and then, so to speak, retired from the scene. Thereby it also subverts the hegemony of the past over the present and confers theandric value on the strivings of our people for a more humane society. Besides the recognition that the Divine continues to confront humans signals the return of prophecy, which Institution had all but smothered.

2. Theandric practice calls for a revolution in our discourse about the Divine. Traditional theology speaks of God as though he were a subject already known to which predicates may be attributed, as when we say God is love, God is truth, God is the defender of the orphan and the widow, and so on.

   But this manner of discourse becomes problematic when it is realized that the truth about the Divine is what humans have yet to create in the course of history. The Divine can be known only as a predicate of the human, as the depth dimension of human history in the making. What we encounter here and now is no more than pointers, invitations to the Divine.

   This perspective requires that we reformulate our earlier statements and say, Love is divine. Truth is divine and Caring for the widow and the orphan is divine. In doing so, we are rejoining Gandhi who wrote that for a long time he used to say, God is truth, but subsequently came to realize he should rather say, Truth is God.[8] This manner of theological discourse will put an end to the arrogant wordiness of Christian theologians and set the Divine free from the dead concepts in which it has been encapsulated. Further, it will restore to theology its lost credibility. Tell the slum-dwellers of Bombay or Calcutta that God is the defender of the poor, and you are lucky if they don't lay hands on you. Not so if you tell them, if you love one another, when you strive to shake off your shackles, you are under the grip of the Divine.

3. If the self-revelation of the Divine continues in History the conception of Jesus as the definitive revelation needs to be revised. Jesus will be seen from now on for what he really is: a unique, intense, hitherto unparalleled manifestation of the Transcendent as immanent in the flow of history, a sure way, and guide to humanity's ultimate future. The meta-historical 'Christ' seated at the right hand of the Father will give way to Jesus the wayfarer on the road to Jerusalem. With that, the worshippers of 'Christ' will become once again the disciples and followers of Jesus. Putting Jesus back where he belongs, in history, will bring to a close the ideological imperialism of Christianity which legitimized colonialism and imposition of the so-called 'Christian civilization' on the peoples and nations.

4. Not until Christians relinquish customary stance of self-righteous intolerance will they be able to engage in concerted action for a better world in a pluralist society like ours. The standpoint of theandric practice alone can throw light on the personal destiny of Jesus. Experience shows that the struggle against injustice and oppression inevitably exposes one to reprisal from the powers that are. The Christian involved in transformative action is, therefore, better attuned than the worshipping Christian to perceive the truth that Jesus did not die but was murdered by those intent on maintaining the status quo in Palestine. It was a perverse theology that converted that murder into death, and the death into a ritual,

and the ritual into a mere stepping-stone to the resurrection, itself ritualized. It begot a Christianity which for all practical purposes eliminated the cross and the crucified, a Christianity suited to the affluent West that has 'risen and ascended' to the heaven of conspicuous consumption.

5. Only Christians who harken to the divine call to march forward from slavery to freedom can grasp the original character of the church as the community of disciples, conscious, like Jesus, of the mission to preach the good news to the poor. That community was truly ex-centric, having its centre outside itself in the absolute future of mankind. Only those had a place in it who sought first the kingdom of God and its justice and were prepared to contest the forces of injustice and oppression. In contrast, the current notion of the church as a community of worshippers of a Christ who remains supremely neutral before the slave and the master, the exploiter and the exploited, has no foothold in contemporary theandric practice.

6. Since the Second Vatican Council many Christians — priests, nuns, and laypersons — have taken to politicizing and organizing slum-dwellers, the rural poor, and the tribals. In the process, they found it necessary to form wider groups including Marxists and people of other religions. In such groups, members share the same socio-political and humanist goals but derive inspiration from different sources, religious or secular. These activist groups already enjoy theological legitimacy in so far as they constitute a response to the divine call conveyed through the concrete situation. But the Christian cannot but ask whether they have any foundation in the teachings of Jesus? A positive answer may be found in that Gospel narrative where, pointing to the crowd that came to listen to him, Jesus said,

"Look, here are my mother and my brothers! Whoever does what God wants him to do is my brother, my sister, my mother."[9]

What Jesus envisions here is a community based not on discipleship or on any set of doctrines, rituals, and laws, but solely on doing the will of God which, for him, meant loving one's neighbour in deed. Since its focus is on the reign (= *basileia*, in Greek) of God to come, one might call it, basileic community. In religiously pluralist societies like India, such communities are a necessary mediation between the Jesus-community and the reign of God to come. In truth, the primary mission of the ecclesial community is to create basileic communities.

7. Theandric practice calls for a re-appraisal of authority in the church. Where the Divine reveals itself through events and situations, it at the same time authorizes those who respond to it. This is authority in its most original, unconditional manifestation. Of it, institutionalized authority is but a historical concretization. The latter must derive from and subserve the former. More, institutionalized authority can bind and loose only in so far as it lets itself be bound by the call of the Kingdom. The same applies to the sacramentality of the ecclesial community. It is sacramental, that is, it signifies and communicates the Divine only in so far as it, in obedience to the Divine, takes a stand against the forces opposed to the reign of God and is committed to the total liberation of humans. Sacramentality is not a magical prerogative but an ethical quality of the community of believers. Nor is it exclusive to Christians. Basileic communities, too, are sacramental, even more so than any ecclesial community as they alone constitute effective agents of transformative action.

8. Encounter with the Transcendent as immanent in history undermines the dualism of the sacred and the profane, of the material and the spiritual, which provided the official churches both a convenient alibi for sordid involvement in the affairs of the world and an excuse for culpable inaction in the face of manifest inhumanity.[10] Contemporary Christians are impelled by their secular experience of the Divine to return to the Gospels and recapture the holistic perspective of Jesus, who saw the inbreaking of the Kingdom in the visible, tangible realities of history: as when the blind see, the deaf hear, the oppressed are set free, and the poor take possession of the earth.

We have thus far reflected on some aspects of the Gospel and tradition in the light of theandric practice. We shall now reverse the process and direct the searchlight of the Gospel on to the Indian reality. Here too we must be on our guard against certain presuppositions that might vitiate the approach.

From the Gospel to Theandric Practice

Our starting point here must not be just orthodoxy but the Gospel, already reinterpreted along the lines indicated above. It is here that academic theologians go wrong. They often start with the assumption that Christianity is a cultic religion and then proceed to integrate into it elements from Hindu rituals. Thus the estrangement of the prophetic movement of Jesus into a cultic religion as that movement spread to the Greco-Roman world is further accentuated on the Indian soil. As a result, Christianity loses its identity, having nothing specific to offer which Hinduism cannot. Similarly, those theologians who take it for granted that theirs is a religion of individual salvation will end up singing hymns to the notorious religious individualism of the Hindu. Here, again, the specificity of the revelation of the Divine in Jesus is given the go-by. Equally misleading is to approach the Indian reality from the standpoint of the so-called 'mystical Christ'. This theological construct along with the notion of 'anonymous Christians' enabled Christians to integrate whatever is true and good in non-Christian religions and peoples into their own religious universe. This is Christian imperialism under a new guise, seeking to annex the non-Christian world through an act of ideological aggression, as though to offset the bankruptcy of the theology of conversion. At least, so it will be construed by the Hindu population.

We should also get rid of the notion that the Gospel is an essential prerequisite for transformative action on Indian society. Long before Christians took the initiative in organizing popular struggles, Indian communists had done so for decades particularly in Kerala, Andhra, and West Bengal. Hundreds of men and women have laid down their lives in the cause of justice, and only a few among them were Christians.

The majority drew inspiration from the situation of oppression itself or from other religions or ideologies. What is essential for transformative action is obedience to the unconditional call of the Divine, though one might not name it so. This is not to devalue the Christian presence in India but to see it in the proper perspective. What the Gospel can bring to the scene is its own power to illumine and to inspire. Its role is one of reinforcing "the energies of the new age" that are already fermenting in Indian society.

Academic theologians often entertain the notion that secular society follows the cyclic rhythm of institutional life where nothing new happens. They, therefore, fail to see that society and culture in India are undergoing rapid changes under the impact of science, technology, and the spread of capitalism. Taking the religion of the written scriptures for lived religion, they engage in the futile attempt of salvaging elements from tradition, which Hindus themselves have long since left behind. Still worse when they take the Sanskritic tradition for the whole of Indian tradition, whereas the former is largely the creation of the dominant castes to protect their own interests."[11] The temptation is all the greater when the theologian's own standpoint is that of a Christian faith which has itself degenerated into an ideology of the status quo.

With these caveats in mind, let us, from the standpoint of Jesus, examine the creative response of the Indian people to the liberating challenge of the Divine.

The light of the Gospel will enable the Christian and the Hindu alike to discern the working of the Divine in contemporary history. That mankind's self-creation in time and space has a theotic dimension is not something obvious to the average Indian who is inclined to look for the Divine either in natural phenomena or in the mythical universe of gods and goddesses or in the realm of the metaphysical. If more and more Hindus are beginning to recognize that human history has a religious dimension, and religion a historical dimension, it is largely due to the influence of the Gospel.

In the same way, it is the historic contribution of Christianity to have reminded Indians that authentic religiosity has a social thrust and involves loving one's neighbour irrespective colour, caste, or creed. It has inspired Hindus to start service institutions like hospitals, orphanages, and schools. One may hence hope that as Christians become progressively radicalized and take up the cause of the exploited, it will open the eyes of Hindus to the realization that no faith is authentic unless it inspires struggle for a more humane social order.

The Gospel can also help distinguish between genuine and spurious responses to the divine will, revealed in history. Jesus' teaching that, where the Divine presents itself in time and space, the hungry are filled, the thirst for justice is quenched, and all humans made free for love and universal communion, shows that the humanization of the world is the only sure index of its divinization. Only that response of the human community bears the stamp of truth which results in the full development of the individual. The theologian will, therefore, be wary of all attempts at social transformation which rely on violence and hatred, which use the masses as mere tools to power or sacrifice the individual to some estranged collective will in the hope that society can be restructured through dictates from above. His sympathies will rather lie with the way of non-violence which, however, does not rule out organized resistance to unjust social structures.

The Indian Christian theologian who looks for a point of insertion in the Indian heritage for Jesus and his message will find it not so much in the Brahminical scriptures as in the dissenting voices from the past.[12] True, the scriptures contain a theology of release from bondage (*mukti*). But what they envisage is the liberation of the individual only. They know nothing of the liberation of the human community, much less of nature or of human history. In this perspective, the world of human creation has no ultimate value. Further, that from which liberation is sought is conceived as sin (*papa*) or the cycle of existence (*samsara*) or ignorance (*avidya*). In the scriptures, there is no mention of what we would today call structural sin, that is, sin embodied in laws, customs, and institutions. As to the manner of achieving liberation, tradition speaks of three ways (*marga*) of ritual action (*karma*), devotion to a personal God (*bhakti*), and gnosis (*jnana*). Since structural sin is not recognized, there is no recognition either of collective striving, let alone struggle, as a valid liberative practice. On the contrary, the scriptures in their present form are geared to maintaining the supremacy of the male and the caste system of institutionalized inequality. They hold out the promise of freedom in some heaven above or on the plane of transcendental being, while ignoring the real fetters here below.

A refreshing contrast to the conception of liberation just described is the tradition of dissent in India, whose earliest and the most powerful spokesman was Gautama Buddha who flourished in the sixth century before Christ. Though there is much that is enigmatic and mystifying in his teaching, it is remarkable that in many respects he anticipated the concerns of the prophet from Nazareth. This great Asian was the first to repudiate the hierarchy of caste and the supremacy of the Brahmins; the first to denounce the worship of gods, goddesses, and spirits good and evil, along with the superstitious practices accompanying it; the first to point out the economic roots of violence and social anarchy; the first to remind his fellow-humans that they must each be a light unto himself; the first to project a future society in which the rule of kings will give way to the rule of ethics (*dharma*); the first to preach universal love and compassion as the eternal law of life. The Buddha also founded communities (*samgha*) open to all, including outcastes, communities meant to act as mediating points between the present age of sorrow (*dukha*) and the kingdom of righteousness to come.[13]

But this powerful upsurge of the Asian spirit toward love and freedom could not maintain its original radical thrust. A militant Brahmanism succeeded in neutralizing it. But the liberative energies Buddhism released were to emerge once again in medieval India, this time in response to the growing feudal exploitation. Its spokesmen were the saints of the devotional movement (*Bhakti*). They attacked not only economic exploitation but also the prevailing religious formalism and the evils of the caste system, and, for that reason, were persecuted by the priestly class.[14] But the new religion of devotion, too, eventually succumbed to caste Hinduism, itself assuming the form of a caste. Again, in the 18th and the 19th centuries, when colonial exploitation became intolerable, there arose messianic movements from among the tribals and the outcastes, some drawing inspiration from folk traditions regarding the Golden Age, others from the Christian message. They were all ruthlessly suppressed by the colonial rulers with the support of the local ruling castes. Then came the innumerable peasant struggles spearheaded by the Communist movement.[16] Finally, we come to the struggle for Independence under the leadership of Gandhi. In him, the Buddhist doctrine of non-violence, a re-interpreted Hinduism, and the message of the Gospel blended to form a powerful ideological weapon to fight colonial rule. It was the unifying power of religious symbols that enabled him to rally the peasant masses. He is second only to the Buddha in laying the foundation for a theology of liberation. His genius consisted in harnessing religion to liberative political praxis. However, Gandhism failed to radically restructure Indian society, mainly because an irrational commitment to the unity of Hinduism coupled with theoretical ambivalence regarding capitalism prevented it from recognizing the reality and the necessity of caste-and-class struggle.[17]

Clearly then, the light of the Gospel subverts the current reading of the history of India's religious quest, just as the light of theandric practice subverts the dominant reading of the Gospel. Only from the fusion of these two subversive readings of the Gospel and of the Indian religious tradition will emerge a genuinely Indian and Christian Theology of Liberation. Understandably, the breeding ground of the new theology will not be closed Christian communities but what we earlier referred to as open basileic communities.

(Paper presented at the ninth annual seminar of the Indian Theological Association at Poonamallee, Madras, 28-30 December 1985; Puthenangady 1985, pp. 301-318; Wilfred 1992, pp. 146-157; Kappen, *Jesus and Culture*, Chap. 10)

4

From Religious Ideology to Prophetic Religiosity

Let me first comment on the term, religious ideology. Ideology is often taken to mean the sum of ideas shaping the life of a community. In this broad sense, ideology may be good or bad, true or false. The term is also used in a restricted sense to mean a partial view of the world emanating from a particular class but projected as the total view and therefore as valid for all classes. It is in this latter sense that I am using the term. The term 'religious ideology' would then pose a problem. Religion is born of faith. And faith is man's response to the ultimate ground and goal of human existence. It involves being taken hold of by the Absolute, being challenged to march forward to the fullness of being and loving, leaving behind all that is relative, partial, and one-sided. Religion and ideology, therefore, tend in opposite directions. This makes 'religious ideology' a contradiction in terms. Should we then refuse to qualify any ideology religious? By no means. For, the contradiction in terms is also a contradiction in reality. All religions have become ideologies; they propound partial conceptions of God arising from particular cultural-historical contexts as wholly and eternally true. Similarly, they teach as universally beneficial ideas and beliefs formed by the ruling classes to further their own interests. They thereby enable the past to hold sway over the present, the favoured few to lord it over the many.

Religious Ideology and the Will-to-Power

Religion becomes an ideology when God is reduced to a mere tool in the hands of man. For God to become a tool, he must first be mastered. Now, what is that mechanism whereby man gains mastery over God? It is, above all, abstract, discursive reason. Reasoning is different from genuine thinking. Genuine thinking is akin to thanking, adoring, communing, merging with all that is. It never severs the link between the thinker and the flux and fullness of reality; it is throughout governed by that which is thought about, in the present case, God. Reason, on the other hand, abstracts the essence from the existent and forms concepts meant to represent reality. Having done so, it turns its back on what originally provoked thought. It dissects the one into many disparate concepts to be neatly pigeonholed. It arrests what is ebbing and flowing, waning and waxing, in order to transpose it into eternal and immutable truths. Similarly, it reduces the unspeakable, unfathomable mystery of God into manageable concepts. With that, the living God is eclipsed and his place is taken over by the man-made deity. Called into being by man, the deity is ever at his beck and call. He is God broken in and made to bear the burden of man's love and hatred, his lust for wine and women, his craving for power and glory. He is an alienated man, magnified into infinity.

The attempt to master the Numinous must be seen in conjunction with man's striving for mastery over the environment: nature and other men. For early man, nature was a mother. Every fibre of his being resonated with the rhythm of nature, before whom his compartment was marked by wonder, fear, reverence, and love all in one. Over time, with the growth of science and technology, nature too was reduced to abstractions: mass, weight, energy, quantity, quality. Science opened up possibilities for manipulating the processes of nature. Parallelly, there developed institutions for dominating other men. Chief among them was the state which came to replace the tribal organization of yore. The growth of capitalism also saw the birth of social technology for engineering the conscious and the subconscious of human beings.

The three forms of mastery — over nature, man, and God — do not run along parallel lines but are closely interlinked, forming a unity in tension. On the one hand, mastery over God is a precondition for mastery over man and earth. How can you lay hands on your brothers and sisters as long as God's "Thou shall not kill" rings in your ears? How can you violate nature, when you know that divinity runs through her veins? On the other hand, the attempt to have command over God is nothing but the logic of mastery over men and things pushed to its final conclusion.

Nowhere else did the will-to-power run its fateful course more fully than in the West, where it ensouled a culture and a civilization and spawned up monstrous forces of death and destruction. True, in Asian countries too there have been similar tendencies. Our forebears did try to have control over the numinous through magic, myth, and concepts; but at no time did they lose sight of the symbolic character of all discourse about God. Nor did conceptions of God crystallize into dogmas to be adhered to under pain of eternal damnation. Similarly, on the socio-political plane, the subjugation of man by man did not carry with it such naked use of force as it did in the West. Under the pre-capitalist mode of production, the king did not directly interfere in the day-to-day life of the village communities. Domination was achieved less through force than through psychic violence institutionalized in caste. Again, in contrast to the West, the Asian mind retained something of that primordial sense of wonder and reverence before nature. Despite the ravages of capitalism, there still exists among our people a certain sensuous, intuitive, flesh-and-blood relationship with God, man, and nature.

One might ask: Is not an outright denial of God better suited to the conquest of the world than the taming of the Divine? So it might seem at first look. A little reflection will show that, for the aspiring wielders of power, a mummified God is better than no God. Because, the violent need to legitimize the use of violence, before themselves and other men. And ultimate legitimization can come only from God. Hence the only way out is to get rid of the living God that his semblance still lingers on the horizon. Thus a brand of theology came into being which succeeded in neutralizing God without eliminating him.

Deity as Provider of Legitimation

Religion legitimizes the political subjugation of the masses either by deifying the king or by king-ifying God. Instances of the deification of the king abound in the history of religions. Let me confine myself to the Judeo-Christian tradition. Here, what we notice is not so much deification as sacralization. According to the Psalmist, Jahweh, establishes the king in Sion as his anointed, adopts him into sonship, seats him on his right hand, confers on him the scepter of power, and declares him a priest according to the order of Melchisedech. The ruler, divinely empowered, proclaims Jahweh's own decrees and wages wars on his behalf (Ps. 2, 110). Coming to our own era, we need only to recall Pope Gelasius' (492-498) theory of the two powers, according to which the emperor receives the temporal sword from God either directly or through the Pope. Hence the emperor's claim to being "imperator a Deo coronatus" (emperor crowned by God) and "*rex et sacerdos et vicarius Christi*" (king, priest, and vicar of Christ). Even Luther held the view that temporal power derived from God, which made the State "God's functionary and the servant of his anger" (*Gottes Amptmann and seyns zorns diener*).

The same Judeo-Christian tradition also bears witness to the search for political legitimacy through the king-ification of God. The Israelites transposed to Jahweh their own lust for power, their own itch for aggression and violence. Jahweh is said to assemble troops (IS 17: 26), engage in war (IS 18: 17; Nb 21: 14), march in the van of the army (Jos 3: 6; 6: 6 ff; 2 S 11: 11), scatter the enemies (Nm 10:35-36), throw them into confusion, and order men and beasts to be put to death (Jgs 4:17; 7:22: Dt 7:22; IS 17: 47). The Deuteronomist sings in exultation:

> "Happy art thou O Israel — who is like thee? People victorious through Jahweh, whose shield is thy help, whose sword is thy victory. The enemies will stoop low to worst thee, but thou shalt trample on their backs" (Dt 33:29).

One may not excuse Jahweh on the grounds that the wars he led were defensive. For, wars of conquest too there were, as when the Hebrews carved out a territory for themselves out of the land of Canaan. God here appears as the enlarged version of a tribal chief or mundane ruler.

The same tendency showed up in the history of Christianity. Jesus, no doubt, consistently refused the role of a messianic king. He lost his life in the struggle against political power, Roman as well as Jewish. Nor did he think of God after the manner of a universal king. He, of course, preached the kingdom of God. The term, however, meant the final coming of God to save all men, not to establish the sovereignty of one privileged nation over the rest. But already from very early times, the community of believers tended to identify Jesus with the kingdom of God (Mt 16:28; 19:29; 21:9; Lk 9:27; 18:29; AA 8:12; 28:31). Over time, such identification even found liturgical expression in the devotion to 'Christ the King'. This indeed has profound implications. While the reign of God did not involve the superiority of the Christian community over the rest of mankind, the Kingship of Christ does because the blessings of his kingly rule accrue only to those who believe in him. This community, therefore, shares Christ's sovereignty over all peoples and nations. Those who do not belong to it are reduced to being God's step-children, if not His enemies.

Understandably, Christ, the conqueror of souls, found it congenial to join hands with the powers and principalities of this world. In the fourth century of our era was formed that fateful alliance between the cross and sword, between the imperial Christ and the Christian emperor, an alliance that polluted the mainstream of Christianity down to our own days. Later, the imperialism of the word and imperialism of the sword undertook the joint venture of colonial conquest. The soldier and the missioner marched hand in hand, shoulder to shoulder, urged on by the 'noble' mission of annexing territories and saving souls. Natives were subjugated, if not wiped out; their cultures uprooted, their economies ruined — all with the blessings of Pope and priest. Violence and bloodshed were invested with a sort of religious halo as though it formed some kind of '*preparatio evangelica*' (evangelical preparation).

Religious Legitimation in a Secularized World

With the secularization of society brought about by the development of productive forces and the spread of science and technology, the close link, between the deity and the State broke down. The State became autonomous, deriving its authority not from God above but from below, from the people. What people — which in practice meant the majority - willed came to be held reasonable, rational. Reason was thus installed as the ultimate legitimizing principle of the modern State. Its counterpart on the economic plane was technological reason governing the development of productive forces. At the bottom, both are forms of unreason. Political reason wrongly assumes that the majority is always right. Majority decisions can be manipulated as is done in all bourgeois democracies today. Political reason also ignores the uniqueness of the individual, reduces him to an abstract citizen, a mere subject of rights and duties. No less unreasonable is technological reason. What it seeks is not the satisfaction of the genuine needs of the community but the profitability of enterprises.

Be that as it may, with political and technological reasons usurping the throne of the supreme legitimizer, the deity was forced to make a shameful retreat into the Holy of Holies. This does not mean that religions exercise no more any legitimizing function. The deity continues to play the same role even today, though for other reasons and in other ways. For one thing, due to the uneven development of capitalist science and technology, there are vast sections of people on whom secularization has had little impact. Besides, even in the industrially advanced countries, there are areas of the human psyche untouched by secular reason. What is more, even the secular man is not that cocksure of his own moorings as he pretends to be. Deep down he is insecure, frightened by the forces of death he has released through science and technology. All the more so, when he sees the same forces recoil upon himself and endanger his very survival. He, therefore, still feels the need to invoke the God of yesterdays to still his inner qualms and to legitimate his wrong-doings.

If it is true that the secular world is still in need of divine legitimation, it is no less true that the deity is constrained to provide that legitimation for his own survival. Though he has been relegated to the outskirts of the secularized world, he is very much tied up with the same world through the immense wealth of the religious bodies he presides over. The need to maintain and expand the economic base of institutionalized religion constrains him to side with whoever happens to be in power.

Such legitimation need not necessarily be expressed in the form of official teachings. When organized religions expect the State to guarantee their property, that itself is a legitimation of State power. They are also driven to confer legitimacy on the prevailing economy. Because the laws governing their own internal economy are the same as those underlying the macroeconomic system (commodity exchange, profit-seeking, supply and demand, and so on). No wonder if the deity finds the political and technological reason underpinning secular society eminently reasonable. What else can he do, himself being God cut down to reasonable proportions! To declare State power reasonable is a more effective way of legitimizing it than to declare it divinely ordained. In the first case, the deity as legitimizer can maintain at least a semblance of neutrality, whereas, in the second, his good faith is suspect, since he would be overtly identifying himself with the oppressor. In this sense, the secularization of society has only enhanced the legitimizing role of religion.

The God of authentic religion is partial to the poor and the powerless. The deity of theocratic society is partial to the rich and the powerful. The deity of the contemporary secularized world is neutral in principle but in practice partial to the ruling classes. Hence the need to tear the mask of neutrality off his face and expose him for what he is. Only then will the living God, the defender of the downtrodden, once again rise in the horizon of history.

The Political Function of Cult

Man gains mastery over God not only through discursive reason but also through symbolic actions, of which the chief is cult. Cult originates from the discernment of life and death. To our forebears, it was crucial to distinguish the life-giving from the death-dealing as they could survive only by pursuing the former and avoiding the latter. It had also dawned on them that life and death, though opposed to each other, formed a unity. They saw the seed die and sprout into fresh life; the decaying carcass gives birth to swarms of living creatures, the treeless and flowerless winter transform itself into the luxuriant vegetation of springtime. In short, they saw life emerge out of death, but only to lapse again into the lap of death. They went further and identified the life-death process at the microcosmic level with the same at the macrocosmic level: the eye with the sun, breath with the wind, sexual reproduction with cosmic reproduction. From this arose the notion that one can determine the macrocosmic process of life and death by re-enacting it microcosmically. And what is a cult but the attempt to promote cosmic well-being by inflicting death on a chosen victim? This explains why, in times of famine or epidemic, primitive peoples immolated an animal or one of their kind so that life may once again surge up in abundance. Sacrificial cult re-enacts the primordial emergence of the cosmos from chaos, of life from death. In religions based on the belief in a personal God, the immolated victim passes over into the sphere of Divine life; and the sacrificing community along with it.

What has all this to do with political change, one might ask. Very much indeed. For what is politics of class society but the art of ensuring abundant life for the few at the cost of inflicting death on the many? To grasp the implications of this statement it is necessary to set out on another train of reflections. In all human beings, there are two fundamental drives: the will-to-life and the will-to-power. The first seeks pleasure, enjoyment, freedom, self-expression, and communion with the universe of men and things; the second seeks mastery over self and environment. But mastery over anything is possible only by limiting and curtailing, in other words, by inflicting death, understood in the broader sense of the term. (The will-to-life corresponds to the libido and the will-to-power to the death instinct, of Freudian theory). Now, in class societies, the majority have no chance to satisfy their will-to-life, deprived as they are of the means of production and consumption. Will not the frustration of such a fundamental urge lead the oppressed masses to turn their will-to-power into violence against the oppressors? If that does not happen, it is because the ruling classes use certain devices to neutralize the potential of violence embedded in the collective subconscious. They do this in various ways. One is to divert people's will-to-power to the object of work. All work involves the destruction of an earlier form and the creation of a new one. In the work-place, the will-to-power exhausts itself in a manner useful to the owning classes. Yet another device is to educate the masses in directing their urge for mastery against themselves, against their own will-to-life. They are persuaded to accept a culture of asceticism and self-castration in the name of patriotism or 'the common good.' To this end is geared the entire educational system. Thus the dominated are made accomplices in their own domination. Finally, they are provided with means to expend their collective resentment and anger in socially 'innocent' ways. Such are sports and games of violence; sexual permissiveness (sexual intercourse is akin to death); films depicting violence, sadism, masochism, and rape; occasional feasts when customary social taboos are lifted (Carnival, Holi).

These and other cultural outlets, however, are effective only up to a point. The escape they provide is limited, transient. Besides, they leave the deprived and the powerless in the same material conditions as before. They do not open the door to the unbounded and the infinite, to the everlasting pastures beyond. Here cult comes in to meet the need. In a sacrificial cult, the victim and those it represents are drawn into the sphere of the divine. The immolation of the victim represents also the political immolation of the masses at the hands of the rulers. Thus the experience of oppression itself becomes 'salvific.' Through the mediation of cult, the oppressed regain a semblance of unity with God, man, and the universe. Of course, in real life, exploitation and domination continue. But that is compensated for by the spiritual 'freedom' won and the spiritual 'riches' accumulated in heaven above. More, the mystery of death giving rise to life, which is symbolically enacted in cult, has its counterpart, at the psychic level, in the orgasm of fervour and frenzy that takes hold of the devotees. Their psychic energy is drained out in the ecstasy of sacrificial immolation. Thus tamed, they will now return, tail between legs, to the work-place, ready to bend their back to those who hold the whip. Only when all such ways of neutralizing revolt fail, does the state resort to the use of force through its machinery of repression.

In the contemporary world, however, even cult is seen as an inadequate means of release from social oppression and regimentation, particularly so in the technically advanced countries. Why? Because the deity of cult is a reasonable being. He is a stickler for law and order, a lover of the golden mean; and he cannot tolerate the free play of instincts within the precincts of his abode. He must impose strict norms on cultic behaviour. Thus cult, meant to be an escape from systems of oppression, becomes itself systematized. Hence the growing tendency to find means of escape other than those provided by State and institutionalized religion. Here is the reason for the proliferation of esoteric religious groups on the margin of society (Pentecostalism, Charismatic movement, Satan worship and the like) and the increasing recourse to psychedelic drugs, sexual orgies, and the Hippy culture.

It might be objected that the explanation given does not account for the fact that cult appeals to all classes in society. My answer is that any social system, once developed to a point where it moves on its own axis, tends to become autonomous in respect also of the ruling classes, which is particularly true of capitalism. As a result, the oppressiveness of the system is experienced by all. There are, also, existential bondages — the burden of sin and guilt, the vulnerability of freedom, and the inevitability of death — which torment all human beings to whichever class they belong. From such bondages, too, one finds release in cultic celebrations.

Back to Origins

It follows that religion as it exists today, stands in the way of political emancipation, either by legitimizing oppression or by smothering dissent through cultic compensation. This does not mean, however, that religion is evil pure and simple. All religions contain unused reservoirs of creative energy which could be mobilized for the humanization of politics. Some of them like Buddhism and Christianity arose as protest movements against prevailing socio-political systems. And at no time in history was the original critical impulse, which is inherent in genuine faith, totally suppressed.

Today we are witnessing a development of world-historical significance within Christianity itself: the growing struggle between faith and dogma, between prophecy and institution, between the Jesus of history and the Christ of traditional faith, between the living God and the man-made deity. The voice of the Angry God, vehicled through the demand of millions for bread and freedom, has found new spokesmen even within the pale of orthodoxy. So much so, even diehard conservatives are compelled to resort to radical rhetoric to regain lost credibility. The success or failure of this new quest for relevance will decide whether Christianity will become a force that changes the political face of the earth. It augurs well for the future that in other religions too attempts are being made to return to the radicalism of origins.

5

Towards an Ecumenism Without Domination

Ecumenism may mean theory and practice relating either to the unity of the churches or to the unity of all mankind. In this paper, the stress will be on ecumenism in the broader sense, since the unity of the churches assumes meaning only in relation to the unity of mankind as a whole. As I shall show in what follows, commitment to the *unity-in-freedom* of all human beings is an essential prerequisite for unity among Christians.

The perspective adopted here is also dictated by the specificity of the Indian situation. Though the search for a universal humanity is found in all cultures and among all peoples, its urgency is experienced all the more intensely in India where we are confronted with a vast humanity fragmented on the basis of caste, colour, and religion. The problem before us is to create a climate of solidarity in which people of different communities recognize their oneness as members of the human family while respecting each other's differences and address themselves to the common task of creating a new social order based on justice and mutual concern.

It is generally believed that ecumenism is something good in itself. This needs to be called in question. Whether it is good or bad depends on the goal in view and on the strategy adopted for realizing it.

Seen from this angle, one may distinguish two types of ecumenism — ecumenism of domination and ecumenism of freedom. By ecumenism of domination, I understand every attempt by a human group — caste, community, or race - to impose on others its own particular vision and way of life as valid for all. Domination may be exercised by the use of force or by means of economic and religious sanctions. Where the attempt fails to eliminate all opposition, it may resort to the strategy of co-optation, that is, integrating the dissenting view into the dominant culture by according it a subordinate place. Where even that strategy proves futile, efforts will be made to marginate the dissenters. In any case, the aim is to create a universality under conditions chosen by the ruling classes. In so far this kind of ecumenism denies, those outside, the right to maintain their otherness, it is but a form of totalitarianism.

The ecumenism of freedom, on the other hand, seeks to create a universal community in which the different races, castes, cultures, and religions will be able to develop each according to its own specific genius and tradition, while at the same time enriching and being enriched by one another. What it envisions is a union that diversifies and a diversity that unites. It stands for the oneness of all achieved through the otherness of each. The freedom it promises to individuals and groups will consist in their being recognized by the community as absolute values, in other words, it will be a freedom born of justice and love.

Of the two types of ecumenism, only the second is genuine. All ecumenism of domination is self-defeating. For, it has for its essential condition the division of the human community into the rulers and the ruled, the teachers and the taught. It is a search for unity based on disunity. Besides, by its very nature, it is conservative. Because it is in the interest of the ruling classes to maintain and reinforce the conditions which have conferred on them the privilege of ruling. As such, they will be opposed to any radical change in society and culture. The ecumenism of freedom, on the contrary, cannot accept the status quo of exploitation and domination. It has to overthrow the prevailing conditions to create a new society in which there will be neither exploitations nor domination. And this is because it has for its social agent those sections of the community in whose interest it is to do away with all conditions of domination.

Ecumenism as a historical force whether of domination or freedom — operates both on the level of consciousness and social being, of theory and praxis. The ideas, values, and beliefs associated with it condition and are conditioned by the mode of production (economy) and by the system of decision making (politics). The interaction between the two levels admits of infinite variations depending on time and place, and are to be empirically verified. In what follows, the stress will be on religio-cultural ecumenism, while not altogether neglecting the economic and political dimensions.

Ecumenism of Domination

The earliest attempt in India to establish a universal community - which is what the word '*oikoumene*' means - came from the Aryans who invaded the country around 1800 B.C. Thanks to their possession of cavalry and superior methods of warfare, they were able to subjugate the original inhabitants of the land and settle down in north-western India. The conquered pre-Aryan tribes were reduced to the position of slaves condemned to render menial service to their conquerors. They, in course of time, became the lowest castes and outcastes. The racial hegemony of the Aryans is reflected in their religion as embodied in the *Samhitas* (collection of hymns to the gods), the *Brahmanas* (sacrificial rituals), and the *Upanishads* (philosophical aphorisms and anecdotes). The Aryans used religion to legitimize and reinforce their domination. It is significant that the chief of the Vedic pantheon, Indra, was invoked as the "protector of the Aryan colour" and the "destroyer of the dark skin" (i.e. the pre-Aryans). The nascent theology, clothed in the language of myth, also provided religious sanction to the social supremacy of the Brahmanas and the Kshatriyas over the lower castes. For instance, the *Purusha-sukta* of the *Rigveda* narrates how the four castes emanated from Purusha, the highest deity - the Brahmana from his mouth, the Kshatriya from his arms, the Vaisya from his loins, and the Sudra from his feet. Even in later times, the gods would continue to fulfill their function as the guardians of the interests of the dominant race and castes. In the *Bhagavat-gita*, Lord Krishna claims to have himself founded the caste system. The bias in favour of the upper castes may be seen also in the way of salvation propounded in the Upanishadic writings, which consisted of gnosis i.e. in the knowledge that one's deepest self (*Atman*) is identical with the Absolute (*Brahman*). But to attain that knowledge, one must study the *Vedas*, and, significantly, the study of the *Vedas* was forbidden to the lowest caste, the Sudras. They could attain salvation only through the performance of menial service to the higher castes.

The attempt of the dominant castes to impose on others a social and cultural unity on terms suited to maintain their hegemony provoked a protest from the dominated castes and tribes, a protest spearheaded by Jainism and Buddhism around the 6th century B. C. From out of the struggle between Vedic religion and these heterodox religions, there arose the Hinduism of today. The emergent Hindu orthodoxy continued the policy which Vedic Arians had initiated of bringing about unity through domination. In this, it was greatly helped by the patronage of the Hindu kings of the Gupta period (319-540). The means it employed may be grouped under the following heads:

1. *Elimination by use of force.* Orthodox Hinduism colluded with the rulers that were to wipe out the religions of the dominated classes. Buddhists and Jains were persecuted. Buddhist viharas were demolished and looted. There is evidence to show that in the 6th century A. D. about eight hundred Tamil Jains were put to death by militant Hindus.

2. *Co-optation*: The social integration achieved through the caste system was reinforced by the co-optation of alien gods and goddesses into the traditional Pantheon. Krishna of popular religion was identified with Vishnu and Siva with Rudra. Just as the lower castes were made to serve the upper castes, the gods of the former were made servants

of the higher gods. Thus Hanuman, the monkey-god, was made a servant of Rama; Nandi, the Bull, became the beast of transportation of Rudra-Siva; the Cobra, till then an independent object of popular worship, became Vishnu's bed. Similarly, the female deities of the subjugated matriarchal tribes were married to the male deities of the Hindu pantheon.

3. *Religious legislation*: The most powerful weapon orthodoxy fashioned to enslave the minds and hearts of the common people was the religio-legal code devised by Manu. It re-affirmed the sacred origin of the caste system, conferred economic and social privileges on the Brahmanas and the Kshatriyas, stabilized the system of ritual purity, thus degrading millions to the position of untouchables and outcastes.

4. *Marginalization.* Such tribes and communities as refused to be integrated into Hindu society were relegated to a position inferior to that of even the lowest castes and were socially and ritually discriminated against. Marginalization was itself a way of ensuring the all-inclusive unity of the social organism.

The search for a Hindu *oikoumene* based on institutionalized injustice and inequality reached a new stage of intensity with the advent of colonialism. The colonizers bolstered up the power of the dominant castes by conferring on them absolute property rights. With the connivance of the rulers, orthodox Hindus started Hinduizing the tribals all over India. Their attempt met with greater success in southern India than in the north where the indigenous tribes, by and large, managed to maintain their cultural identity. The policy of Hinduization has, in part, a reaction to Christian missions, aimed as it was at preventing the tribals and the outcastes from joining the Christian fold. However, with Independence and the formation of a secular State, militant Hinduization was all but given up. Nor was it any longer needed. The subaltern castes had so internalized the values of their masters that they began on their own to assimilate the habits and practices of the latter as a means of improving their social status. This process, however, has in recent years slowed down, thanks to the spread of capitalist culture.

Hindu militancy is still very much alive in contemporary India. The threat from the economic power of the Christian churches, the new forms of upward and downward social mobility induced by money economy, the secularization of economic and political life, and the impact of Marxism on the Hindu intelligentsia: all this has put the majority community on the defensive. And this defensiveness has taken the form of a concerted offensive whose goal is the creation of a theocratic Hindu nation that would marginate the followers of other religions into aliens.

Christian Ecumenism: An Ideology of Conquest?

Paradoxically, Christianity which proclaims the equality of all human beings came to India with its own project of domination. The advent of European Christianity on the Indian soil coincided with colonialism, which itself was largely determined by the requirements of mercantile and industrial capitalism. And imperialism is essentially an attempt at establishing a political *oikoumene* using the sword. It is not by accident that Christianity of the colonial period manifested tendencies which smacked of cultural imperialism. True, it did not resort to the use of force either to take root in India or to expand its fold. But it had developed a theology of ideological domination. Particularly relevant here is the theory and practice of conversion prevalent in the churches till recently. It had for its premise the belief that those outside the Church cannot reach salvation. It divided mankind into the spiritually privileged and the spiritually disprivileged and made a virtue out of ideological violence against the latter. Just as the colonial capitalist saw in the produces of India so much raw material to be transformed into finished products, just as the imperialist rulers saw in the native rulers so many centres of power to be conquered, so, too, the churches looked upon non-Christians as but human raw materials to be converted into members of her own fold. Understandably, during this period it was the image of 'Christ the King' that occupied the centre of Christian consciousness and piety.

Dogma, cult, and religious law as they developed in the West were made normative not only for Christians but also for non-Christians if these wished to be saved. In short, Christianity entertained the dream of a unity of faith for the people of India according to patterns it imported from abroad. In essence, therefore, what it envisaged differed little from the ecumenism of domination pursued by the dominant castes in India. What is worse, the Christian pursuit of unity tended to reinforce the colonial rule. Nehru was not entirely wrong when in his Autobiography he accused the churches of having "served the purpose of British imperialism and given capitalism a Christian covering". With the collapse of colonial rule, a new relationship continued whether through unfair trade relations or through International organizations like the World Bank. With this, there came about a change in the attitude of Christianity to people of other religions persuasions. The theory and practice of conversion were all but abandoned. Christians reconciled themselves to the prospect of having to live with people of other religions for ages to come. However, this did not amount to a renunciation of the Christian ecumenism of conquest. For, there arose a new theology which sought to achieve theologically what the policy of conversion sought to achieve in practice, namely, the Christianization of the world. It 'baptized' all men and women of goodwill of other religions as 'anonymous Christians'. While it recognized that the followers of other faiths can be saved, it hastened to add that such salvation as was gained by them was due to the fact of the Church existing as the sacrament of universal salvation. In tune with this development, the image of 'Christ the King' was replaced by that of the 'Cosmic Christ' presiding over the destiny of all nations and cultures. Christians could thus nurse the comforting illusion that they are the nerve-center of an invisible spiritual empire encompassing the entire universe. They could maintain their privileged position while, at the same time, being a permanent minority. In reality, this kind of Christian self-awareness and the theology corresponding to it constitute a way of preemptively annexing the non-Christian world to the Christian domain and, for that reason, are forms of covert ideological imperialism.

Church Unity — for What?

The period of competitive capitalism saw the various Christian denominations pitted against one another, each claiming to establish its own *oikoumene*. Under such conditions, their unity could not have become a live issue. But competitive capitalism has since given way to monopoly and multinational capitalism based on the co-ordinated sharing of raw materials and markets. Similarly, on the political level, the industrialized nations have learned to work together in exploiting their own labour and the labour of developing countries. I suggest that this has created a climate favourable to efforts towards the unity of churches. No wonder, the movement for Christian unity originated in the West and only subsequently became an issue in the peripheral countries like India. How are we to evaluate this new development?

If the ecumenism, pursued by the individual churches, is one of domination, their unity can only reinforce that domination. A unified front of ideological aggression on the part of Christianity will be seen as a much greater threat by non-Christians who wish to maintain their own religious identity than the existence of churches at variance with one another. Furthermore, where the churches are in league with the exploiting classes, their unity will render the necessary structural changes all the more difficult. This is particularly true of India where the church leadership, on the whole, tends to support whoever happens to be in power.

Certain conclusions follow from our discussions thus far:

1. All ecumenism of domination whether through force, co-option or marginalization denies the equality of all humans as children of God, and, as such, should be eliminated.

2. Church unity within the framework of a theology of domination and of alignment with the ruling classes will only serve to accentuate the disunity and conflict already existing in society.

3. There is, therefore, a need to look for a new basis for the unity of the churches. What is that new basis? And what is the ecumenical practice it calls for?

The Ecumenical Perspective of Jesus

The new basis, we are looking for, finds its clearest expression in Jesus' message of the reign of God. His concern was not founding a community with himself as its centre but the realization of a universal humanity centred upon the God who comes and becomes in history. He looked forward to a new age of freedom in which the poor will possess the earth, in which justice and love will bind all men and women into an abiding communion. In the age to come, neither ideology nor power nor wealth will fragment the human community; not ideology, because humans will have seen God and in seeing Him discovered their true visage and that of their fellow humans; not power, because it will have given way to service; not wealth, because there will no more be exploitation. Jesus spoke of the new age in symbolic language as a festal meal where people will come from east and west and sit at the table with Abraham, Isaac, and Jacob, thus forming an all-encompassing togetherness of nations, peoples, and cultures.

Membership in the new humanity will be determined on the basis not of adherence to any set of dogmas, cultic practices, or religious laws but of doing the will of God which consists of loving one's neighbour. Significantly, the Jesus of the Synoptic Gospels never required faith in him as a prerequisite for belonging to the reign of God. What he instead enjoined on his hearers was faith in God, faith as a creative response to His beckoning presence in history. There is, therefore, nothing sectarian about his project of an *oikoumene* of freedom. That is why commitment to it can provide a new basis for the unity not only of churches but also of different religions. This Jesuan approach calls for a radically new theory and practice of ecumenism.

Liberative Ecumenism

To begin with, let me state first in what liberative ecumenism does not consist. It does not consist in merely carrying on dialogue at the theoretical level between theologians of different religious persuasions. Such dialogue can only have a marginal value so long as the deeper causes of conflict are not eliminated. Nor can an *oikoumene* of freedom be established through the conversion of all men and women to any one faith, whether Christian, Hindu, or Muslim. For, all peoples have the right to maintain each the specificity of its own experience of God. What genuine ecumenism demands is the conversion of all religions and peoples to God, to the God who confronts man in history with His unconditional demands. Conversion in this sense does not presuppose the superiority of any one culture over the others or of any religion over other religions since people of all religions and cultures need being inwardly purified and transformed by the spirit of God that renews the face of the earth. What superiority any religion may have must be measured in terms of its capacity to change the world in response to the ever new challenges of God mediated through history. Further, the conversion to God, we are advocating, will not level down all differences nor impose any sterile uniformity on all. What it will achieve is unity in diversity: unity, because it is the same Spirit that takes hold of all humans; diversity, because both the divine challenge and the human response will be clothed in different religio-cultural traditions.

Conversion unto God means further that we let ourselves be taken hold of by his Spirit so that in the strength of the same Spirit we preach the good news to the poor, release to captives, and give sight to the blind. This means waging a relentless struggle against all forces — economic, political, and cultural — that cripple life. Only through such struggle can liberative ecumenism be realized. Understandably, the agent of struggle cannot be any closed Christian community. The means must conform to the end. The all-inclusiveness of the new humanity envisioned must be reflected in the local communities of struggle. These must consist of men and women of different religions and cultural traditions but united on the common basis of overcoming all social and cultural antagonisms. It is encouraging to note that such truly ecumenical communities are already springing up in different parts of India. They need to be linked up with similar groups in other parts of the world so that a broad international front is created for global collective action.

Conclusion

The participation of Christians in the struggle for unity in the sense explained above will have profound repercussions on their faith and practice. Let me enumerate some of them:

1. A new theology will emerge which focuses not on tradition but on God encountered in history. In so far as this encounter involves both the divine challenge and the human response, theology will become the articulation of ecumenical praxis.

2. Since the divine challenge in any one country will be basically the same for all its people, theological reflection carried on in the context of different religio-cultural traditions will tend to converge.

3. The new theology will recapture the original perspective of Jesus centered upon the reign of God. It will thus rejoin prophecy to become a world-transforming force. Purely academic, conceptual theology will be left behind once and for all.

4. The dominant image that will shape specifically Christian consciousness will be neither 'Christ the King' nor the 'Cosmic Christ' but 'Jesus the Prophet and Servant of Jahweh'.

5. In the measure in which Christians creatively respond to the ever new challenges of the living God, they will realize that He cannot be housed in dead concepts inherited from the past. The new wine will burst the old wineskins of dogma and tradition. With that, an important barrier that separates the various Christian denominations will have fallen to the ground.

6. The community in which Christians will have to insert themselves to work for the *oikoumene* of freedom will be modeled not on the Parish but on Jesus' table fellowship with social outcasts. In other words, it will be a community open to all who are open to the new age to come.

7. Finally, as popular struggles for the socialization of wealth gather momentum, the churches will be forced to sever their links with the ruling classes and once again become capable of the divine option in favour of the poor. Similarly, the demand for people's control over all levels of decision making will initiate a process within the churches in the direction of ever greater decentralization and democratization. Freed from conflicting socio-economic vested interests, the churches will find it easier to achieve unity among themselves.

(Paper read at the International Congress of Jesuit Ecumenists held in Barcelona, September 1979; Jeevadhara, May-June 1980, No. 57, pp. 217-29)

6

Church, Liberation Theology and Marxism

I

The Second Vatican Council marked a turning point in the history of the Catholic Church. It set in motion a process of self-criticism accompanied by an openness to other churches, religions, and to secular society in general. It initiated a quest for Christian relevance in the contemporary world. A significant outcome of it has been the Theology of Liberation. The official Church now sees in the new theology "the practical negation" of its faith. This means Christianity has arrived at a critical stage where orthodoxy may be said to have begotten its own opposite. But beneath the opposition, there is also a certain unity. This is clear from the fact that the Theologians of Liberation now under attack are still seen by the Church as coming within its pale. It is in this context of the unity and struggle of opposites that we must situate the "Instruction on Certain Aspects of the Theology of Liberation" issued by the Sacred Congregation for the Doctrine of Faith (henceforth, SC). (First published in Vaidikamitram, Pattanakad, Vol. 18, No. 4, Apr. 1, 1988; reprinted in International Communications Quarterly, Bruxelles, June 1985, No. 34.)

From the Standpoint of the Kingdom

In order to evaluate the Document, we need a correct standpoint which cannot be that of the SC itself. History shows that the official Church has gone wrong in the past and was forced to retract what it had earlier taught as in the case of withholding the Bible from the laity, the legitimization of colonialism, the condemnation of democracy, and so on. Nor may we assess the Instruction from the standpoint of an uncritical acceptance of Liberation Theologies, since these too may propound ideas which may have to be eventually discarded. The point of view, we adopt, must be one whose validity will not be questioned either by the official Church or by Liberation Theologians. That, in my view, is provided by Jesus' message of the kingdom of God. It involves, in fact, a bifocal criterion: one looking to the past, to the life and teaching of Jesus; the other to the future, to the God who comes in history. Hence the relevant question is: How far does the position of the SC and the Theologies of Liberation conform to Jesus' message and to the divine challenges vehicled through our historical situation? Before we tackle this important question it is necessary to make a detour and discuss at some length the Vatican view of Marxism and its impact on Liberation Theologies.

The Bogy of Marxism

The SC does not censure all Liberation Theologies but only such as propose "a novel interpretation of both the content of faith and Christian existence which seriously departs from the faith of the Church" (6:9). It goes on to allege that the departure from orthodoxy is the result of an "uncritical borrowing of Marxist ideology"(6:10). There is here an implicit recognition that a critical use of Marxism is legitimate, which makes sense only if Marxism also contains valid insights. But what is granted with one hand is taken away with the other. For, in the subsequent analysis, the document says that "atheism and the denial of the human person, his liberty and his rights are at the core of the Marxist theory" (7:9). Clearly, one cannot critically use a theory that denies the human person, particularly so when that theory forms "an epistemologically unique complex" so that if one tries to take only one part, say the analysis, one ends up having to accept the entire ideology (7:6). Thus, in effect, any, even critical, use of Marxism is ruled out. It is this position of the document which needs to be called in question as it preempts all dialogue with Marxism.

Let me begin with a general observation. In one sense, the document gives Marxism more credit than is due in so far as the latter is presented as a unified whole whose parts hang together. This is largely true of the Soviet version of Marxism which is Marxism congealed into a dogmatic system. But it is not true of the writings of Marx, Engels, or Lenin. In them, we find varying stresses, approaches, and formulations, which have not fused into a synthesis. They contain insights fully worked out along with others whose implications are left unexplored. This leaves room for varied, if not conflicting, interpretations. The Instruction addresses itself to one such interpretation recognized as the orthodox one and equates it with Marxism as such. In what follows, I shall show that a more sympathetic and synthetic approach gives us a Marxism that is at once in harmony with the message of Jesus and with the contemporary challenge of radical social reconstruction.

Marxism — a Pseudo-science?

Marxism is charged with subverting the very notion of truth in so far as it holds that there is no truth "except in and through partisan *praxis*"(8:4). As far as Marx is concerned, the charge is absolutely unfounded. To understand why we must reflect on his concept of the relation between theory and practice.

The crucial term is '*praxis*'. Marx uses the term in a twofold sense. In the broader sense, it means man's sensuous experience of, or encounter with, the world.[1] By sense experience, he means not only the activity of the five senses but also the perception of reality through what he called 'the practical senses' like willing and acting.[2] He argued that all genuine thought must originate in, and be tested against, sense perception: "Sense experience must be the basis of all science"[3] In this perspective, neither *praxis* nor the theory emerging from it is partisan, as both are accessible to all human beings. Here Marx's position is in continuity with the entire philosophical tradition from Aristotle to Hegel.

In the narrower sense, *praxis* means revolutionary or "critical-practical activity."[4] It is that activity which, on the basis of a critical understanding of reality, aims at transforming the human subjects. It brings about the transition from *what is* to *what ought to be*. And the full truth of anything that exists is *what it is meant to become*. Seen from this angle, the truth of the present society is the classless society of the future, just as, for the Christian, the truth of the world is the kingdom of God. This is ontological truth consisting of the conformity of *what is* to *what ought to be*. In relation to *praxis* as critical activity, a theory is true in so far as it reflects reality both in its being and its becoming and is itself a factor contributing to the transition from the *is* to the *ought to be*. Put differently, a theory is true in as much as it helps society unfold its authentic possibilities and become ever more human. From this, it also follows that only those can arrive at a correct theory of society who are themselves involved in the task of humanizing the world. Those others who are sitting on the sidelines of history without engaging themselves in the struggle for a better world have no access to the complete truth about man and history. Hence the saying of Marx that "true practice is the condition of a real and positive theory."[5] The truth that derives from the struggle for humanizing the world and must be tested on the basis of the same struggle is not the logical truth of the natural sciences but the truth of the theory of revolution.

If so, the SC is wrong when it attributes to Marxism the notion that there is no truth except in and through partisan praxis. The truth born of sensuous encounter with the world is accessible to all people. What mere sensuous perception cannot give is the true theory of revolution which can only arise from revolutionary practice. But according to the founders of Marxism, revolutionary consciousness is not the exclusive prerogative of the working class.[6] In fact, Lenin would go to the extent of saying that, left to itself, the proletariat can only arrive at mere trade-union consciousness and that it has to learn revolutionary consciousness from an outside source, namely, the Party.[7]

No less unfair is the criticism raised by the SC that Marxism acts as a predetermining principle that distorts the analysis of social reality. On the contrary, it is central to the teaching of Marx that theory must constantly be revised in the light of practice. In its original thrust, Marxism is essentially anti-dogmatic. However, it must be admitted that the kind of Marxism held by the Communist Parties is dogmatic and tends to fit social reality to a preconceived system. Among orthodox Marxists, there is also the tendency to nurse the illusion that the Proletariat and its vanguard, the Party, have the monopoly of truth. This does not prevent the Theologians of Liberation from making their own Marx's profound insights into the relation between theory and practice.

Is Marxism Reductionist?

According to the Vatican document, Marxism teaches "the fundamental law of class struggle" which has a "global and universal character" and, consequently, denies the autonomy of other spheres of life like the religious, the ethical, the cultural, and the aesthetic. The target of the attack here is the materialist conception of history. Here the SC is on surer ground though its own approach is reductionist. It reduces the many formulations of the materialistic conception of history found in the Marxist tradition to the one centering upon class struggle. The more important formulations in this regard may be briefly stated as follows:

1. Being (equated with social existence) determines consciousness.

2. The base (the economic structure comprising both productive forces and relations of production) determines the superstructure.

3. Class struggle (within the relations of production) determines the superstructure.

4. Productive forces determine the superstructure.

5. The law of development of matter determines consciousness and society.

The first formulation is free of all reductionism. It embodies the fundamental insight that human beings do not think in a vacuum but in a specific historical context of economic, political, and cultural relations. This applies also to religions and to their founders. The next three formulations, also found in the works of Marx, are guilty of a certain reductionism when seen in isolation from the overall context of his philosophy, in as much as superstructural realities like religion, ethics, philosophy, and art are presented not only as determined by, but also as derived from the economic base. Such formulations must be seen as partial formulations of the materialist conception of history which, however, can serve as heuristic tools for the analysis of society. For, though religion, ethics, and the like are not derivative but original dimensions of societal life, there is no doubt that they are in various ways and varying degrees shaped by economic life. It must also be borne in mind that Marx admitted that, once arisen, the realities of the superstructure can exercise a determining influence on the economic base.[8] If so, in any social system, the base which determines the superstructure is itself already determined by the superstructure. As for the fifth formulation in our enumeration, it derives not from Marx but from Engels and in course of time became the cornerstone of Marxist orthodoxy. To say that the law of development of matter determines consciousness is to reduce Marxism to a form of crass materialism that Karl Marx would surely have repudiated. For, he qualified his philosophy not as materialism but as a synthesis of materialism and idealism[9] or more aptly, as 'complete humanism.'[10]

It follows from this analysis that the SC has simplified the materialistic conception of history in order the more easily to explode it. For, it knows very well that by recognizing the historically conditioned character of cultural institutions as is demanded by the materialist conception of history it would be undermining the eternal validity it claims for many of its own doctrines and practices.

The Person Sacrificed to the Collectivity?

The Instruction alleges that Marxism misunderstands "the spiritual nature of the person" and subordinates him to the collectivity (7:9). What does "the spiritual nature of the person" mean here? In the same context, there is a question of the eternal destiny of the individual. This would suggest that the spirituality of the person is understood in terms of the immortality of the soul. If so, the SC is thinking in the categories of the Greek dualism of body and soul, which cannot be philosophically justified. Besides, such dualism is foreign to the Hebrew mode of thought which Jesus shared. If, on the contrary, the spirituality of man is understood to consist, as it should be, in his capacity to constantly transcend himself in virtue of consciousness and freedom, Marx cannot be faulted with denying the spiritual nature of the person. In the first volume of *Capital*, he argues in so many words that what distinguishes man from animals is his ability to surpass himself by projecting ever new models in imagination and realizing them in practice.[11]

Elsewhere in the document, it is objected that the practice of class struggle slowly leads to a totalitarian society (7:7), which, by definition, reduces the individual to brute collectivity, thereby denying his spiritual nature. But there is no necessary causal link between class struggle and totalitarianism. Marx, Engels, and Lenin envisioned the outcome of the proletarian revolution after the manner of the Paris Commune, characterized by devolution of power, the primacy of direct over indirect democracy, the revocability of elected representatives, and the replacing of the standing army with a people's militia.[12] This, indeed, is a far cry from the feared subordination of the individual to the collectivity. If subsequently, what came into being under Stalin turned out to be not the dictatorship of the proletariat over a recalcitrant minority of the bourgeoisie, but the dictatorship of the Party over the proletariat, it was due to factors not inherent in the concept of class struggle. The revolution took place under the conditions of the cultural backwardness of the Soviet people and the exigencies of primitive "socialist accumulation in a period of scarcity and famine, and the Leninist concept of the Party as the sole bearer of revolutionary theory."[13] Therefore, to state that class struggle necessarily leads to totalitarianism is as preposterous as claiming that Crusades, witch hunting, and the Inquisition are essential to Christianity.

However, the Vatican document serves a useful purpose in so far as it puts Christians on guard against uncritically swallowing the line of such Communist Parties as justifying the Stalinist version of the Dictatorship of the Proletariat.

Is Marxism Subversive of Ethics?

The SC is convinced that class struggle radically calls in question the very nature of ethics because it denies the transcendent character of the distinction between good and evil. The argument is not valid. What Marx criticized away was not ethics in general but the bourgeois ethics of private property, private interest, competition, and consumerism. Though he did not elaborate on a theory of ethics, the ethical motive is central to his vision of man and society. His prime concern was to highlight the alienating, dehumanizing character of capitalism. And, for him, the recognition of alienation carried with it the "categorical imperative"[14] to overcome it and create a new society of free and fully developed individuals. This new society he called, interchangeably, socialism, or communism. And whatever contributes to the creation of such a society cannot but be moral. Such, pre-eminently, is class struggle. Here it must be kept in mind that, in the Marxian perspective, there is no absolute discontinuity between the end (classless society) and the means (class struggle). Marx saw clearly that "nothing emerges at the end of a process which was not already in its beginning"[15] A class struggle which devalues human beings cannot usher in a humanized social order. It is when the final goal of a classless society is lost sight of and its place taken by immediate, limited goals like electoral gains that class struggle resorts to opportunism, thus sacrificing its ethical integrity. This is just what is happening to the Communist Parties in India.

Nor can Marxism be called unethical for the reason that the class struggle it advocates involves violence. The aim of class struggle is not the physical elimination of the bourgeoisie but the overthrow of the capitalist system. And the capitalist system dehumanizes not only the working class but also their employers. Hence the goal of revolution is the liberation of both capital and labour. Marx wrote:

> "From the relation of alienated labour to private property it also follows that the emancipation of society from private property, from servitude, takes the political form of the emancipation of workers; not in the sense that only the latter's emancipation is involved, but because this emancipation includes the emancipation of humanity as a whole."[16]

And what is seeking the good of humanity as a whole but universal love.

Quite in keeping with this was the position Marx took on recourse to terrorism as a means to revolution. He saw in terrorism the deluded attempt of an impatient minority to bring about a political revolution through conspiratorial methods before the preconditions for revolution have matured. He had only contempt for those who "throw themselves on discoveries which would work revolutionary wonders: incendiary bombs, hell machines of magical impact, emeutes which ought to be the more wonder-working and sudden the less they have any rational ground"[17] In the same vein wrote Engels:

> "Terror implies mostly useless cruelties perpetrated by frightened people in order to reassure themselves"[18]

This does not mean that Marx and Engels ruled out violence under all circumstances or that they posed the problem in ethical terms. Their view of the matter may be summed up thus: Where the conditions for revolution have been realized, violence is superfluous; where they have not been realized, it is useless. If nevertheless, the class struggle came to be associated with violence, it is due to the peculiar course taken by the revolution in countries like the Soviet Union.

The Stumbling-block of Atheism

The Instruction is right in qualifying Marxism as atheistic. Marx rejects the notion of God as "an alien being, a being above man and nature" who determines human destiny from outside, as such a belief, he thought, is irreconcilable with the freedom of man. He wrote,

> "A being does not regard himself as independent unless he is his own master, and he is only his own master when he owes his existence to himself. A man who lives by the favour of another considers himself a dependent being. But I live completely by another person's favour when I owe him not only the continuance of my life but also my creation; when he is its source."[19]

Here the denial of God has for its reverse side the affirmation of the human. What Marx repudiates is the prevailing Lutheran conception of God as one before whom man sinks to the level of an object, being without freedom and creativity. Such a conception needs to be repudiated. However, it would be incorrect to say that Marx denied only an inadequate conception of God and not the Divine as such. For, the essence of his atheism is to be found not so much in his denial of God as in his affirmation of the total immanence or self-sufficiency of man.

At the same time, Marx admitted that the total immanence of man is contradicted by practical experience which shows him alienated, fragmented, a mere creature of circumstances over which he has no control. Hence man's absolute self-sufficiency remains an ideal project yet to be accomplished. Will the project be realized with the proletarian revolution? Not yet. Revolution will end only the pre-history of man and inaugurate his true history. If so, the post-revolutionary man will still be in search of total immanence. And the search will have no end, since history, for Marx, has no end. But what is that total immanence man will be striving after? It consists in his being the ultimate ground and maker of himself and the world, in other words, in being or becoming God. The Divine thus reappears from out of the wasteland of Marxian atheism, this time as an ever-receding horizon. Does not Marx here, in a sense, rejoin Christians who too believe in the divinization of man, knowing full well that the human will never coincide with the Divine?

Further, is not the atheism of Marx closer to Christianity than the theism of many who surrender their freedom to a "God above man and nature"?[20]

The foregoing reflections show that, far from denying the human, the philosophy of Marx provides insights indispensable for the creation of a more humane world. Therefore, no Theologian of Liberation can ignore it without condemning himself to historical irrelevance.

II

From Prophecy to Orthodoxy

The main thrust of the Vatican document is that Liberation Theologies, in practice, negate the faith of the Church. It would be interesting to enquire as to which theologians have deviated from orthodoxy and how far such deviation is due to the influence of Marxism. But that is not my purpose here. I shall instead argue that orthodoxy itself is a product of history and, as such, is ambivalent. Orthodoxy contains both truth and falsehood, faith, and ideology. Therefore, any criticism of Liberation Theologies from the standpoint of a blind and unconditional submission to orthodoxy is itself vitiated.

In its origin, Christianity was a prophetic movement grounded in Jesus' message of the reign of God as mankind's absolute future when man will be reconciled with nature (The poor shall possess the earth), with his fellowmen (You shall be brothers to one another) with God (You shall be sons of God), and with himself (You shall be comforted). The earliest disciples, if not also Jesus, believed in the imminent coming of the Kingdom. But Jesus was done to death, and the hoped-for Kingdom did not come. The world remained much the same as before. This created a crisis of faith among believers. The 'cognitive dissonance' between faith and reality, between hope and fulfillment, had to be solved. This called for a reinterpretation of the faith. One interpretation that came to stay was that the Kingdom had already come in the person of Jesus and was present in the community of his disciples, the Church. With this, the focus of belief was shifted from the future to the past. The God-ahead gave way to the God-above as conceived in traditional non-prophetic religions. The faith of Jesus in the reign of God to come was replaced by faith in Jesus as the bearer of the fullness of revelation and grace.

How then to reconcile the presence of the Kingdom with the existence of division, inequality, and injustice in the world? The answer took the form of spiritualizing the notion of the Kingdom, thereby removing it from the sphere of verification in practice and transferring it to the meta-historical plane. This made it possible for the Apostle Paul to argue that in Christ, that is, on the spiritual plane, there is neither Greek nor Jew, neither slave nor master, neither male nor female, though in reality social discrimination based on such distinctions persisted. Thus came into prominence the kind of dualistic thinking which delights in the opposition between the temporal and the eternal, the spiritual, the profane, and the sacred.

This entire development has had fateful consequences for the subsequent history of the Jesus movement:

1. Once it is assumed that in Jesus God has already come and uttered his last word, He becomes superfluous and can as well retire from the scene, leaving his word to his vicegerents to be interpreted and passed on from generation to generation. In the process, God is reduced to a speechless idol fit only to be washed, anointed, and worshipped.

2. For the same reason, history ceases to reverberate with the voice of God, of the God who confronts, challenges, promises, and judges. Henceforth whoever wants to listen to God must retrace his steps from the profane world and approach the teaching and saving authority of the Church. Thus arose an accredited few who expropriated the masses of all access to the Divine in order to concentrate it in their own hands. The process may be called primary religious accumulation.

3. It was through an act of violence that the God who spoke to our fathers in many and varied fashions was silenced. And violence

has been at work in all subsequent theologizing. Theologians would try their hand at dissecting the very Being of God, reducing it to manageable concepts that can be conveniently tabulated, pigeonholed, and computerized. Thus transformed into eternal and immutable essences, the Divine was further removed from the everyday world of change and turmoil.and from the common man's sphere of intelligibility. This made it all the easier for the teaching Caste to maintain its monopoly of 'saving' truth.

4.   Once tamed, the Divine could easily be made a silent witness and legitimizer of man's mastery over man. The quest after union with God could, from now on, go hand in hand with the quest after Money and Power. No wonder the ecclesiastical bureaucracy has a vested interest in perpetuating the status quo of traditional theology.

Orthodoxy Challenged

From the very outset, orthodoxy contained the seeds of its own dissolution in the Bible which it could not do away with. No wonder, for centuries it forbade lay persons from reading it. But that policy had to be given up. With the spread of literacy and the advance made in printing technology, the common man and woman were able to read the Bible and encounter in it the person of Jesus and his radical message. The emergence of Liberation Theology marks the re-discovery of the prophet from Nazareth. It signals, so to speak, Jesus' penultimate coming in our midst. As of old, he is now pointing to the God ahead, to the living God who calls all human beings to the decision in favour of His reign to come. This has cut the ground from under the feet of the guardians of orthodoxy who claim to be the sole interpreters of God's word.

It is but natural that Marxism should act as a catalyst in the resurgence of prophecy. At a time when prophecy had all but been swallowed up by the Institution, it was Marxism that, in the tradition of the dissenting Christian sects of earlier times, kept alive the Judaeo-Christian hope in the new age of equality, freedom and universal love. This it could do because it was itself an offshoot of Christianity. It was a Christian Utopian association called the League of the Just which eventually became the First Communist International.

Besides, many Christian themes had entered into the texture of Marxism from the philosophy of Hegel and from French socialist thinkers like Saint Simon and Fourier. That is why, of all philosophical traditions, Marxism is the one that comes closest to Jesus' vision of man and history. Marxism also provides the re-emerging Christian prophetism with the theoretical tools to translate itself into historical practice.

The challenge to orthodoxy comes not only from the Bible and Marxism but also from the civilizational crisis described in chapter three. Briefly, due to the progress of science and technology, the notion of an over-world of gods and goddesses has been robbed of any basis in the self-awareness and world-awareness of contemporary humans who are thrown back on themselves to seek the Divine in their own history. At the same time, the awareness that social and political institutions are not God-ordained realities but human creations has given rise to movements for the democratization of institutions, the overthrow of despotic regimes, and the elimination of imperialism. All monopoly of wealth, power, and ideas is being called in question; so too every monarchical concentration of religious power.

We are, in fact, witnessing the birth of a new world and a new genre of religiosity. In this crisis of planetary proportions, the Theologies of Liberation and the Marxian vision of the Total Man are on the side of the emergent, creative forces, and Christian orthodoxy as reflected in the Vatican document on the side of the decaying forces. Those comfortably seated on the Rock of Peter are now awakening to the disturbing realization that the Rock is falling apart and dissolving in the onward rush of a world in total transformation. Seen from this angle, what the SC propounds through the Instruction is an interim theology of survival and self-defense. It is a product of the fear of its losing its hitherto unchallenged monopoly of religious power. The fulminations against Liberation Theologies also serve the useful purpose of diverting public attention from the urgent need for radical self-criticism and renewal within the Church.

In explaining the historical context of the Instruction, I have already exposed its inherent weakness. Nevertheless, it is worth-while responding to some of the specific criticisms leveled against the new thinking in the Church. Here, too, my aim is not to defend any brand of Liberation Theology developed elsewhere but to show how any theologian who concerns himself with the total liberation of man should react to such criticism if directed against him.

III

Orthodoxy versus Orthopraxis

It is alleged that Liberation Theologians set up, in the place of orthodoxy, revolutionary *praxis* as the supreme criterion of truth (10:3). I have already called in question the notion of orthodoxy defined as the rule or official interpretation of faith since it has itself been shaped by socio-cultural conditions. The truth of orthodoxy needs to be tested against a more fundamental criterion, which can only be faith as man's response to the God who unveils himself in contemporary history. The rule of faith must be judged by faith by the rule. But to respond to the self-revelation of God in history is to accept his call to march to the realm of total freedom. Therefore, the struggle for freedom from every alienation is faith become subversive-constructive *praxis*. In this sense, revolutionary *praxis* is the privileged source and norm of theological truth. This does not mean that the teaching authority of the Church is barred from truth. In the measure in which it is responsive to the voice of the living God, its directives are relevant; as is the case when the present Instruction calls upon pastors to accord the highest priority to the struggle for justice.

Immanence versus Transcendence

Liberation Theologies are charged with absorbing the sacred history and reducing the kingdom of God to an earthly kingdom. As was shown earlier, the dualism of the sacred and the profane, the spiritual and the material, was resorted to, in order to reconcile the presence of the Kingdom with the persistence of evil in the world. But this way of looking at the reign of God has no basis in the Old or New Testament. For the Hebrews, Yahweh was one who revealed himself in the history of his people. Jesus, too, saw the coming of the Kingdom in concrete historical events as when, at his bidding, the blind saw, the deaf heard, the mute spoke, the lame walked and the dead rose to new life. Similarly, he hoped the Kingdom would usher in a new state of affairs within our history, one in which the poor will take possession of the earth, prison-houses will be pulled down and the captives let free. This must be seen against the background of his explicit repudiation of the current categorization of things, actions, and persons in terms of the pure and the impure (Mk. 7). If so, Liberation Theology is doing nothing more than returning to the original perspective of Jesus in which the saving dialogue between man and God takes place within our one and only history. This is not reducing faith to 'fidelity to history' as the Instruction alleges. For Liberation Theology, faith is fidelity to God revealing himself in history. What it denies is transcendence above the world not the transcendence of the world.

If nevertheless, the official Church clings on to the obsolete dualism of the sacred and the profane, of the material and the spiritual, it is because it finds in it the basis of its own survival. Just as physicians cannot survive without the sick, lawyers without criminals, and social workers without the destitute, so also the Sacred Office in the Church cannot survive without a profane, Godless world. What need is there for monarchic mediators of truth and grace if ordinary men and women have direct access to God in the heart of their own history? Dualistic Theology also helped the Church absolve itself of the obligation to oppose unjust social and political institutions. If master and slave can be equal 'in Christ' without ceasing to be unequal in real life, what urgency is there in overthrowing the system of slavery? The same theology enabled Church leaders to make the best of both worlds. They could in good conscience pursue wealth, power, and prestige on the ground that the profane must be subject to the sacred, the temporal to the eternal, the material to the spiritual. This is how the subversive faith of Jesus became an ideology of the status quo.

Christ of Faith versus Jesus of History

Now to come to the allegation that Liberation Theologians oppose Jesus of history to the Jesus of faith and that they deny traditional Christology. If all genuine theology must proceed from the assumption that it is in history that human beings encounter the Divine, it is crucial to find out what Jesus as a member of the family of man believed in and hoped for and how he translated that belief and hope into practice. If there is an irruption of the Divine in and through him, it must be discovered in what he actually said and did. To what he said and did his disciples responded in faith. And their faith itself was an interpretation. Nor was that interpretation uniform. In the New Testament, one finds diverging interpretations of the Jesus-phenomenon, reflecting the differences in the life-situation of the early Christian communities. Hence it is important to distinguish between what Jesus was, said, and did, and what the local communities believed he was, said, and did. The theologian of Liberation anchors himself in the actual message and practice of Jesus because he finds in it a historical step forward in mankind's search for freedom from every form of human servitude, one that is at the same time consonant with God's call to freedom in his contemporary situation. This by no means implies that he denies all subsequent interpretations. These he would subject to a stringent criticism to find out how far they are true to the authentic message of Jesus or deviate from it. Because even believing interpretations are shaped by the socio-cultural conditions prevailing at any given time and for that reason may throw a veil over or even distort the original data. The same sort of criticism the theologian should extend to the interpretations of interpretations which in course of time crystallized into dogma and traditional theology. If this is taken exception to the SC, could it not be because it senses a threat to its own survival in a Jesus risen from the tomb of decaying concepts?

According to the SC, the Church is a spiritual reality, 'a gift of God' and 'the mystery of faith'. It is even claimed that it speaks "in the name of truth itself". This is not the Church as we see it but a spiritualized, platonic version of it. Such a version fulfills a definite purpose. Having installed itself 'in excelsis', the Church can with all the greater legitimacy exercise the authority to save or damn. Besides, the spiritual essence Church is said to possess provides it a convenient alibi for collusion with the "principalities and powers of this world". Being "the gift of God" has not prevented it from legitimizing slavery, from sponsoring the Crusades, from sanctioning colonialism, from maintaining a State apparatus and a Bank, or from investing heavily in capitalist enterprises.

Against this ecclesiology of equivocation, the Theologian of Liberation restores the Church to where it belongs, that is, to the heart of the real world, there to be judged by the Lord of history. This is not to reduce the Church to a sociological reality. Nothing can be so reduced, not even an individual human being. Reality has deeper dimensions than sociology can fathom. Nor does seeing the Church as part of history amount to denying its sacramentality. A sacrament is that which at once signifies and communicates the Divine (revelation, grace). Whether the Church is sacramental in this sense or not is to be verified from its actual practice. It is a sacrament in the proportion in which it responds in word and deed to God's liberative call, not if it is in league with big money and oppressive regimes. Nor is sacramentality an exclusive property of the Church. Any human community is sacramental and revelative of the Divine in the measure in which it seeks first the kingdom of God and its justice.

Universalism or Proletarianism?

A Church that has come to terms with the world will pounce upon any saying of Jesus that can be made to buttress its position. Here came handy the beatitude, "Blessed are the poor in spirit." The phrase, 'poor in spirit' is then interpreted to mean those who cast their trust wholly on God to bring in the salvation they long for. One would have expected the SC to be consistent and say that it is only to the spiritually poor that the Gospel demands us to show preference. Instead, the document speaks of the preference given to the poor without exclusion, "whatever be the form of their poverty"(9:9), thus including also the materially poor. But the materially poor need not be poor in spirit. How then can they be en bloc the object of God's preference? The Instruction thus ends up contradicting the very Gospel saying. Such contradictions are inevitable when the desire to accommodate conflicting interests vitiates the interpretation of the Bible.

Who then are the poor towards whom God is said to show preference? It is now widely recognized among New Testament scholars that the original saying of Jesus is the shorter version of the Beatitude found in Luke, "Blessed are the poor", and that the phrase, "in spirit" is an interpretative addition by Matthew, in whose community, social inequality posed no serious problem. If so, what Jesus had in mind, when he pronounced the blessing, are the poor as an objective social category comprising all those who are the victims of exploitation, political domination, and religious discrimination, in short, the 'amhaares' of the Bible. It is the option for these disprivileged sections that made Jesus contest, to the point of shedding his own blood, the social, political, and religious powers that were. However, the Instruction is right in rejecting the identification of the Church with the proletariat of Marx. The Church is the community of disciples who, after the example of their Master, seek first the kingdom of God and its justice. And for that very reason, it is bound to take the side of the poor. But the poor to whom preference is shown need not themselves be disciples of Jesus but may belong to other religions and persuasions. It is understandable if Liberation Theologians in Latin America tend to identify the Church with the proletariat since there the poor are by and large Christians.

If the ecclesial community opts for the poor, it is because it is committed to taking humanity nearer to the justice of the Kingdom. Therefore, only those have a place in it who are dissatisfied with the status quo of a fragmented and mutilated world. And the poor are more likely to be so dissatisfied as they are the victims of unjust social systems. But there may be individuals among the rich who desire the vindication of the poor and are critical of their own involvement in perpetuating injustice. Such persons, too, can belong to the ecclesial community (see the contrast between the Rich Young Man and Zacchaeus). In any case, there should be no place in it for those who fatten themselves on the unpaid labour of their fellow humans.

The Vatican Road to Revolution

The SC solemnly affirms:

> "The Church, guided by the Gospel of mercy and by the love for mankind, hears the cry for justice and intends to respond to it with all her might"(11:1).

This is good news indeed! All the more so when it goes on to exhort pastors to give the highest priority to the problem of justice in the world. More importantly, it is stated that the Church " intends to come to the aid of the noble struggle for truth and justice"(11:5). We are thus led on to expect the dawn of a new era when the Pope along with bishops and priests from all over the world will be at the forefront of the struggle against imperialism, racism, neo-colonialism, and capitalism. But the document takes us to the pinnacle of expectations only to drop us down back on this sordid earth of ours. For, it goes on to say that, if the Church comes to the aid of the struggle for justice, it will be in the light of the Beatitude of the poor of heart (11:5). Which means, the arena of struggle is shifted to the inwardness of the human heart. And the struggle itself boils down to "appealing to the moral potential of the individual and to the constant need for interior conversion"(11:8).

The mountain of radical rhetoric has finally given birth to the mouse of interior conversion! Clearly, what the Church intends to do for the poor turns out to be no different from what it has been doing for the last twenty centuries from the days of Paul of Tarsus who appealed to the masters to be kind to their slaves.

If the SC can do no more than going on mounting the slogan of interior conversion, it is for a twofold reason. On the one hand, it naively believes that 'structural sins' can be reduced to personal sin. Though it is human beings who fashion social systems, how these actually come into being is a complex historical process often beyond the control of individual decisions. It is not as though the people of India somewhere met in conclave and decided to introduce the caste system. The caste system arose out of the confluence of a multitude of factors — psychological, racial, geographical, economic, and cultural. So, too, once a social system has come into being and has developed to a point where it moves on its own axis, it enjoys a certain autonomy in relation to the individuals who live under it. So that it can persist even against considerable opposition from individuals. The system will collapse only when the opposing wills fuse into one and become a concerted struggle. Therefore, to anathematize class struggle, and other forms of struggle, as the SC does, is to effectively abet exploitation and oppression.

It is by no means implied that the leaders of the Church are insincere. But sincerity is no substitute for sound theory. Theory can go wrong despite the goodwill of those who theorize if their thinking is shaped by systemic compulsions. Now, it is a fact that the Universal Church and most local churches are dependent on capitalism and the prevailing centres of political power for their survival. Besides, within the Church itself, there exist semi-feudal relations of power and structures of ideological manipulation. Therefore, any struggle for the total liberation of man will inevitably rebound on the Church itself. This is yet another reason why the framers of the present Instruction fall back upon the impotent strategy of interior conversion.

The discussion thus far leads us to the following conclusions:

1. The Church is very much a prisoner of its own concepts and secular interests. So long as this internal prison is not demolished, it cannot act as an agent of liberation from external prisons.

2. The needed radical transformation of the Church will not come about merely by appealing to the moral potential of its leaders. These need to be challenged by Christians who have the courage to reinterpret tradition in today's context in response to the voice of the living God. Polarization and struggle within the Church are inevitable and necessary.

3. It is an illusion to think that it is possible to work out a theology of freedom while strictly adhering to dogma and tradition. Nor is it possible to respond effectively to the challenge of the struggle for justice so long as one remains within the bounds set by the directives of the official Church.

4. The Theologian of Liberation can integrate the Marxian philosophy of *praxis* — correctly interpreted — within the Jesuan vision of human history. Only such a synthesis can pave the way for meaningful dialogue between Christians and Marxists. But were he to fall in line with orthodox Marxism he would be doing no more than replacing one set of dogmas with another.

IV

A Rejoinder to the Second Vatican Document on Liberation Theology
Since the publication of this article, the SC has come out with another document under the title, "Instruction on Christian Freedom and Liberation," dated March 1986. Latin American Theologians like Gustavo Gutierrez and Leonardo Boff have welcomed it as marking a new phase in the teaching of the Catholic Church. This reaction is understandable. For Latin American Theologians, on the whole, accept the framework of dogma and tradition and on that basis try to develop a liberative theology. In what follows, my concern is to find out whether the new

document answers the questions raised by Asian theologians, who are challenged by the situation of religious and cultural pluralism to subject that framework to a more radical critique. That it does not is clear from the SC's claim that "between the two documents there is an organic relationship. They are to be read in the light of each other" (2). This means the present Instruction does not amend, much less retract, anything said in the previous one. Hence the criticisms I have made of the earlier document continue to hold good. However, I should like to substantiate my position with reference to both the theological approach adopted by the document and some of the doctrines contained in it.

As far as the approach is concerned, it smacks of occidentalism, triumphalism, theological imperialism, and deductionism.

Though the document is addressed to the faithful all over the world, the standpoint from which it speaks is the history of the West as is clear from the reference to the Renaissance and the Enlightenment. Typical is the following statement:

> "Thus the quest for freedom and the aspiration to liberation, which are among the principal signs of the times, in the modern world, have their first source in the Christian message . . . Without this reference to the Gospel, the history of the recent centuries in the West cannot be understood"(5).

So, too, in its analysis of the world situation, it has all but ignored the Asian and the African countries except for passing references to the erstwhile colonies. The document in no way reflects the avowed catholicity of the Church.

What is still more disconcerting is the strain of triumphalism that runs through the entire document, a triumphalism that often borders on the obscene. An instance is the grandiose claim that the Church, since its origin, has never ceased to work for the release, defense, and liberation of the poor (68). The SC has conveniently forgotten that, from the time of Constantine when Christianity was proclaimed State religion till the French revolution, the official Church consistently took the side of the landed aristocracy. If it began to show some concern for the poor, it was much after Communism had taken up their cause. Forgotten, too all the evils it has perpetrated at the time of the Inquisition, the crusades, and the many religious wars, and later, by its collusion with the colonial powers. In order to make its triumphalist claims sound plausible, the SC cleverly exploits the ambiguity of the term, Church, which can mean either the institutional Church or the community of believers. The responsibility for all sins of commission and omission, for all errors and deviations, is passed on to the believers, while the institutional Church takes credit for whatever work of liberation has been accomplished by its members (20, 57, 62, 68). If the official Church is to have any credibility at all, it must muster enough courage to own up to its innumerable past deviations from her prophetic mission.

The SC is correct in pointing out the ambiguities present in the modern process of liberation. About the history of liberation movements, it raises the question,

> "Why does this history, in spite of great achievements, which also remain always fragile, experience frequent relapses into alienation and see the appearance of new forms of slavery?"(19).

Here the reader cannot but pose the counter question, Why has the history of the Church, in spite of its great achievements, often relapsed into alienation, and given rise to new forms of mental slavery? Does not the evil of collectivism, the document vehemently attacks, exist within the Church itself? Does not the concentration of wealth and power in secular society have its counterpart in the Church as well, this time compounded with the concentration of religious power? Is not the monarchial structure of the Church an estrangement of the original prophetic movement started by Jesus?

The triumphalism of this sort, however, is not the result of caprice or bad faith on the part of those who formulated the document. Undergirding it is a Church-centred theology that sees in the Church the beginning of the Kingdom of God on earth (54,58). Evidently, if the church is the Kingdom, it cannot harbour within itself error or evil in any form. If the root of triumphalism is a wrong ecclesiology, the root of this ecclesiology lies in Christology, i.e. in the understanding of Jesus as the full and definitive revelation of the Divine, and as the one who has already accomplished the salvation of mankind as a whole. However, in fairness to the SC, it must be admitted that this kind of Christology is not its invention, but goes back to the times of the early Christian community. It can be overcome only through a radical reinterpretation of the Gospels and a return to the historical Jesus. For, unlike the Church's Magisterium, the Jesus of the Gospels was fully conscious of his own limitations. When, for instance, addressed by the rich young man "Good Master", his reply was, "Why do you call me good? No one is good but God alone" (Mk10:18). So, too, when the sons of Zebedee asked him to be allotted seats of honour in the Kingdom to come, pat came the answer that was not within his competence to grant (Mk 10:40). Not until the Church has recaptured this prophetic language of radical honesty will it be able to encounter people of other religions.

This brings me to the third characteristic of the document, namely, theological imperialism. By theological imperialism, I understand, the attempt to subordinate other religions to Christianity. In its extreme form, it places non-Christians outside the pale of the Kingdom of God. Here is a statement loaded with imperialist connotations: Speaking of the truth that sets humans free, the SC says,

> "This truth which comes from God has its centre in Jesus Christ, the Saviour of the world. From him who is the way, the truth, and the life (Jn 14: 6) the Church receives all that she has to offer to mankind. Through the mystery of the Incarnate Word and Redeemer of the world, she possesses the truth about the Father and his love for us, and also the truth concerning man and his freedom"(3).

Naturally, this truth that sets humans free belongs only to the members of the Church. Those outside are virtually doomed to despair. The document implies as much when it says,

> "Human history, marked as it is by the experience of sin, would drive us to despair if God had abandoned his creation to itself. But the divine promises of liberation and their victorious fulfillment in Christ's death and resurrection are the basis of the 'joyful hope' from which the Christian

community draws its strength to act effectively and resolutely in the service of love, justice, and peace" (43).

The monopoly of truth and grace, which such statements imply, places an insuperable obstacle in the way of dialogue and collaboration with non-Christians. Equally offensive to these is the definition of the task of the Church as spreading "the kingdom of Christ" (note, not the kingdom of God!) and "recapitulating all things in Christ"(80). Christocentrism of this kind inevitably carries with it Christianity's claim to hegemony over other religions and cultures. No wonder, the document speaks of the "intimate transformation of authentic cultural values by their integration into Christianity and the planting of Christianity in different human cultures"(96). Significantly, there is no mention of Christianity having to learn anything from non-Christian cultures, much less of the challenge these pose to radically revise its absolute claims.

What an irony that a document that presumes to teach the theory and practice of liberation itself commits ideological aggression against people of other faiths! If this does not shock Latin American Theologians, it is because they do not have to confront in their day to day life any world religion such as Hinduism, Buddhism, or Islam. Here is proof that a truly liberative and universalist theology can come only from Asia.

The theological approach of the SC is manifestly deductionist. It starts with certain dogmas and then, by way of deduction, arrives at abstract ethical principles, from which in the end, are drawn out practical guidelines. This is diametrically opposed to the approach of authentic Liberation Theology, which, as I have pointed out earlier, starts from below, from the practice of liberation, personal as well as social. Practice, understood in the global sense, is also the point of arrival of theological reflection. The SC almost comes to the threshold of such a reflection when it refers to the so-called *sensus fidei* (sense of faith) of the Christian community. But, curiously, the *sensus fidei* is made to say what the official Church wants it to say, namely, that the most radical liberation is the one from sin, that the Virgin Mary is to be honoured, and so on and so forth. This is all the easier since popular faith is itself largely the product of centuries of catechizing and preaching on the part of the official Church. Hence the sense of faith itself needs to be critically assessed in order to ascertain whether it is in tune with God's contemporary challenge and with the prophetic thrust of Jesus' message.

That the theological approach of the document diverges from that of Liberation Theology will become abundantly clear when we consider the diverse conceptual polarities mentioned in the Instruction. Chief among them are the salvific and the political(23); the Kingdom of God and earthly progress (68); the transcendent and the temporal order (62); the city of God and the city of man (63); heavenly riches and earthly riches (66); the supernatural and the human (80), and grace and nature (52). The SC rightly points out that, between the terms of these polarities, there is only a distinction and no separation. But throughout the document, the movement of thought is from the first term of each polarity to the second. A genuinely liberative theology will reverse the process and see the salvific in the political, the Kingdom of God in earthly progress, the transcendent in the temporal, and the supernatural in the human. In other words, it would begin with human history as we ordinarily experience it and discover within it the depth dimension of the Transcendence. This is the only approach that conforms to the mode of thinking of Jesus who met his God in the heart of the secular world. This shows that the official Church has not really learned anything from Liberation Theology. It has done no more than accommodate certain concerns of Liberation Theologians within the traditional dogmatic theological framework. It has appropriated the rhetoric of Liberation Theology but not its spirit. This explains why the document is riddled with ambiguities, inconsistencies, and even contradictions.

To come to the Church's analysis of the world situation and the strategy of liberation it puts forward, the pronouncements are all too general and vague, if not mystifying. No less than the earlier document does the present one reduce all structural evils to personal sin. Similarly, in explaining the option for the poor, the focus is still on the spiritually poor. In one place, poverty is called a sign of original sin! This sort of language can only emanate from an ecclesiastical authority that has lost touch with reality. The strategy of change indicated is manifestly reformist. What is more, the document evinces an almost pathological fear of revolution which it calls a myth.

These criticisms notwithstanding, the Instruction is to be welcomed in so far as it affirms the legitimacy of armed resistance under certain conditions, advocates the simultaneity of personal conversion and structural change, stresses the priority of work over capital, repudiates both totalitarianism and the theory of "the national security state", highlights the need for cultural change through education and, above all, recognizes liberation as an essential Christian concern. What remains doubtful is whether these principles can be translated into meaningful practice within the framework of the checks and restraints imposed by ecclesiastical authorities and, in Asian countries, within the framework of dogma and tradition as well. This impression is reinforced by the fact that there is not even a hint anywhere in the document of the need for radical reforms within the Church!

(In Parts I, II, and III the Arabic numbers with a colon, like 11:5, refer to the sections and paragraph, respectively, of the Vatican document. In part IV, Arabic numbers at the end of sentences refer to the subsections of the second document.)

(Vaidikamitram, 18, 1979, 97-122)

7

The Marxist and the Christian Dialectics of Liberation

Introduction

In comparing Marxism and Christianity, it is necessary to keep in mind that their axes lie on different planes. Marxism is at once a philosophy, a sociology, a methodology of knowing and acting, and an economic theory. Christianity, on the contrary, is neither a philosophy, nor a sociology, nor a methodology, nor a theory of economics. The prime concern of Jesus was the absolute meaning and value of life, the ultimate goal of human existence. If he concerned himself with the concrete problems of this world, it was because God and his reign had a stake in them.

However, that Christianity and Marxism move on two different planes is only part of the truth. It is equally true that they have much in common, whether we consider their origins or their structure and dynamism. Marx's parents were Jews who joined the Christian fold not out of conviction but for reasons of expediency. It is more than probable that their Jewish origin had a profound impact on their children as well. Probably, too, Marxian messianism bears the imprint of Jewish messianic hopes. Besides, Marx was a disciple of Hegel, whose philosophy is but a rationalistic interpretation of Christian faith. He was so greatly influenced by his master that even when he subsequently weaned himself away from the latter, his criticisms were still couched in Hegelian terms. He inherited from Hegel not only, as is commonly believed, the dialectical method but also much of the content of his philosophy. His originality consists in this that he re-thought Hegelianism in the context of the real world of man and nature, and made use of the dialectic to go beyond Hegel himself. This is especially true of his early writings. The other great influence on Marx, Feuerbach, was also a Christian theologian who tried to re-interpret the essence of Christianity for his contemporaries. Finally, Marx's thought evolved and matured in the context of confrontation with the teaching and practice of the Christianity of his time, and, as it happens often in such cases, the denial of existing versions of Christian faith mounted to an affirmation of original Christian truths and values. For these reasons, Marxism, both as a vision of the world and as a socio-political movement, retains a certain family resemblance to Christian beliefs and practices. This will become clearer in the course of our analysis.

In the discussion that follows, when I speak of Christian humanism, I do not mean the system of thought regarding man and his destiny that prevailed at any one stage in the development of Christianity. I mean by Christian humanism the vision of man implicit in the life and teaching of Jesus of Nazareth. That the prime concern of Jesus was God and his reign does not mean that, for him, the realm of the Absolute began where that of the relative ended. Far from it. He saw the Ultimate as a dimension of the proximate, the eternal as a dimension of the temporal, the absolute as a dimension of the relative. It is in this concrete world of ours that he sought and met God. Loving one's neighbour was for him the same as loving God. Hence Jesus' faith in God is implicitly an affirmation of the supreme value of the human. Only in this sense may we speak of a Christian humanism, not in the sense of a developed and coherent system of doctrines regarding the nature and destiny of the human being. Similarly, by Marxist humanism, I do not mean the understanding of man embodied in any of Marxism's historical versions, but the one represented by the original thought of Marx. At the root of this approach lies the conviction that the original teachings of Jesus and of Marx are more relevant today than much of what subsequent interpretations have to offer. One might even say that contemporary Communism and contemporary Christianity are largely alienations of what Marx and Jesus, respectively, taught. This does not mean that all that we have to do is to repeat parrot-wise what these great men said. They were themselves products of their age and had the limitations of their respective thought-world. Hence, in certain respects, we may have to go beyond them if we want to be totally relevant today.

In the following pages, I shall first indicate the basic dimensions of Marxist humanism and then proceed to offer my reactions as a follower of Jesus. No claim is made that my views represent the position of the official Church, or even of the rank and file of Christians.

Man in Alienation

For Marx, man is not a finished product who can be defined once for all. He is essentially a process, a becoming, a quest, a movement. History is nothing but the becoming of man.[1] Of this process the dynamic principle is the dialectic of negativity; more precisely, negation and the negation of the negation. Capitalism is the negation of man, human alienation at its worst. Communism as the negation of this negation is the process of dis-alienation. One of the greatest contributions of Marx is that he made an exhaustive analysis of the alienations inherent in capitalist society. Here, a few reflections on the nature and scope of these alienations are in order.

Alienation is a term with many dimensions of meaning. In general, it may be described as the process whereby man exteriorizes his essential powers either in the world of objects or in that of phantasy in such manner that these same powers eventually become autonomous and, in their turn, begin to dominate and enslave him.[2] It involves privation, division, conflict, and servitude. Of these, the last may be taken as the key concept. In capitalism, man is enslaved economically, socially, politically, and ideologically. He is enslaved by what he has brought into being — by the world of products and the means of production; by the ruling classes who own the means of production; by the 'political' State which, while professing universal goals, in reality pursues the interests of the privileged classes; and by false ideologies. Of these, economic alienation is basic and sets the pattern for all other alienations. Its suppression, therefore, amounts to the total liberation of man. In the words of Marx,

> "This material, directly perceptible private property, is the material and sensuous expression of alienated human life. Its movement — production and consumption — is the sensuous manifestation of the movement of all previous production, i.e. the realization of the reality of man. Religion, the family, the state, law, morality, science, art, etc. are only particular forms of production and come under its general law. The positive supersession of private property, as the appropriation of human life, is, therefore, the positive supersession of all alienation and the return of man from religion, the family, the state, etc. to his human, i.e. social life. Religious alienation as such occurs only in the sphere of consciousness, in the inner life of man; but economic alienation is that of real life and its supersession, therefore affects both aspects"[3]

Alienation means man is not what he ought to be, and, for that reason, it is at the same time a fact and a challenge, a challenge to shake off all shackles and achieve freedom. This is what makes Marxism a humanism of liberation. The abolition of economic alienation, as embodied in private property, is the prerequisite for man's transition from the realm of necessity to the realm of freedom.[4] Marxism thus comes as a message of salvation with its own demand for 'conversion' understood as a turning away from capitalism and its values and a turning to genuinely socialist goals.

The Marxist concept of alienation finds an analogy in the Christian concept of sin. Sin is alienation not only from God but also from man, nature, and oneself. Naturally, one may not look in the Bible for a sociological analysis of alienation. In the theocratic world of his day where religion directly shaped the social system as a whole, Jesus could not have thought of socio-structural alienations as we understand them today. But, for the Christian of the 20th century, living in a secular, scientific age, an adequate grasp of structural alienations is not only possible but also necessary. Hence he can integrate into his worldview whatever is sociologically verified and verifiable in the Marxist analysis. He must recognize the truth highlighted by Marx that capitalism and its values are essentially dehumanizing.

However, there are certain inadequacies in the Marxist analysis, which the Christian cannot but view critically. First, Marx was so exclusively preoccupied with structural alienations that he failed to note those at the personal-existential level. Of these, the most important is the ambivalence of human freedom, that is, man's capacity to use his freedom to love as well as to hate, to destroy as well as to build up. To argue that this alienation is only derivative and is bound to disappear once man is inserted in truly socialist structures is to deny his autonomy which Marx explicitly affirms when he says that human beings are not only the creatures but also the creators of circumstances.[5] So, too, he did not grapple with the alienation of death and the related problem of the ultimate meaning of individual life. Second, while it is true that economic life conditions all spheres of life and thought, it is an exaggeration to hold that it is the matrix of all other alienations. The relative autonomy of the aesthetic, moral, and religious dimensions of human experience is not sufficiently recognized. This problem will be discussed more fully later in the article.

Marx's concern for human liberation, which logically follows from the recognition of alienation, should find a positive echo in any authentic Christian. For he shares the mission of Jesus whose message is equally a manifesto of human liberation. The reign of God that Jesus proclaimed and to which he was committed is, in the last analysis, the reign of justice, love, and peace.[6] It is the full flowering on this planet of a universal community bound by love and united with the ultimate ground of all, God. As such, it is the realization of freedom not only from death and sin but also from all alienations. But, whereas Marx believed that mankind can achieve freedom through its own resources, the Christian is convinced that it can be realized only within the framework of dialogue with God.

Alienation is a value-laden concept and, as such, presupposes a certain understanding of what man ought to be, of his true essence. Conversely, any understanding of his true essence presupposes some grasp of existing alienations. In what follows, we shall consider the dialectical polarities which constitute man as he ought to be. In our analysis, we assume that these polarities are realized in the capitalist society only in an alienated, distorted form. What we explicitly concern ourselves with is Marx's prospective vision of man.

Man and Nature

For Marx, man is not a stranger on earth. He is but a part of nature. His history up to now is one of his emergence from the womb of nature. Nature has meaning only as a longing for man. And man exists only as oriented to nature. He is not a being complete and well defined in himself, who only subsequently relates himself to the world around. Rather, this relationship is constitutive of his essence. In other words, he is a natural essence.[7] One with nature, he is also different from it. For he makes nature the object of his free, conscious, and creative activity.[8] He is, therefore, not only a natural essence but also a human natural essence.

As a human natural essence, he works upon objects of nature and thereby gives them a new name and form, a new unity and meaning. He shapes them in his image so that they become the extension of his being in time and space. He thus humanizes nature. In doing so, he develops his consciousness and needs and becomes progressively more human. In humanizing nature he humanizes himself.

But all work is essentially social, social in its origin and its nature. The individual works only as a member of a community and with tools provided by it, whether these be spiritual (language, traditions) or material (implements, machinery). Similarly, the products he creates are meant to satisfy the needs of the community. They are but so many bonds he fashions between man and man. In consequence, the humanization of nature is at the same time the socialization of man.

Through work, man produces society and is, in turn, produced by it.[9] Of course, the human essence of nature and the natural essence of man exist today only in an alienated form. Under capitalism, in humanizing nature man becomes dehumanized; in creating products that go to form private property, he erects so many barriers between him and his kind. With the abolition of private property, the naturalism of man and the humanism of nature will fully be realized.

The Christian has no difficulty in accepting the Marxist conception of man and nature. He, too, sees man as emerging from nature. The story of creation, divested of its mythical garb, only means that this emergence is in response to the call of God, who is both the point of arrival and the point of departure of the process. Man's self-creation in history through work is at the same time the unfolding of the creative work of God. In the Christian vision, too, it is man's task to "fill the earth and subdue it, rule over the fish in the sea, the birds of heaven, and every living thing that moves upon the earth."[10] He is destined to "possess the earth."[11] The revelation of the glory of man is also the fulfillment of the mute longings of the earth for total liberation from the shackles of mortality.[12] The New Heaven and the New Earth are nothing but our heaven and our earth filled with the power and the glory of God and man. However, living as they did in the pre-scientific world, neither the writers of the biblical books nor Jesus could have fully recognized the creative meaning of work. Besides, the original earthliness of the Gospel was largely forgotten when subsequently it passed through the Greek mould of thought with its dualism of matter and spirit, of this world and the other world.

Man and Society

The second basic polarity in the Marxist conception of man is that between person and society. We have already seen how man is bound to his fellowman through production and the product. This relatedness to society is of the essence of man. No man is an island. Nor is man's relationship to other men something added from outside to his already constituted essence. Marx goes to the extent of saying that he is nothing more than the totality of his social relations.[13] Each man is related to the community both practically and theoretically — practically in as much as by working on nature, he binds humans together, and theoretically in so far as he makes other men the object of his experience, thinking, and willing.[14] He is related to others not only actively but also passively. They satisfy his need — the highest of all needs — for human togetherness.[15] In a true sense, therefore, each man is all men.

> "Though man is a unique individual — and it is just his particularity which makes him an individual, a really individual communal being — he is equally the whole, the ideal whole, the subjective existence of society as thought and experienced."[16]

Hence, too, society is not an aggregate of monadic individuals, "but the sum of the relations in which these individuals stand to one another."[17] This does not, however, mean that the individual is dissolved in society. The individual, understood as the person, is the central concern of Marx despite certain popular versions of his philosophy. Significantly, the Communist Manifesto defines Communism as an association in which the free development of each is the condition for the free development of all.[18] The Marxist vision of man, therefore, goes beyond both primitive collectivism in which the individual is sacrificed to society and bourgeois individualism in which society is made a means to individual ends.

This understanding of man and society is basically in harmony with the teachings of Jesus, though he expresses it less in philosophical than in ethico-religious terms. For him, too, the true being of man is being-for and being-with others. Love for one's fellowmen is the sum of all prophecy and Law. The individual is called not to seek his private salvation but to belong to the 'people', God is gathering to himself in history. The Reign of God, whether we consider it in its final flowering or in its emergence in history, is the reign of the family of man united with one another and with God. However, Jesus does not sacrifice the individual to the community. The individual remains the inviolable centre of decision. It is he who has to opt for or against God and his people.

> "Whoever does the will of God is my brother, my sister, my mother."[19]

However, this basic harmony between the Marxist and the Jesuan vision of man reveals a divergence when human destiny is seen against the background of history as a whole. Who, according to Marx, is the subject of the historical development from alienation to dis-alienation? It can only be humanity, not the individual. More precisely, it will be that privileged section of humanity which happens to survive the revolution. What about the millions of individuals and groups who lived and died without enjoying the fruits of the revolution? Are they not reduced to the state of being means to an end? This problem is all the more acute if the classless society remains a dream and is never realized. In that case, generations of men will have died for a useless cause. The Christian on the contrary lives in the assurance born of faith that the God who is to come is already at work in history gathering all who surrender themselves to him in serving their fellowmen and investing their lives with a meaning that survives death. But he too has no easy solution to the problem as to how individual and collective salvation is to be reconciled and made intelligible. Nor does he claim to be able to give any such explanation, since he, unlike Marx, hold that there are realms of truth which can only be known through faith.

Being and Knowing

The polarity of being and knowing is more than a methodological one. It is equally an essential structure of man whether considered individually or collectively. The being in question is not an abstract concept as in scholastic philosophy. It means, rather, the concrete life-process of man, the process whereby he transforms himself in transforming the environment. In other words, the being of man is praxis i.e. his creative activity having for its object nature as well as other men. Understood thus, praxis is the source and the determinant of consciousness and theory. To quote Marx,

> "The mode of production of material life determines the general character of the social, political, and spiritual processes of life. It is not the consciousness of men that determines their being, but, on the contrary, their social being determines their consciousness."[20]

In respect of theory, praxis is not only the determinant but also the criterion of truth: Man must prove the truth, i.e. the reality and power of the this-sidedness "of his thinking, in practice."[21]

This does not mean that consciousness is a mere reflection of reality or that it is not creative. Its creativity consists of this that it can form "projects", i.e. conceptual models to be realized through subsequent praxis. Marx sees in this capacity one of the distinctive and essential attributes of man.

> "But what distinguishes the worst of architects from the best of bees is this, that the architect raises a structure in imagination before he erects it in reality. At the end of every labour process, we get a result that already existed in the imagination of the labourer at its commencement."[22]

In translating the projected model into practice, one realizes that it needs to be revised. The revised model then becomes the basis of further praxis which in turn leads to still another revision of the model, and thus indefinitely. This spiral movement is the mainspring of history.

Viewed in general, the dialectic of being and knowing does not pose any serious problem for the Christian. He, too, recognizes the fact that the world of ideas, values, and beliefs are conditioned by the concrete life-process of man. Religious beliefs, too, are largely influenced by the socioeconomic infrastructure. Their truth also needs to be tested based on praxis. A belief, which in no way changes the quality of life, cannot be fully true.

But does not Marx's affirmation that being determines consciousness amount to materialism and undermine the very basis of religion? We do not think so. Marx uses the term "materialism" to contrast his position with that of Hegel, whose system begins with the Absolute Idea, conceived as prior to man and nature. Against this, Marx argues that our reflections should have for their point of departure the concrete, objective world of immediate experience. Besides, he does not say that consciousness is determined by brute matter. When he speaks of "material conditions" determining consciousness, he has in mind not matter in the usual sense of the word but the social life-process of man, i.e. praxis in the sense explained earlier. This is borne out by his words:

> "The great achievement of Feuerbach is … to have founded genuine materialism and positive science by making the social relationship of man to man the basic principle of theory."[23]

More positively, in saying that it is his capacity for self-transcendence which distinguishes men from animals, Marx is equivalently affirming the reality of the spirit. For these reasons, it would be more correct to qualify Marxism as humanism rather than as materialism.

However, there are some ambiguities in the Marxist dialectic of being and knowing which raise serious problems for the Christian. The being of man, his social life-process, includes consciousness. Hence to say that being determines consciousness is equal to saying that conscious life determines consciousness. Besides, what is this consciousness inherent in the social life of man? Marx seems to understand it solely as immediate sense-experience comprising both perception and need.[24] If so, the implication is that the other modes of consciousness, especially the moral and the religious, are not original but derivative. But a phenomenological analysis of sense experience will reveal that it is shot through with intelligence and meaning. What our senses normally reveal are not mere material stimuli but 'meanings' which in turn are related to other meanings, not excluding the ultimate meaning of life. If this is the case, moral and religious awareness is not mere reflexes of pure sensation but original components of our primordial relationship to nature and society. In other words, they have more originality than Marx would accord them.

Finally, a word about the role of praxis as the criterion of truth. Unfortunately, Marx is neither precise nor consistent in his definition of terms. The Christian can accept praxis as the criterion of truth if by praxis is meant the primordial, global, active-passive relationship of man to his environment. But the term is often used in a narrower sense to mean man's conscious economic activity. A further narrowing down of meaning occurs when it is taken to mean the revolutionary activity of the proletariat. The narrower the meaning of the term the less valid is it as a universal criterion of truth. How can economic praxis, for instance, be the criterion of aesthetic truth? Besides, if the criterion of the truth of a theory is 'true praxis', do we not need another criterion to distinguish true praxis from false one? What else can it be but theory?

Man and Transcendence

Man alone of all animals can be what he is not and not to be what he is. He *is* only in the measure in which he transcends himself. Transcendence in this sense belongs to the essence of man and is recognized as such by Marx. But, whereas the Christian believes that man's self-transcendence has God for its absolute term, Marx denies the value of any such belief.

Marx makes three basic affirmations regarding religion. The first is that the idea of God is an alienation. It is nothing but the true essence of man projected on to the realm of phantasy. Therefore, affirming God means denying the human. To believe in a creator is to deny man's creativity. To accept God as a master is to condemn man to the condition of a slave.[25]

The second affirmation is that the root of religion is to be sought in the alienations of political and economic life. Religion arises either as a reflection and legitimization of reality or as a protest against it.[26] To the poor, it provides illusory compensation; to the rich, an instrument of legitimization. The third basic affirmation concerns the supersession of religion, which is thought of as taking place in three stages. The first is theoretical atheism which consists of the criticism of religion as an alienation with a view to unmasking its profane roots. The second involves removing the economic conditions which give rise to religion. It represents practical atheism or practical humanism. The third stage is positive humanism where man is so conscious of his self-creation and self-sufficiency that the need for denying the existence of God no longer arises.

"Since, however, for the socialist man, the whole of what is called world history is nothing but the creation of man by human labour and the emergence of nature for man. He, therefore, has the evident and irrefutable proof of his self-creation, of his own origins."[27]

An exhaustive evaluation of Marxist atheism is not possible here. What is offered is nothing more than a few preliminary reflections. First of all, it is a fact that many historical forms of religion are dehumanizing and alienating. This is true also of contemporary Christianity, in spite of the fact that Jesus opposed, at the risk of his own life, the oppressive practices and beliefs of the Judaism of his days. At the same time, one cannot but reject the notion that religion is essentially an alienation, a notion that cannot stand the test of the criterion of truth Marx himself proposes. It is not based on adequate reflection on historical praxis that he arrived at atheism. If he had studied history objectively he would have seen that religion has played also a positive role in the liberation of man. Many religious movements were, in their original intention and impact, socialist revolutionary forces. This is particularly true of Buddhism and the Bhakti movement in India, with their staunch opposition to caste inequality. Has not Christianity contributed to the dissolution of slave society? It is true that these religious movements eventually became reactionary forces. But has not the same fate befallen Marxist political Parties?

If nevertheless, Marx concluded that religion is essentially an alienation, it is because he learned from his erstwhile master, Hegel, who explained the man-God relationship in terms of the dialectic of master and slave. The slave cannot be free so long as the master remains. So too man cannot be free so long as God exists. But this way of explaining religion is but a caricaturing of it. For the believer relates himself to God as to one who loves. And it is love that makes man free, a truth recognized even by Marx, who wrote that man can achieve freedom only in a community.[28] If so, cannot community with God be a source of freedom? Should we not go a step further and claim that God is the condition for the possibility of total freedom for man? If the love and recognition of others make him free, the Absolute love that is God frees absolutely.

What is original to Marx is not his qualification of religion as an alienation but his analysis of its economic basis. While admitting that economic realities do influence religious doctrines and practices, the Christian will maintain that religious consciousness is not derivative but an original component of man's primordial global experience, of which economic activity is only an aspect. It is against the horizon of an absolute concern that man works to satisfy even his immediate physical needs. In reacting against Hegelian idealism, Marx failed to see the depth-dimension of man as well as his existential alienation. The supersession of this fundamental alienation cannot be achieved merely by restructuring the economic base of society. For it, nothing less than a *being-taken-hold-of* by the absolute is needed.

The supersession of any alienation means for Marx three things: abolition of what is dehumanizing, preservation of what is positive in the state of alienation, and the realization, on a higher level, of the positive. Hence, the abolition of religion is also its preservation and sublimation. This is possible only if the attributes of God are realized as attributes of man. Hence, the denial of the transcendence of God amounts to the affirmation of the transcendence and absoluteness of man. To this, we shall turn our attention now.

The Marxist man achieves transcendence in a two-fold manner: The first consists of the abolition of private property and the ushering in of the socialist society. This is a radical and qualitative change, implying the end of man's prehistory and the beginning of his true history. It is "the definitive resolution of the antagonism between man and nature, between man and man."[29] The classless society is one that has left behind not only alienation but also the possibility of alienation. It is the final resurrection of man and nature. That such a society will be realized is more an object of hope than of scientific forecast. For, if alienation was necessary for the historical development of man, one does not see why the same law will not operate also in the classless society and generate new alienations. If, on the other hand, it was not necessary but contingent upon the arbitrary will of individuals, for the same reason new alienations could emerge in the future. The classless society, therefore, is no more than a secular version of "the new heaven and the new earth" and of Christian hope. In this sense, Marxist and Christian hopes converge. Recognition of this by Marxists and Christians could provide a basis for dialogue and collaboration.

But the classless society is not humanity come to rest. It is but the beginning of man's authentic history. Though all alienations have been overcome, the dialectic of work, of self-affirmation through self-objectivation, will continue. It will be society still on pilgrimage in search of its own fullness. This is the second sense in which the Marxist man achieves transcendence, but this self-transcendence has no point of arrival. It is a search for fullness which will never be fulfilled. Thus the historical optimism of Marx conceals a certain pessimism. But this very belief in indefinite progress after the inauguration of the classless society can be a much needed corrective to the popular Christian understanding of "the new heaven and the new earth." Christians are wont to think of heaven as a state of absolute possession, of total quiescence.

If creativity is of the essence of man, should it not continue in the totally liberated man? Again, looking at the problem from the point of view of God, does He not cease to be God the moment he is totally possessed by finite man? Hence, Christians would do well to think of mankind's ultimate future in terms not of quiescence but of quest. The difference between the classless society and the Kingdom of God would consist in this that in the case of the latter the quest will be in indefectible dialogue of friendship with God, whereas in the case of the former it will take the form of a collective monologue.

We have seen that the Marxist and the Christian vision of liberation converge on many points despite radical differences. I should like to conclude this article with two remarks: First, both Christians and Marxists should recognize the provisional character of the formulation of their respective positions. They should show a willingness to revise them in the light of the global experience of man today. Second, theoretical problems have to be solved practically, namely, through a common commitment to the total liberation of man. It is by committing themselves to concerted action for the creation of a better home for the family of man that they will discover the truth that sets men free.

(Published in Journal of Dharma, Bangalore, January 1977, Vol, II, No. 1, pp. 53-67)

8

Marxist-Christian Dialogue

"Religion is the opiate of the people", said Marx. Is this characterization still valid?

Marx's charge that religion is an opiate of the masses is to a degree valid even today. When religion loses sight of the truth that called it into being, it becomes a way of escape into an illusory world-above of gods and goddesses or a heaven of disembodied souls and antiseptic angels or into the world-within in search of an *Atman* which is not there or, again, into the frenzied world of ecstatic piety. To add to these, ever new forms of psycho-technology are being imported from the West and popularised here under the guise of religion, with their fervent apostles preaching the good news of "I am OK and you are OK" and shouting from rooftops that the world we live in is the best that can be imagined. Amidst the welter of these conflicting recipes of salvation, the real challenge is forgotten, which is to create a society where one need not wish one were born a pedigree dog and not a member of "mankind."

But there is another side to the picture which is often ignored. And that is, religion can be a humanizing force.

The Buddha was the first to protest against caste, priestly domination, ritualism, and magic. He envisioned the future in terms of a casteless, stateless society. In fact, on many points he anticipated Marx. His voice was echoed later in the medieval *Bhakti* movement. As for Christianity,

Engels was right when he wrote that originally it was a religion of the poor and the oppressed in the Roman empire. And it continued so until the day when the cross was welded to the Roman sword. As a movement started by a man who was killed for his opposition to the prevailing structures of power, Christianity is essentially a religion of protest. It is this awareness that has given birth to a radical Christianity in some countries of the Third World. Today even Marxists are beginning to recognize that religion can release creative energies for the restructuring of society.

> *Marxism has been a powerful source of hope for the masses of our time, even if that hope has sometimes been tarnished with disillusionment. Is the Christian hope parallel to it?*

Marx's was indeed a philosophy of hope capable of generating revolutionary practice. But I wonder whether the same thing could be said about Marxism as it has developed since his days. What was a philosophy of hope has all but degenerated into a science of the necessary 'laws of motion' of society. Where the iron law of necessity rules, hope gives way to fatalism, and revolutionary practice is rendered superfluous. One can then conveniently transfer to the dialectic the responsibility for ushering in the classless society and quietly settle down to the flesh-pots of bourgeois politics and capitalist consumerism. The dialectic then plays the same role which divine providence did in traditional Christianity. It explains everything, legitimizes everything, achieves everything, while man does nothing. Moreover, where hope is lost, the horizon of the Absolute vanishes, and the notion of the classless society becomes an impotent myth. But man cannot live without an Absolute. So he looks for surrogates. And he finds one in the Party, which is now set up as the new Absolute and buttressed with infallible dogmas. The good of the Party is identified with the good of the people. An inevitable consequence is a dictatorship of the Party over the proletariat and the people.

A similar development may be noticed in the history of Christianity. With the loss of hope in the coming of the reign of God, the community of believers, the Church, came to be equated with mankind's absolute future. The growth of the Church meant the expansion of the kingdom of God. Thus arose in medieval Europe the totalitarianism of the Church over the faithful and the world. Luckily, this situation is now a thing of the past, though vestiges of it still persist. Recent decades have witnessed an upsurge among Christians seeking to return to their prophetic moorings in the liberating message of Jesus. It has brought in its wake greater freedom of thought and expression within the churches. This indeed is a heartening development, though there is now a disturbing move in certain circles to take Christianity back to the stagnant waters of earlier days.

> *Unlike many contemporary philosophies, both Christianity and Marxism are future-oriented and basically optimistic. Therefore, should there not be co-operation between them for forging the future of mankind?*

True, in their original thrust both Christianity and Marxism are future-oriented and optimistic. And they should join hands in the task of making a better home for the family of man. It is an illusion for either to think that it can construct the future ignoring the other. But what is desirable is not always feasible. In their historical development, both Marxism and Christianity have deviated from their origins and have congealed into rigid dogmas and institutions. This has created innumerable psychic barriers in the way of meaningful collaboration. How can Marxists collaborate with Christians when they doubt the latter's sincerity or, still worse, take them to be agents of the C.I.A, out to subvert Communism from within or without, or if they claim revolution as their private property which no one else may dare espouse? Collaboration is all the more difficult when Marxists follow the policy of all-or-nothing. Either you join the Party and swallow the Party line or you remain out and be counted as an enemy of the revolution. Christians, too, have to get rid of many mental blocks before they can collaborate with Marxists. Till a few decades ago, they tended to see in Marx the Anti-Christ, the embodiment of all that is evil and odious. They also labour under the inhibitions of a colonial theology which render them, political eunuchs.

Collaboration is genuine only when it flows from a certain community of vision and strategy. To arrive at it, there is a need for self-criticism and dialogue. Today there seems to be more self-criticism and serious soul-searching among Christians than among Marxists. As for the dialogue, I have the feeling that Indian Marxists are too unsure of their own philosophical foundations and, consequently, too much on the defensive to be able to discuss theoretical issues with Christian thinkers, especially when these also happen to be students of Marxism. Confronted with so many obstacles to dialogue and collaboration, some committed Christians find an easy way out by accepting the Party line. But that amounts to abdicating the critical role which their faith enjoins them.

Can one be both a Marxist and a Christian at the same time?

It all depends on what you understand by the labels. Naturally, a Christian deeply entrenched in his dogmas cannot be a Marxist of the dogmatic type. The two systems of dogmas repel each other. But the Christian who is critical of his own tradition and has appropriated the original revolutionary perspective of Jesus will find much in the theory and practice of Marxism that is in tune with his own world-view. Without disowning his faith, he can make his own the Marxian hope in the overcoming of all human alienation and the emergence of the Total Man. He can make critical use of Marx's materialist conception of history, his analysis of exploitation and alienation under capitalism, and his theory of revolution. An encounter with Marxism will help the Christian make his faith concrete, contextual, and geared to transformative action. Only in this sense can a Christian be also a Marxist.

Maybe, you are posing a pseudo-problem. For, in the end, what matters is not labels but commitment to fashioning a future of creative freedom. Besides, all labels are odious. We are on the threshold of a new age which challenges us to dream new dreams and see new visions while holding fast to what is valid in the perspectives of Jesus and Marx.

The Church presents a new face today. It speaks of social equality and justice, among other things. But critics say that the new face is only a mask representing nothing more than a device to stay in business. May I have your comments?

I am pleasantly surprised to hear you say that the churches present a new face today. But in paying that compliment, you are possibly overshooting the mark. It is true, the churches have left behind the kind of theology that functioned as an ideology of the status quo. They have come out with a social teaching that is in many respects revolutionary. But, more often than not, their practice lags far behind. It is this wide gulf between theory and practice that has forced many radical Christian groups into the periphery of the churches. Within the framework of official Christianity, one can be radical only up to a point. At one time or another, one's political involvement comes into conflict with the institutional interests of the churches. This means that the new face that Christianity turns to the world is not that new after all; it still bears too many marks of the old. It is amusing to see the official churches basking in the reflected glory of committed Christians whom they marginate and all but disown.

Nevertheless, it is true that, on the whole, Christianity now presents a new face. But I do not think this development is the result of a conspiracy to stay in business. For one thing, as Christians become radicalized, they cease to concern themselves with maintaining inherited traditions and institutions. Their concern is rather to have done with the 'business' of religion and the religion of business. (One wonders, though, whether Christian radicalism is not itself becoming a lucrative business!) It is those who want to stay in business who desperately cling to age-old institutions. Imagine how many priests, nuns, and laypersons would be thrown out of job and forced to take to the streets if the churches suddenly turned radical and broke loose from big money and business. No, the radical stance of contemporary Christianity is not a tactic of survival. It derives from an attempt to recapture the prophetic spirit of Jesus and his early followers. Christianity is on the verge of a historic mutation. Something new is struggling to be born. Let it be born.

You say in your book, Jesus and Freedom, that liberation can come only through a total revolution. Will that revolution be peaceful or violent? Is revolution, violent or nonviolent, allowed to Christians?

By revolution, I mean the planned, radical restructuring of a social system. Revolution is total when it seeks the transformation not only of structures but also of persons. Whether total or partial, it does not involve as an integral part the use of violence, meaning actions resulting in the destruction of persons. In virtue of their very faith, Christians are committed to revolution. But the same faith demands that they eschew all violence. Even the founders of Marxism were critical of violence as a means to revolution.

However, I can understand — which does not mean justify — the violence of the frustrated few who in the name of the mute majority take to the gun. What I cannot understand is the obscene violence of an obese minority who, for safeguarding their own interests, seek to maintain by all means a social system that condemns millions to death from hunger, disease, and exposure to heat and cold. Nor can I accept the violence of those who administer a law-and-order that enables the same minority to loot the masses legally and in a right orderly fashion, and use every conceivable means to smother dissenting voices. How well we have learned the wisdom of our ancient seers and saints! Who needs them any longer when we have guns chanting, *Ahimsa paramo dharma, om Shanti, Shanti!*

(Part of an interview given to P. N. Benjamin, and published in Sunday Herald, Bangalore, December 25, 1983)

PART - 2
ESSAYS

9

The Spirit Descended Upon Him

John was preaching the baptism of repentance for the forgiveness of sins. People were flocking to Jordan by the hundreds. The news reached the carpenter's home in Nazareth. Jesus too felt the urge to heed the call from the wilderness. Come to the scene of baptism, he stepped into the cool waters and dipped himself. As he came up, he saw the Spirit coming down upon him in the shape of a dove and heard a voice speak from heaven, Thou art my son, my beloved; on thee my favour rests.

The Spirit that descended on Jesus was the power of God which brooded over primal waters before time was, the power that fashioned cosmos out of chaos, form out of the formless, name out of the nameless void. The Bible speaks of the Spirit in the language of symbols, comparing it to a wind that blows mightily over the land tearing up trees and leveling down mountains; to a fire that consumes and purifies smelting crude ore into pure gold; to a sword that pierces to the very place where life and spirit, bones and marrow, divide. These symbols, however, do not adequately represent the working of the Spirit. They derive from a patriarchal view of the world where the father is supreme as the source of power, order, and discipline. Today, we are witnessing the collapse of patriarchal civilization. Motherhood is once again coming to the fore: motherhood of the woman, of the earth, of the waters. And motherhood is the matrix of unconditional love and compassion and the source of the sense of the equality of all. Though Jesus was not wholly free from the male bias of Jewish society, his self-awareness burst the bounds of male symbolism. He spoke of himself not only as one sent to wield the sword and cast fire on earth but also as a hen gathering her young under her wings. Truly, the Spirit that worked through him was at once father and mother, wind and womb, fire and water, sword and peace, power, and compassion.

The descent of the Spirit is not just an event of the past. The Son of Man is WE, the sons and daughters of men. What happened to Jesus happens to all men and women of every age and culture. So, the Spirit must be at work in our society and in our history as well. But where in our midst do we find the insufflation of the Spirit?

Let us go into the cities, towns, and villages and tarry among the toiling masses. What do we see there? No dove divine brooding over the human continuum but vultures perched in high places itching to swoop down on the defenseless, man feeding on the flesh of man, the rich sucking the marrow from the bones of the poor, mothers cursing their womb for the young they cannot feed, fathers selling the shame of their daughters at crossroads, children vying with dogs for the refuse of food in wayside dumps while the scholar looks on impassively taking down notes for his dissertation and paunchy priest passes by muttering imprecations!

Could it be that the Spirit not finding a foothold in the masses has withdrawn to the more congenial sequestered islands of modernity? In fact, in the more posh areas, a different picture awaits us, a picture seemingly more like the handiwork of the Spirit of God: chubby little children, each a blithe poem wrought in flesh and blood, flitting about in well laid-out lawns and gardens; teen-aged cuties tiptoeing in high-heeled shoes as though wary of the defiling touch of the earth; muscular boys and girls nursing dreams of spiraling up from conspicuous to more conspicuous consumption; sleek, presentable, antiseptic ladies and gentlemen exuding seductive perfumes and sweet reasonableness; palatial residences resounding with laughter and rejoicing to the accompaniment of exotic music and dance. Dazzled by so much wealth and well-being, we might exclaim: Here indeed is the land flowing with milk and honey, here are the bearers of the Spirit, the creators of the New Humanity. But on a closer look, the vision vanishes, the hope collapses. What looked like the Spirit of God proves to be the spirit of Mammon. The creators of the future turn out to be but scavengers of demon-dung, money. The hilarity and the merry-making show, for what they really are, so many devices to drown uneasy consciences and anguished groanings. In this world of make-believe, love is at best a sentiment confined to one's kin or class, at worst a commodity bought in the market-place; and religion a convenient means to bridge the gulf between profit and loss.

Disenchanted, we wend our way to the world of religion, the acknowledged domicile of the Divine. Here, in temples, mosques, and churches, the routine of prayers and offerings and incantations and libations go on without a hitch. But what these confer on the devotees is no more than a private consolation for public sins. They leave the world untouched, as mutilated and fragmented as ever before. Religion even feeds the irrational forces of death and violence as happens in every communal riot. As for the accredited mediators of the Spirit - priests, pastors, and god-men - they can only trot out impotent words, mere vacuous shells from which the Spirit has long since fled. What is worse, they speak at cross purposes. Some say that the Spirit is the spirit of science, technology, and progress; others that the Spirit is the spirit of flight from the world of time and space; others that the Spirit is concentrated in the navel within the navel; still others that the Spirit is brewed in the genitals! But all of them have one thing in common: they know the magical art of condensing the Spirit into gold and silver and real estate. Few know of the Spirit that uproots and plants, demolishes and builds up; of the Spirit that roams about roaring like a lion to avenge the blood of the innocent.

Does this mean the Spirit has deserted the world for good, leaving a broken humanity to shift for itself? Is man fated to spend his days licking his wounds in eternal loneliness? No. That cannot be. The very fact that we now pose these questions is proof enough that the Spirit of God lives and is at large. For, our questioning is at the same time a quest born of concern for mankind's ultimate future and, as such, instinct with compassion. More, it is a quest straining to become the saving deed. And what is such questing but the Spirit stirring within us? What is concern and compassion but the Spirit unfolding? What is striving for a new creation if not the Spirit empowering the powerless?

Now to come back to the question, we set out from, Where do we find today the Spirit of God brooding over the waters of human existence? In all those men and women - young or old, rich or poor, learned or unlearned - who dare question the inhumanity of the world we live in, who are ready to translate their questioning into contesting, who have made their own the cause of the deprived and the unwanted, who long for a new world in which all men will weep when one man weeps. The Spirit reveals itself in our workaday world in many and varied fashions whether as nostalgia for lost oneness and wholeness or as prurience of the inner self which can find relief only in a total giving or as a new light in which truth stands raw and naked or as an invading presence that ennobles and fulfills. It makes its presence felt now as a healing touch, now as a defiant NO to the rules of the game framed by the haves for the have-nots, now as concerted action to right the wrongs done to the dispossessed. In every case, the Spirit is a spirit of transcension urging men and women to reach out to the other shore of freedom whole and entire.

Seen in this light, the picture I drew a moment ago of the wasteland of a Spiritless world represents only part of the truth. All is not gloom and darkness. There are also points of light flashing out "wherever the just exchange their messages". And the just who exchange messages are to be found not only among the poor but also among the rich. Not all the rich have mortgaged their souls to Satan. Nor are all men of religion peddlers of divinity. From the subterranean roots of decaying religions fresh shoots are sprouting. We are on the threshold of a new post-religious religiosity of the Spirit which will make dead bones prophesy, muted tongues wax eloquent, and hope blossom in the midst of despair. The earth will be riven in two, releasing new waters for the coming baptism of the Son of Man.

(Anawim No. 34, Jan. 1984)

10

Jesus Beyond Jesus

Our age is marked by a profound concern for the future. Envisaging the future, planning for it, projecting alternatives - these have become matters of absorbing interest. Not merely interpreting history, but creating it, occupies the minds of men. Paradoxically, this concern for the future has generated its opposite, namely, a concern for the past, a tendency to return to the origins. In philosophy, this tendency has found expression in the slogan: 'Back to things themselves', i.e. back to the world of our original experience, the matrix of all truth. This trend is also observable among the Marxists, especially of the West, who are trying today to return to the early writings of Marx. This can also be noticed among the adherents of various religions: Hindus today are striving to recapture the original insights of the rishis and seers of old. Christianity is no exception. Luther's was the first attempt to free faith from the accumulated traditions of the past and to root it directly in the message of the Gospel. In our times, Catholics are returning to the New Testament writings, to drink there from the clear spring of the earliest traditions. This trend has of late become further radicalized in so far as the aim is to get behind the Gospels to the original phenomenon of the historical Jesus and his teaching.

Why this tendency especially at a juncture when our primary concern is with the future? It can only be because it has dawned on us that we cannot leap into the unknown future unless our feet are solidly planted in what is perennially valid in the past. Implied is also the recognition that, for us today, the origins of historical movements are more relevant than their subsequent developments and accretions. This means further that the history of ideas and movements has not been one only of progressive clarification but also of self-alienation and deviation. This is true even of contemporary Marxism which has developed along lines which Marx would never have approved of. The deviation had set in even during his lifetime, as is clear from a letter he wrote to a friend, in which he pleaded not to be called a Marxist and disclaimed being one. A process of alienation can be discerned also in the history of Christian faith. Would not Jesus of Nazareth, if he were to come in our midst once again, disown much of what today is being done in his name by Christians?

Jesus Bound

The alienation of Christian faith and practice from the historical Jesus took place along three principal lines - cultic, dogmatic, and institutional. For an adequate grasp of this process, it is necessary to go back to the very sources of Christianity and from there trace its development right up to our day. This is not possible within the limited scope of this article. What is attempted here is nothing more than a schematic and, admittedly, a simplified outline of the salient features which even a cursory study will reveal.

Cultic alienation was the first to set in. The historical Jesus devalued cult by subordinating it to justice, mercy, and love. He did not project himself as an object of worship. He did not institute any rite which may be called cultic in the traditional sense of the term. What we call the Eucharist today was originally a prophetic gesture that looked forward to the end of present history when God would invite his children to sit at table with him. But no sooner had Jesus died than there developed a cult centred upon him. However, the focal point of this cult was not the Jesus of history but Jesus risen from the dead and seated at the right hand of the Father. Jesus who was part of our history was replaced in Christian piety by the risen Christ who is thought of as above history, as eternal and immutable. The same piety removed him from our midst, from the common run of everyday life, and installed him in the tabernacle. It built a separate home for him furnished with flowers, candles, holy water, incense, and the like. It projected him as a stickler for ritual purity, who avoided publicans and sinners and looked down upon the 'profane' world of everyday life. Cult also started a process of abstraction. The death of Jesus was dissociated from his historical life or reduced to a mere prerequisite for resurrection. Jesus was further fragmented into many formal aspects, each of which in its turn became the object of a new devotion. Thus we had a plethora of devotions having for their objects, 'the Precious Blood', 'the Crown of Thorns', 'the Five Wounds', 'the Sacred Heart' etc. By the Middle Ages Christianity had become a cult-centered religion. Mercy, justice, and love took second place to the Eucharistic cult and the devotions. The circle was complete. A non-cultic prophetic movement ended up as a cultic religion.

The history of dogma and catechesis shows a parallel process of alienation. Jesus as pictured in the Synoptic Gospels is a man among men, a member of the family of man. He was less word made flesh than flesh become word, matter endowed with a tongue. Flesh of our flesh, blood of our blood, bone of our bones, he learned to love in being loved by others and gained knowledge of himself in being acknowledged by others. It is in meeting his kind that he learned kindness and compassion. He loved man. He struck roots in others to such an extent that all this became a need for him especially in moments of crisis. Exquisitely attuned to everything human, he valued the friendship of women; he loved children, wine, and flowers. He would rejoice with those who rejoiced and weep with those who wept.

Like any man, he too had to grow in wisdom and in favour with God and man. He was a quester after truth: after the God who made him; and he found God on the banks of Jordan. On the day of his baptism at the hands of John the Baptizer, he was taken hold of by God. He was swept off his feet, uprooted from his familiar world, and transplanted into the realm of the Divine. There he was given a new mind and a new heart, and he began to see the world in a new light, in the light of the reign of God. But his search did not end there. He had still to come to terms with God and reach a point of clarity regarding his mission in life. The consequent inner struggle with light and darkness is represented in the Gospels as the temptation in the desert.

Jesus was also fully conscious of his limitations. Asked about the final coming of the Kingdom, he replied,

> "But about that day or that hour no one knows, not even the angels in heaven, not even the Son, only the Father" (Mk. 13:32).

So too he admitted openly that he could not dispense the blessings of the age to come just as he liked. The sons of Zebedee who sought from him the favour of being allowed to sit in state one on his right, the other on his left, were told bluntly that to sit on his right or left was not for him to grant, such privileges were for those to whom it had already been assigned (Mk. 10:40). Though the Divine in him radiated its power, he did not think of snatching at equality with God (Phil. 2:6). When a stranger called him 'good master' his answer was:

> "Why do you call me good? No one is good except God alone" (Mk. 10:17-18).

Like any man, he too was subject to varying and conflicting emotions. The woes he uttered against the hypocrites of his day betray a spirit that was quick to flame with indignation. He was filled with anger at the sight of the trafficking that went on in the temple, the house of his Father. The destiny he was to meet in Jerusalem set every fibre of his being in tension.

> "I have a baptism to undergo, and what constraint I am under until the ordeal is over." (Lk. 12:50)

The prospect of death was to him a source of infinite sadness which he tried to share with his friends:

> "My heart is ready to break with grief." (Mk. 14:34)

> It filled him with fear and anguish. To quote the writer of the Letter to the Hebrews:

> "In the days of his earthly life, he offered up prayers and petitions, with loud cries and tears, to God who was able to deliver him from the grave" (Heb. 5:7).

What a far cry from this Jesus, who is so much like us and in his very likeness stands out as the wholly 'other', to the Christ of dogma! The latter is Jesus transmuted as he was made to pass through the Greco-Roman mould of thinking. He came out of this mould fragmented into abstractions like person, nature, hypostasis, body, soul, substance, quality, quantity, essence, and existence. What cult did at the level of action, theology did at the level of thinking. Jesus was reduced to a mere sum of formal concepts. Seen from the human side he is a man with two natures subsisting in one divine person. Seen from the divine side, he is the second person of the Trinity identical in nature with the Father and the Holy Spirit. Controversies raged as to whether the Spirit proceeds from the Father only or from the Father and the Son. What is worse, in this process of sterile philosophical reflection, the humanity of Jesus was downgraded. Of course, dogma as well as theology affirmed his human nature but not without denying him the status of a human person, a mode of reasoning which sounds so odd to us. This had its repercussion in popular catechesis. For the mass of believers, Jesus appeared as God under the guise of man: he knew from early infancy all there is to know. Though they recited the official creed which said that Jesus suffered under Pontius Pilate, they assumed well enough that he could not have really suffered, endowed as he was on earth with the beatifying vision of God. If ever they read the Gospels they slurred over the passages which affirmed the human condition of Jesus or, if they were clever enough, managed to put dishonest interpretations on them. In short, if cult segregated Jesus from the company of man and settled him down in Churches on the fringe of the real world, dogma banished him to the world of ideas. In the process, the real Jesus of history became a forgotten person.

No less than cult and catechesis, institutionalism distorted the image and the teachings of Jesus. The Gospels picture him as one who, right from the outset of his public life, rejected power, whether economic or political, as a means to usher in a New Age. The historical movement he set in motion was supposed to be for the poorer classes in Palestine and the Graeco-Roman world who had no political ambitions. But with Emperor Constantine, who declared Christianity the state religion, the leaders of the Christian community began to enjoy economic and political privileges. The temptation that Jesus overcame in the desert, his disciples succumbed to, all too easily. The Church began to exercise control over every sphere of life. This led to a proliferation of institutions. Though in course of time political life regained its autonomy, the Church held on to its institutions, its schools, colleges, hospitals, and orphanages, and even started new ones. Every local Church today has its institutional empire. What is still more saddening is that most of these institutions have not even an umbilical bond with the Gospel of Jesus. By and large, they embody the values of capitalism: private interest, competition, aggression, and lust for power. Besides, in so far as they violate the legitimate autonomy of secular spheres of life, they have become many instruments of domination. Thus by a curious development, the Good News of liberation preached by Jesus gave rise to structures of unfreedom. Institutionalism has in this manner disfigured the image of Jesus and neutralized the revolutionary, disruptive force of his teaching.

The tragic consequence is that he is the most forgotten person among the very people who claim to be his disciples. He lies buried under the weight of accumulated layers of rituals, rubrics, laws, concepts, legends, myths, superstitions, and institutions. He lies bound hand and foot by innumerable cords that tradition has cast around him. His voice is smothered, his spirit is stifled. If he still acts and makes his presence felt in history, it is less through the official Church than through honest dissenters among Christians.

It is the duty of all who cherish the vision and hope of Jesus to set him free from the prison-house of cult, dogma, and institutionalism so that he can freely go about pointing, as of old, his accusing finger at the Scribes, Pharisees, elders, priests, and Herods of today. To this end, it is necessary to remove the many veils which historically conditioned faith and tradition have put on him, and let his visage shine forth in its original splendour, and his words ring out in their untamed incisiveness.

What we have said thus far should not be interpreted to mean that the history of Christianity until now has been one only of progressive alienation. Admittedly, the development of Christian theory and practice in the West contains also positive elements in harmony with the teachings of Jesus. These have to be clearly distinguished from others at variance with them. A critical study of this question may be useful, and even necessary, up to a point, but should never be made an absolute for people who do not share the Western tradition. If we Indians have no other way to meet God as revealed in the life and teachings of Jesus than by mentally reenacting the history of Western Christianity, we are, of all human beings, the most to be pitied!

It is necessary to go back to the historical Jesus. But is not the attempt doomed to fail, if the Gospels are not historical documents in the usual sense of the term but the expression of the faith of the early Christians? This is a serious problem of which an adequate discussion, though necessary, is not possible here. This much, however, may be said. The nature of our sources indeed renders futile any attempt to write a biography or to describe the psychology of Jesus. It is impossible to reconstruct the sequence of events in his life. But to go further and say that no understanding of the historical Jesus at all is possible is unwarranted. The Gospels are the concrete embodiment of the response of the early Christians to a historical reality, namely, to the life, words, and deeds of Jesus of Nazareth. Hence, we can have a real encounter with the historical Jesus in and through the Gospels. Using the criteria provided by contemporary Biblical criticism, we can arrive at an adequate grasp of the person and teaching of Jesus, which are themselves events in history, and perhaps also, of a very broad outline of his life. Nothing more is presupposed here.

However, this is no plea for rediscovering the historical Jesus to mimic him or to repeat his teachings parrot-wise. For he was a product of his culture, and his thinking bears the mark of the world that bore him. Both his message and the language in which it is couched need to be brought up to date so that they may be relevant for us.

Jesus Beyond Jesus

To appreciate fully the need for such a reinterpretation, a change affecting ideas and beliefs may be useful. No man thinks in a vacuum nor is he born into the world with innate ideas. He finds himself inserted right from the dawn of consciousness into society with its specific system of ideas, values, norms, and goals. These he assimilates from early childhood as mediated by the institutions of society like the family, school, and temple. He internalizes the ideas and beliefs currently held by the people at large. What was objective thus becomes subjective and influences his attitudes and decisions.

But the ideas and beliefs of a people at any given time are intimately interwoven with everyday practical life - with the prevalent mode of production, the structures, and institutions of society, the political organization, and cultural activity. Ideas influence the social base and are in turn influenced by it. In other words, they mutually condition each other. In normal times there is a certain equilibrium between ideas and their social base. Crisis, however, may develop during which this equilibrium is disturbed and society is thrown off its balance. This may happen in two ways. The first is when ideas change without any corresponding change in the social base. It happens when people assimilate new ideas either from outside sources or from an internal elite. In such conditions, one begins to question the value of the existing social structures and institutions. The other mode in which a crisis develops is when the social base undergoes radical change without a corresponding change at the level of ideas. In such a situation what is called into question is the relevance of traditional ideas. In either case, society is in birth pang bringing forth a new truth. It is in periods of crisis that exceptional individuals arise who play a prophetic-creative role. They give articulate expression to the revolt against the past and the longing for the new, which exists inarticulate and confused among the masses. In the tensions maturing in the heart of society, they discover the call of God. The masses on their part love and hate the new, at the same time. The burden of the past makes them welcome the new. But the fear of the new drives them to conform to the past. The same ambivalence is found also in their attitude to the prophets in their midst, these being heralds of the new. They slay the prophets, and then hasten to erect monuments to the memory of the slain!

The prophets who rise up in periods of crisis are essentially heralds of the future. They are men who dream of new dreams and see new visions. Their destiny is to leap into the unknown future and carry the masses with them. They are gripped by an ultimate concern, and their message necessarily has something of the unconditioned. Both in their revolt against the status quo and in their commitment to the *not-yet*, there is much that is valid for human persons of all times. All the same in the very break-through they achieve the level of a total vision of man, they remain conditioned by the status quo they revolt against. The new they can envisage only in the language of the old. The very content of their message exhibits this tension between the not-yet and the already, between the absolute and the relative, between the perennially valid and the historically conditioned. Lonely in the sweep of their vision and in the passion of their commitment, they remain very much men of their age.

Jesus of Nazareth was one such prophet, transcendent in his vision and immanent in his world, perennial in his appeal but rooted in his age, absolute in his demands yet conditioned by his environment. The universal in his message comes to us, cast in a cultural mould we have long left behind. This poses a two-fold challenge to us: We have first to ascertain in the teachings of Jesus the perennially valid aspects as distinguished from their historical conditioning. Next, we have to bring to light their deeper implications for the man of today and clothe them in our idiom. To do this is to set free the spirit and thought of Jesus from their original mould and thereby release their revolutionary energies for the creation of a better world. This is to allow Jesus to respond to our historical situation in our patterns of thought and speech. Only then can the Jesus of yesterday be a creative force in the world of today and tomorrow.

But in trying to re-interpret Jesus for the men and women of today, are we not committing the same mistake as the early and subsequent generations of Christians? Are we not distorting his image to suit our tastes and safeguard our interests? That there is such a danger cannot be denied. And the only way to avoid it is to see to it that our interpretation is not naive but critical. But what are the criteria that should guide such criticism? They are twofold: fidelity to the original Jesus-phenomenon and responsiveness to the God who reveals himself to us in history. The Christians of the first centuries could not have applied the first criterion, for they lived in an age in which the boundary between myth and reality was blurred. Reality tended to be mythicized, and myth, to be looked upon as history. Consequently, it was natural for the early Christians to raise Jesus to the status of a mythical person. Criticism in our sense of the term was therefore not possible to them. Our situation is quite different. We have gone beyond the stage of myth. We also know that any valid interpretation has to be like a response to the historical phenomenon as we encounter them. This obliges us at every stage to subject our subjective prejudices and preferences also to criticism lest they colour our interpretation of reality.

As for the second criterion, in the message of Jesus, there is an absolute and a relative dimension. The absolute dimension can be explained only based on his encounter with the Absolute, with God. But precisely because this encounter was enfleshed in a historical situation, it is possible and even natural that the total significance of it overflowed the limits of what was explicitly perceived by Jesus himself. This is true of all aesthetic and religious genius. However, any further interpretation has to be in line with the fundamental thrust and implicit dynamism of the original datum. Now the fundamental dynamism of Jesus' message pointed to God working in history. If our reinterpretation of Jesus is to be authentic, we must encounter in history the same God whom he encountered two thousand years ago. It is our responsiveness to the God of today that guarantees our fidelity to the original Jesus-phenomenon. The demands which God in history makes on us today help us understand the deeper meaning of the teaching of Jesus. Conversely, the demands of Jesus help us interpret the signs of the times and decipher the divine challenges inscribed in history. In this way, the Jesus of history enters into dialogue, in and through us, with the God of today.

However, the encounter with God is not to be understood solely in a mystical or esoteric sense. Any man gripped by an absolute concern for his fellowmen has encountered God. It is possible, even likely, that the extreme radicals who are in prison today for the sole crime of having opposed an unjust society had a more authentic encounter with God than many professedly religious men and women who devote themselves to prayer and penance. For the same reason, the former may understand the significance of Jesus much better than the latter.

If we retrace our steps to Jesus of Nazareth it is not to pitch our tent with him in the past but to go beyond him. We go beyond him when we free him from the historical conditioning of the Judaism of the first century, re-interpret his message in the context of our contemporary concerns, and translate it into today's language. Put differently, we can make it possible for Jesus to go beyond himself and discover his true identity in our age. He can slough off the past to come alive in the present, with whatever in his past has an abiding value. Thus we raise him from the dead and give him a new name and habitation. Seen in this light, the resurrection of Jesus is a continuing process achieved through our re-interpretation of his message and our commitment in response to it.

A re-interpretation of the entire message of Jesus along the lines indicated is an urgent need of our times. This, however, is beyond the scope of this article. No more can be done here than to illustrate, by way of conclusion, the approach set out here with a few reflections on the Kingdom of God which is central to the preaching of Jesus.

He believed that God would come to free man from every kind of bondage and usher in a new age of justice, freedom, love, and universal brotherhood. His concern for the ultimate future is of supreme relevance for us today and will be so for men and women of all ages. but to be fully operative it has to be stripped of its historical conditioning. One form of conditioning concerns the belief in the imminence of the Kingdom which most scholars attribute to Jesus. If he entertained such a belief it might have been under the influence of the apocalyptic literature of his days, which found a favourable soil in frustrated nationalism. Be that as it may, for us today, the horizon of ultimate fulfillment has receded into the unknown future, a future handed over to the mysterious working out of two freedoms - the freedom of man and the freedom of God. However, belief in the imminence of the Kingdom brings out a truth that is valid for all times, namely, that the ultimate destiny of man will be settled by his decision here and now. In this sense, God and his Kingdom are always imminent.

Historical conditioning can be traced also in Jesus' conception of how the reign of God comes into being. Though he called for human response in the form of repentance, faith, and love, the stress is perhaps unduly on the character of the Kingdom as a gift of God. Nowhere does Jesus explicitly call upon his hearers to collaborate with God in constructing the Kingdom. All that he demands is that they dispose themselves inwardly for it and pray for its coming. Should this attitude be normative for his disciples today? Probably not, for he lived in a pre-scientific age, when the conditions which make it possible for man to envision and create the future, did not exist. Hence, he could not have realized fully the role of man in bringing about the reign of God. In this scientific age, we are in a better position to understand that the future of humanity depends on our freedom as much as on God's. We know that God's gift comes to us not as something ready-made but as a call addressed to us to create the future, which when responded to, brings freedom and creativity to fulfillment. Therefore, when we today call upon men and women to commit themselves to the creation of a new Heaven and new Earth we are, in a sense, going beyond Jesus, but going beyond him in the spirit of creative fidelity to him.

It is along these lines that we have to re-interpret his response to the challenge of the Kingdom which, in more than one respect, will be found embarrassing by contemporary radicals. Jesus did not condemn slavery though he knew of its existence among the Jews. Though there was, in his time, accumulation of wealth in the privileged classes, on the one hand, and unemployment and poverty, on the other, he did not call for any economic revolution. Nor did he join the nationalist liberation movement led by the Zealots. From all this, it has been argued, by many Christians, that revolutionary commitment of any sort is opposed to the Gospel. They err because they set up a historically conditioned attitude of Jesus as normative for all ages. Jesus who lived two thousand years ago could not have envisaged a social revolution since its socioeconomic and cultural pre-conditions did not exist. As for political liberation, his non-involvement probably resulted from his own reading of the times and from his understanding of the divine challenge as revealed at that particular juncture of history. But this is no justification for social conformism today. On the contrary, the basic thrust of his message demands radical commitment where the social system is unjust and oppressive, as in India. One cannot believe in the reign of God as the total liberation of man from every kind of bondage, a liberation to be brought about by human initiative, and at the same time remain neutral to structures of oppression. Similarly, Jesus' affirmation of the primacy of man over the Sabbath can in no way be reconciled with perpetuating the domination of man by structures. When, therefore, Christians commit themselves to social revolution today, they are not going against, but along with Jesus. It is through them, only through them, that Jesus comes alive in the twentieth century.

(Jeevadhara, 5, 1975, pp. 169-181; *Jesus and Society*, Chap.27)

11

The Man Jesus: Rupture and Communion

Reflections on the Gospel According to Mark

There are beautiful things; but beauty itself never appears as a thing, except perhaps in a work of art. Similarly, there are men and women who are human; but humanness itself never appears to us in the form of a man, except in the man Jesus from Nazareth. He reveals to us what it means to be truly human. To know him is to know what all men ought to be. And to know him we have to remember not only what he said but also what he did. For with him, word and deed were not two things. His word was power and deed; and his deed was a message. In this paper, we shall dwell, though briefly, on the structure and movement of his life as revealed in his word and deed.

The patterned dynamism of Jesus' life may be characterized as rupture and communion: rupture of the navel strings that bound him to the society in which he lived; and communion with nature, man and God. His life was a permanent being-born from the womb of a dying Judaism into the light of a new togetherness with man and God, a birth that was consummated only when he died on the Cross, only when the veil of the temple ruptured in two. He was the piece of unshrunk cloth sewn on the old garment of Judaism which as a result was torn asunder. He was the new wine poured into the old wineskin of Jewish Law which, for that reason, was burst, letting the content spill and soak the earth. Twenty centuries have passed since that new wine was spilt on the Cross. Yet, even today, those who claim to represent him are bent on forcing his spirit into old wineskins, into obsolete laws and institutions which they have brought into being to satisfy their insatiable lust for power.

Disrupting the Reign of Satan

The power that went out of Jesus healed all so that his contemporaries spoke of him:

> "He has done all things well; he even makes the deaf and the dumb speak." (7:37: unless otherwise indicated the chapter and verse refer to the Gospel according to Mark.)

In his eyes, the practice of healing meant the subversion of the reign of Satan over man and his destiny. Positively, it sought to promote the well-being of man. And the well-being of man is his full-being in the sense of his being-fully-with nature, his kind and his Maker. The healed regained mastery over their bodily nature and, in that measure also, over the law of decay and death governing external nature. Further, they were reintegrated into society as equals among equals. He told the leper:

> "Go, show yourself to the priest, and offer for your cleansing what Moses commanded, for a proof to the people" (1:44).

Similarly to the paralytic:

> "I say to you, rise, take up your pallet and go home" (2:11).

To the demoniac of Gerasenes, his words were:

> "Go home to your friends, and tell them how much the Lord has done for you and how he has had mercy on you" (5:19).

Here the healed is not only restored to his community but also invested with a saving mission. The woman, who had a flow of blood for twelve years and for that reason was rendered impure and outside the pale of ordinary social intercourse, was, thanks to the cure, readmitted into the community. So too, the daughter of Jairus, on being healed, was reintroduced to the fellowship of the table. "He...told them to give her something to eat." (5:43) Reconciliation with the community is implied in all the miracles of healing and exorcism in so far as the sick and the possessed were looked down upon as defiled and defiling and were therefore ostracized. That miracles have been the revelation of a power that built up the community is particularly evident in the multiplication of the loaves which brought into existence a new fellowship of the table.

Man was made in the image of God. And he is God's image only in the measure in which he fills the earth and subdues it. Now sickness and possession meant that it was nature that subdued him, not his nature. Through his miracles, Jesus restored to man his divine image as lord over the earth and thereby brought him nearer to God. This truth, implied in all the miracle stories, is made explicit in the words of Jesus to the paralytic: "My son, your sins are forgiven." (2:5) Sin in this context is to be understood as the alienation of God's image in man.

From an Economy of Having to an Economy of Giving

The new wine that was Jesus could not be contained in the then prevailing economic system either, which was an unholy combination of the Asiatic mode of production and the slave economy of the Roman Empire. It was an economy in which a privileged few grew richer and richer at the expense of the many poor. At the root of it lay man's aggression against his neighbour. How could therefore the rich, whose hands were soaked with the blood of the innocent, belong to the new humanity which God's coming was to usher in? How could those who worship the idol of wealth be at the same time worshippers of the true God? Hence Jesus' pointed criticism of the rich:

> "How hard it will be for those who have riches to enter the Kingdom of God?... It is easier for a camel to go through the eye of a needle than for a rich man to enter the Kingdom of God" (10:23-25).

It was an illusion for the rich to think that they can belong to the new humanity while remaining within the economic order that made them rich. This is the burden of the story of the rich young man as recorded in Mark. The young man in question was one who observed all the commandments but continued to remain within the system of private property. "Teacher, all these I have observed from my youth." To which Jesus answered:

> "You lack one thing; go, sell what you have, and give to the poor, and you
> will have treasure in heaven; and come, follow me" (10:17-22).

Paradoxically, what the man lacked had something to do with what he had in plenty, namely, riches. How could he inherit eternal life - which was the question he put to Jesus - so long as he clung to an economic system which violently deprived the many of their inheritance of the earth? To become a member of the community of the future, he had to sell what he had and give it to the poor; in other words, he had to break with the economy of private property and embrace an economy of giving. This he was not prepared to do. Hence, his departure with a sad face.

Contrasted with him, the disciples of Jesus were prepared to rupture the bonds that tied them to the system of private property. Simon and Andrew 'left their nets (the instruments of production) and followed him' (1:18). The sons of Zebedee 'left their father Zebedee in the boat with the hired servants and followed him' (1:20). Similarly, Levi, the tax-collector, relinquished his lucrative job and followed Jesus empty-handed. The other disciples too did the same, as is clear from Peter's claim: "Lord, we have left everything and followed you" (10:28). What they did at the outset of their discipleship was to determine also their subsequent mission to preach the Good News, work cures and drive out demons. They were instructed not to rely on the economy of private property in the form of bread, bag, money, or even an extra tunic, but to depend on hospitality, i.e. on the economy of giving (6:7-13). On the two occasions, when he was faced with a large famished crowd, Jesus rejected the disciples' suggestion that they buy provisions from the villages nearby. Instead, he asked them to give what they had, being sure that what was given in love would multiply and satisfy all. And this is just what happened (6:34-44; 8:1-10). He also taught his disciples to devalue money economy as seems to be implied in his comment on the widow's mite:

> "Truly, I say to you, this poor widow has put in more than all those who
> are contributing to the treasury. For, they all contributed out of their
> abundance; but she out of her poverty has put in everything she had,
> her whole being" (12:43-44).

Here too we meet with a paradox: She who gave least gave most. What mattered for Jesus was not the exchange-value of what she put in (which was but little) but its use-value (which was everything, her whole being). Rejection of the mercantile economy seems to be implied also in Jesus' prophetic gesture of cleansing the temple. (11:15-15) Who were the ones he chased away, whip in hand? - the vendors and the money-changers whom he further qualified as robbers. It is significant that the Greek word used to mean 'driving out' is the same as used elsewhere to describe the casting out of demons. One cannot but hazard the conclusion that, in the eyes of Jesus, an economy in which everything human and divine could be bought and sold was as opposed to the reign of God as the rule of Satan.

It follows from our analysis that the preaching and practice of Jesus were subversive of the prevailing economic system. However, for him, subversion was not an end in itself but rather a prerequisite for marching ahead to a new order of things. Hence the demand: "Follow me." And the new order to which his disciples were to commit themselves was an economy of giving whose guiding principle is well expressed in the saying:

> "Take heed what you hear; the measure you give will be the measure you get, and still more will be given to you." (4-24)

The still more that is promised represents the fullness of the age to come, a fullness which is to be understood also in the material sense. In an economy in which each gives what he has, each also receives the whole of what the community has. Here lies the secret of the superabundance that characterizes the community of the future. The seed buried in the ground which produces first the blade, then the ear, then the full grain in all ear (4:28); the loaves which 'on being multiplied, satisfied all' (6:42: 8:8); the mustard seed that becomes the greatest of all shrubs (4:32); the seed that fell into good soil and grew up yielding thirtyfold and sixtyfold and a hundredfold - all these are symbols of the plenty that will mark life in the new humanity. The disciples who left everything are likewise promised a hundredfold in terms of economic and social fellowship:

> "Truly, I say to you, there is no one who has left house or brothers or sisters or mother or father or children or lands, for my sake and the Gospel, who will not receive a hundredfold now in this time, houses, and brothers and sisters and mothers and children and lands, with persecutions, and in the age to come eternal life." (10:29-30)

It is disputed whether the phrase 'and in the age to come eternal life' is part of the authentic saying of Jesus. Even if it were, it could not have meant a spiritual world above this world of ours, since such a concept was alien to the Hebrew mode of thinking. For Jesus, the age to come is both continuous and discontinuous with this age: continuous because it is our earth (land, houses) and our society (mothers, brothers, sisters) filled with love; discontinuous, because it is the definitive superseding of all alienation including the economic.

The earliest community of believers understood very well the call of their master to relinquish the economy of private property and commit themselves to an economy of giving which multiplies the given and satisfies the needs of all. Their practice is the best commentary on that future which Jesus envisaged.

> "Now the company of those who believed were of one heart and soul, and no one said that any of the things which he possessed was his own, but they had everything in common. And with great power, the apostles gave their testimony to the resurrection of the Lord Jesus, and great grace was upon them all. There was not a needy person among them, for as many as were possessors of lands or houses sold them, and brought the proceeds of what was sold and laid it at the apostles' feet; and the distribution was made to each as any had need" (Acts 4:32-35).

From each according to his ability; to each according to his need - such was the creed of primitive Christian communism, which those Christian leaders, who traffic in the blood of Jesus, choose to write off as an exercise in adventurism and utopianism. They forget that they represent the same forces that killed Jesus as well as primitive Christian communism.

Not Class but Communion

Subversion of the economy of private ownership necessarily involves a repudiation of the distinction between the rich and the poor, of class domination and exploitation. But the preaching and practice of Jesus were disruptive not only of the social relations of production but also of the social relations of reproduction and ritual purity. By the relations of reproduction, we understand those existing between husband and wife, parents, and children, and between members of the family as a whole. Regarding the first, Jesus abrogated the practice, sanctioned by Moses, which allowed any man to put away his wife by merely writing her a bill of divorce, a practice rooted in the domination of woman by man. He reaffirmed the original purpose of the Creator which required that 'man shall leave his father and mother and be joined to his wife, and the two shall become one flesh' (10:7-8). To become one flesh is a unique mode of loving one's neighbour as oneself. The disruption of the status quo is therefore at the same time the reaffirmation of authentic communion between man and woman. More, it looks as though Jesus looked forward to the supersession of marriage itself with its two-in-one-flesh-ness and to the emergence of a new mode of man-woman relationship which may be termed all-in-one-flesh-ness, which the creative power of God would bring into existence. This would seem to be the meaning of his reply to the Sadducees:

> "You are mistaken, and surely this is the reason: you do not know either the Scriptures or the power of God. When they rise from the dead, men and women do not marry; they are like angels in heaven" (12:24-25).

Jesus brought about also a reversal of the respective status of parents and children. In Jewish society, children were considered of no importance. For Jesus, on the contrary, they were the ones nearest to the Kingdom of God.

> "Let children come to me, do not hinder them; for to such belongs the Kingdom of God." (10:14)

Why? Because they, in contrast to the adults who had their hearts hardened by the seductions of the prevailing ideology, were open to whatever the future had in store for them, and therefore also to the coming reign of God. In fact, are not the youth of any country, of any age, closer to a social humanity than the adults with their mildewed minds and atrophied hearts? Finally, Jesus challenged the primacy which kinship relations enjoyed in Jewish society, as is clear from his reply to the crowd when they brought to his notice that his mother and brothers were asking for him:

> "Who are my mother and my brothers? Whoever does the will of God is my brother and sister, and mother." (3:33-35)

The communion of men resulting from a common commitment to the reign of God outweighed all other loyalties including those of kinship.

No less radical was Jesus' attitude to the social relations of inequality introduced and maintained by the prevalent ideology of ritual purity. In his time, people belonging to certain professions were held impure. Such were, for instance, publicans, shepherds, tailors, barbers, tanners, and prostitutes. Their company was scrupulously avoided by the respectable classes, i.e. by those who observed every detail of the written law and the oral tradition. This had made a deep rent in Jewish society. The self-styled pure had put up a wall around them lest they are defiled by the touch of the impure and the ungodly. Jesus set about pulling down this wall. Defying all social taboos and accepted norms, he invited the outcasts of society to sit at table with him and thereby assured them that God was with them and not with the walled-in hypocrites. To the Scribes who were shocked and angered at this, he replied in bitter irony:

> "I came not to call the righteous, but sinners." (2:17)

Paraphrased, his words would run: 'I came not to call you, the self-righteous, but those others whom you despise as sinners; for these alone are open to God and his future, not you.' Among the ritually impure, lepers were the ones most excluded from the company of men. They had to shout 'unclean, unclean', wherever they went, lest they defile such pure as might chance to pass by. It must have therefore required tremendous courage of conviction on the part of anyone to have any social contact with them. And courage indeed Jesus had. He had no hesitation in touching lepers or in sitting at table with them (1:41; 14:3).

In sum, the social teaching and practice of Jesus, while disrupting the existing relations of production, reproduction and ritual purity, projected at the same time the horizon of a new humanity in which things will mediate man's self-giving to his neighbour; in which love will replace the violence of sex and the violence of aggression.

Through Political Subversion to a Community of Service

The teaching and practice of Jesus were such as to undermine the very foundations of political power, whether it be of Herod, of the Sanhedrin, or of Rome. Equally, it went counter to the ideology and strategy of the Zealots. We shall begin with this last point since it throws light on the political stance of Jesus as a whole.

The Zealots were determined to throw out the Romans by force and restore the kingly rule of David and Solomon. They looked forward to the coming of a political Messiah who would help them achieve their goal. Ruthlessly crushed by the Romans more than once, they bided their time for decisive action, but meanwhile resorted to sporadic acts of violence in a guerilla-style. They had their stronghold in Galilee where Jesus was brought up and grew into a young man. Does the Gospel according to Mark provide any hint as to his grappling with the challenge of Zealotism? At the beginning of his Gospel, Mark records the temptation in the desert. "And he was in the wilderness forty days, tempted by Satan" (1:13). That the temptation in question was the ordeal of having to make an option either for or against Zealotism is clear from the other two Synoptic Gospels. Mathew tells us:

> "Again, the devil took him to a very high mountain, and showed him all
> the kingdoms of the world and the glory of them; and he said to him, 'All
> these I will give you if you will fall down and worship me." (Mt. 4:8-9)

What Satan held up before Jesus was the Zealot ideal of an Israel ruling over the kingdoms of the world. But that ideal was against the original divine revelation which forbad Israel to have anyone but God to rule over them. Hence Jesus' reply: "Begone, Satan! For it is written: You shall worship the Lord your God and him only shall you serve." (Mt. 4:8-10). It is in the light of this reply that we should understand the saying of Jesus in Mark: "For what does it profit a man, to gain the whole world and forfeit his life?" (8:36). What use gaining universal political power if its final result is the denial of each man's right to lead a full and rich life?

In the desert, Jesus made a definitive option against political Messianism. And Satan retreated for the time being, but only to reappear and confront him with the same temptation at various points in his life. He did so first through the people who by and large shared the Zealot hopes. There are indications in the Gospel that the crowd, on seeing the marvels he worked, began to nurse the hope that he would come out in the open and proclaim himself the political Messiah they were looking for. This explains their persistent efforts to pursue him wherever he went. Equally persistently he withdrew from them. He took refuge in private homes (1:29; 2:1, 15; 3:19; 7:24), in desert places (1:35; 6:31), by the seaside (2:13; 3:7; 4:1), in boats (4:35; 5:21; 6:45; 8:10; 8:13). The contrast between the nationalist hopes of the people and the role Jesus assigned to himself comes out clearly in the narrative of his entry into Jerusalem. On this occasion, the crowd shouted:

> "Hosanna! Blessed is he who comes in the name of the Lord! Blessed is the kingdom of our father David that is coming! Hosanna in the highest!"

The acclamation shows that the people expected Jesus to restore the kingdom of David. This conclusion imposes itself all the more if 'Hosanna in the highest' meant, as a recent interpreter has tried to show, 'save us from the higher-ups', i.e. 'save us from the Romans'. That any such plan was foreign to Jesus follows from the fact that he chose for his means of conveyance a colt, a common means of transportation, in preference to a horse, the beast of war par excellence.

Satan confronted Jesus once again, this time in the person of Peter, to dissuade him from his option against political Messianism. Disappointed at Jesus' prediction that he would have to face death at the hands of his enemies, Peter took him by the arm and began to rebuke him: "No, Lord, this shall never happen to you." Which earned the severe reprimand: "Away with you, Satan, you think as men think, not as God thinks." (8:35) No better were the thoughts of the other disciples, as may be seen from their quarrel as to who should be the greatest in the Kingdom of God (9:33-34), from the request of the sons of Zebedee to be allowed to sit one on his right and the other on his left when he came in glory (10:37), and from the fact that one of the disciples betrayed him and another resorted to violence and struck off the ear of the High Priest's servant. Seen in the light of his initial option against political Messianism, the agony Jesus underwent in the garden of Olives becomes especially significant. It looks as though the ideological rift between himself, on the one hand, and the disciples and the crowd, on the other, assumed on the eve of his death the form of a chasm in his own soul between what he willed (the thoughts of men) and what God willed (the thoughts of God):

"Abba, Father, all things are possible to thee; remove this cup from me;
yet not what I will, but what thou wilt" (14:36).

The agony ends with his final acceptance of the thoughts and the purposes of God as opposed to those of men. The decisive victory won, he surrendered himself to his enemies.

Having defined Jesus' stance regarding Zealotism, let us now examine how his words and deeds posed a threat to the political powers that be. Among these, Herod comes first, whose territory was the main scene of Jesus' activity. He had John the Baptist beheaded because the latter had criticized his taking his brother's wife. If so, he had ample reason to get rid of Jesus too who taught the indissolubility of marriage. The Gospel according to Luke explicitly states that some Pharisees came to warn Jesus that Herod was out to kill him (13:31).

Jesus posed a threat also to the religio-political power-structure of the Sanhedrin with its headquarters in the temple of Jerusalem. And this for the following reasons: First, his radical reinterpretation of the Law, his rejection of the distinction between the sacred and the profane, his re-affirmation of the primacy of love over cult, and his prediction of the destruction of the temple, undermined the religious authority of the priesthood. Second, in chasing away the vendors and the changers of money from the temple premises, he challenged the economic infra-structure of the political power of the Sanhedrin. Third, the universal character of the new humanity he preached contradicted the nationalist particularism of Jewish political power, much as its guardians rejected the hopes and the strategy of the Zealots. Last, the priesthood had a vested interest in maintaining the status quo since they were ruling by the favour of Rome.

We now come to the final question: Did Jesus do anything to disrupt Roman imperialism in Palestine? True, he rejected the reformist, nationalist aspirations of the Zealots. This, however, does not mean that he was indifferent to the political slavery of his people. There are indications to show that he opposed the Roman rule. Very much to the point is the well-known saying of his: "Render to Caesar the things that are Caesar's, and to God the things that are God's." (12:17) To understand the passage we must keep in mind the creation story of Genesis according to which man was made in God's image, and the fact that Jahweh had forbidden Israel to make images of anything in heaven or on earth. To use coins bearing the image of Caesar was therefore contrary to the will of God. Hence, 'render to Caesar what is his' can only mean: 'Let Caesar collect his coins and quit the land. Have nothing to do with him, nor with the economic and political power he wields. But man, unlike the Roman coin, bears the image of God, and therefore belongs, and shall be subject, to God alone. No one else shall exercise dominion over him, not even Caesar.' Naturally, the meaning Jesus wanted to convey could have been grasped only by those 'who had ears to hear'. For such as have ears to hear the subversiveness of his teaching extends beyond the Jewish and the Roman political power to all states which reduce men to the status of mere objects which can be dictatorially manipulated. It is in this light that we have to understand his saying:

"You know that in the world the recognized rulers lord it over their subjects, and their great men make them feel the weight of authority. That is not the way with you; among you, whoever wants to be great must be the willing slave of all." (10:42-44)

In another sense too, Jesus was a threat to the Roman empire. The Romans needed the support of the religio-political power-structure of the Jews to maintain their rule in Palestine. Therefore, in so far as Jesus' preaching and practice called in question the very foundations of Judaism and of the priestly class in particular, indirectly he became a danger also to the stability of the Roman power. Such being the case, it was in the interest of the Zealots, of Herod, of the Sanhedrin and of the Roman authorities to get rid of the man from Galilee.

In the light of these reflections, we may further define the new humanity Jesus hoped for as a transpolitical communion of people, the term political understood in the pejorative sense of 'having to do with structures of power dominating the people as a whole'. Its principle of unity will not be the exercise of power but love as *being-for-others*, as service. The greatest in it will be the least of today, namely, the oppressed masses, the wretched and the dispossessed of the earth. It will be a form of human togetherness which recognizes no barriers, one in which man will meet his neighbour on the basis of what is most divine in him, namely, the human.

We have seen how rupture and communion formed the dynamic pattern of the life of Jesus as it evolved in response to the challenge of the rule of Satan, property, class and state. Admittedly, the analysis offered here needs to be supplemented with a discussion of rupture and communion as verified in his attitude to the religion of his forbears and in his own personal existence as a member of the family of humanity. However, even the limited analysis we have made is enough to show that the Jesus of the Gospels is more relevant for us today than that the Christ of tradition whom men have created in their own image to safeguard their vested interests and to legitimize their wrongdoings.

Are we not called upon to do today what he did twenty centuries ago, namely, to break the fetters that weigh heavily on us so that we may attain a new communion of men and women?[1]

(Paper read at the seminar, held in YMCA Hall, Tiruvalla, Kerala, to felicitate Dr. M. M. Thomas on the occasion of his *shashtiabda-purthi*, 60th year, in 1976; *Religion and Society*, Bangalore, 23, 1976, pp.66-76; *Jesus and Society*, Chap. 28)

12

A Lesson in Socialism

To teach is to lead someone to a fuller awareness of what he already, though but confusedly, knows. Where the teacher is a prophet as well, he also calls upon his disciples to act upon the knowledge gained, to translate theory into practice. Such a one, indeed, was Jesus. He made people recognize the contradictions in themselves and society and showed how to resolve them by opting for the radically new. An apt illustration of this may be found in the story of the rich young man. The following is a running commentary on the narrative as found in Mark 10:17-22. "And as he was setting out on his journey, a man ran up and knelt before him."

The journey Jesus was about to undertake was not just one among the many he had made in the course of his work as a prophet and teacher. It was to be his last and decisive journey, closely bound up with his destiny and with that of all men. "Nevertheless I must go my way...for it cannot be that a prophet should perish away from Jerusalem" (Lk 13:33). This very setting shows that the Evangelist viewed Jesus' dialogue with the rich young man as revealing something central to his message.

Who was this rich man? We know nothing about his background. We are only told that he had great possessions. The Greek word for possessions, *kremata*, meant property in land. We may, therefore, surmise that he was a landlord, and, as such, belonged to the upper stratum of Jewish society. This, however, did not prevent him from prostrating himself before Jesus. What brought him to his knees could only be the power that went out of the prophet from Nazareth. "And asked him: Good teacher, what must I do to inherit eternal life?"

In class societies, what matters is not what one *is*, but the class one belongs to. Consequently, each person will tend to attach a class label to everybody else. No wonder the rich man addressed Jesus as one belonging to the class of the rabbis. However, his evaluation of the latter was not determined by class-bound consciousness, as is clear from the qualifying term, good. He did see something unique in Jesus which marked him off from the other teachers who used their learning to damn rather than to save, to impose heavy burdens on the faithful rather than to set them free. He must have known from hearsay that the Galilean prophet taught like one having authority, that his word was deed and power.

The questioner wanted to know what he must do to inherit eternal life, in other words, to gain entry into the Kingdom of God. His was a quest after knowledge not for its own sake but the sake of correct practice, for deciding what he should do. He knew well enough that faith without practice availed nothing. The question further implies that he was dimly aware that not all was well with his own practice. However, his self-criticism was not radical enough, as the sequel will show. Jesus' reply was aimed at further radicalizing his self-awareness. "And Jesus said to him. Why do you call me good? No one is good but God alone."

At first blush, these words sound curt, if not totally unwarranted. But this is not the case. Jesus is trying to bring home to the questioner that there was something basically wrong with his attitude, which would stand in the way of his gaining entry into the New Age. To grasp this we must remember that in contemporary Judaism the term, good, had come to mean holy, divine. Hence in addressing Jesus good, the man was attributing to him what is a prerogative of God alone. Herein lies also the motivation behind his prostrating himself on the ground, a posture, which in the Orient, one usually assumes only when at prayer. Now, whoever raises man to the level of God will end up degrading God to the level of an alienated man. Jesus would, therefore, repudiate any suggestion that he was God. Hence the curtness and the vehemence of his reply. His words are also a warning to all those who seek the fullness of life. They should beware of identifying the given - whether the given is a thing, a person, or a situation - with the Ultimate and the Absolute. Only those who are prepared to transcend the given can hope to see the face of God. Having thus admonished the questioner, Jesus addresses himself to his question. "You know the commandments: Do not kill; Do not commit adultery; Do not steal; Do not bear false witness; Do not defraud; Honour your father and mother."

All the precepts enumerated here, except the last but one, are from the Decalogue (Ex 20:12ff. and Dt 5:16ff). The command, Do not defraud, is found in Lv 19:13 and Dt 24:14, and probably meant, 'Do not keep back the wages of your hireling'. Significantly, there is no mention of the other prescriptions of the Law such as those regarding cult, ritual purity, and Sabbath. For Jesus, neither cult nor law can guarantee entry into the Kingdom. What matters is man's relationship with his fellowmen. It is in the human community that the God who comes can be encountered. Here we meet with a profound paradox. He had just told the young man that to meet God he must seek to go beyond the given, whether man or thing. But now he tells him to seek God in the given reality of human relationships. This tension between *beyond-man* and *in-man* is not a contradiction but the ultimate truth regarding the God of Jesus. God is the Beyond that reveals itself wherever men and women gather together in love to work, to create, to sing, to play, to laugh, and to mate. "And he said to him, Teacher, all these I have observed from my youth." The reply reveals a certain self-complacency bordering on self-righteousness. True, it might have been that he had never killed, committed adultery, stolen, borne false witness, defrauded, or failed to honour his parents. But how could he be so sure that he had never been wanting in mercy, compassion, love, and justice? The words of John are relevant here: "If we say we have no sin, we deceive ourselves, and the truth is not in us" (1 Jn. 1:8). Jesus would explode his self-complacency and lead him to see the sin lurking beneath it. But this did not prevent him from appreciating his sincerity and earnestness. "Jesus looking upon him loved him." "And said to him, You lack one thing; go, sell what you have, and give to the poor, and you will have treasure in heaven."

What was it that the rich lacked? Here we meet with a second paradox: What he lacked was what he had no lack of, namely, wealth. Wealth was what stood between him and the Kingdom. How so? Because, wealth is not something neutral. It is the accumulated unpaid labour of others. The wealth of a few is bought at the cost of the poverty of many. It is the fruit of aggression, whether personal or institutionalized as slavery, serfdom, or wage labour. In class societies, all wealth is soaked with the blood of the innocent. Therefore, whoever would enter the Kingdom of God must restore his riches to those who produced them. Hence the injunction, "Sell what you have and give to the poor", is not an exhortation to charity but a demand for justice. This shows how hollow was the man's claim that he had all along observed the commandments. This comes into full relief in the version of the story found in the Gospel according to the Hebrews. There Jesus' reply runs:

> "How can you say, I have fulfilled the law and the prophets when it is written in the law: You shall love your neighbour as yourself; and lo, many of your brothers, sons of Abraham, are clothed in filth, dying of hunger, and your house is full of many good things, none of which goes out to them?"

True, our young man had from his early youth observed the commandments. But he had done so within the system of private property. He had never stopped to question the justice of the system itself, which is just what Jesus wanted him to do. This was something he had never bargained for. To be told, that what he so far considered his was but ill-gotten wealth to be restored to the poor, was indeed shattering. All the more so, since giving up wealth meant renouncing power, status, and prestige - the concomitants of wealth. As a rich landlord, he must surely have been a member of the local council of elders, the lowest administrative unit of society at that time. (In fact, Luke refers to him as a ruler: 18:18). Furthermore, he had shared the popular belief that wealth was a sign of divine favour and had been nursing the comfortable feeling of being God's favoured one. And now, that God too he must do without. In short, he must de-class himself to have treasures in heaven. Even that would only be the first step. Between opting out of his own class and participating in the fullness of the New Age there is yet another task to be accomplished, and that is contained in the call: "And come, follow me."

On the surface, there seems to be a discontinuity between *selling-what-one-has* and *giving-to-the-poor* and following Jesus. But the discontinuity is only apparent. For the journey on which Jesus has set out seeks to achieve precisely what he enjoined on the young man - the radical repudiation of wealth, power, and the God of the privileged classes. The temple in Jerusalem was the seat of all three: of the accumulated surplus of the labouring classes in Palestine as well as of commerce and conspicuous consumption, of the political power of the Jewish state, and the God who stood guard over "the den of thieves". Anyone seeking entry into the Kingdom must follow in the footsteps of Jesus and like him contest the powers that be - economic, political, and cultural. Such a huge price our young man was not prepared to pay. The Evangelist concludes, "At that saying his countenance fell and he went away sorrowful; for he had great possessions."

(Anawim No. 17, *Jesus and Society*, Chap. 9)

13

Table-fellowship as Socialist Praxis

The measure of a person's greatness is his sensibility to whatever is true, beautiful, and wholesome in his environment. And the more refined his sensibility, the more intense is the revulsion he feels against all that mars the beauty of living: unlove, hatred, injustice, aggression, and social fragmentation. He experiences every blow dealt with the least of his kind as dealt with himself. The agony he feels inevitably becomes word, protest, and contestation. He thus becomes a subverter of the status quo, thereby inviting reprisal from the guardians of law and order. Such a person, however, is no nihilist. The no to the evil that he sees is at the same time a powerful affirmation of life. More than the prudence of the wise, it is the daring of such prophetic individuals that changes the course of history.

If ever there was a man fully attuned to the least revelation of beauty, goodness, and love, and for that very reason sensitive to every mutilation and fragmentation of the human, that was Jesus of Nazareth. His soul rejoiced at the sight of the birds of the air and the lilies of the field; his heart warmed up to the laughter and innocence of children, to the generosity of love, to whatsoever made life lightsome and joyous. And the price he had to pay for such exquisite sensibility was the pain, the anguish and the indignation he felt for everything around him that served to stifle the human and fracture social existence. No wonder he went through life as a sign of contradiction to all, a contester whose defiant no cuts more keenly than any two-edged sword. But such courage to defy and denounce was not to be tolerated by the rulers that were. They got rid of him in the prime of his life.

Eating with Tax-gatherers and Sinners

A telling instance of Jesus' sensibility to social wholeness and of his courage to protest against the mutilation of man is his table-fellowship with social outcasts. To grasp its significance we must consider the social conditions then prevailing. Gone were the days of tribal unity when social relations among the Israelites were founded on kinship and common property. Society had become fragmented under the system of private property, money economy, and state power. No less sharp was the division brought about by the theory and practice of ritual purity. Pure were those who scrupulously observed every detail of the written and the oral law; impure those who did not. Impurity was attached to various categories of people such as those engaged in unclean professions (shepherds, barbers, tanners, tailors, tax-gatherers, etc.), the illegitimately born, and, above all, the gentiles. Contact with them was shunned by the respectable classes; much more so sitting at table with them.

This state of affairs Jesus could not tolerate. He openly taught that purity or impurity is not a thing inhering in objects and persons and that nothing that enters a man from outside could defile him. His protest, however, was not confined to oral denunciation. It also took the form of counter-praxis. In defiance of prevailing taboos, he went out of his way and sat at table with tax-gatherers and sinners, a term which in the Gospel denotes such social groups as were ritually unclean. Thus we find him sitting at table with the tax-gatherer Levi and his colleagues in the profession (Mk 2:15-17). The Gospels also present him as playing host to the impure multitude, as when he fed them in the desert (Mk 6:30-44). There is no reason to think that the multitude in question consisted only of Jews.

It is likely that eating with social outcasts was a recurring feature of his life. Else it is difficult to understand how his enemies could have accused him of being 'a glutton and a drinker, a friend of tax-gatherers and sinners.' (Mt. 11:16)

The same conclusion may be drawn from his reply to the Pharisees who were scandalized at his conduct: "It is not the healthy that need a doctor; I did not come to invite virtuous people, but the sinners." (Mk 2:17). If his mission was directed exclusively to sinners, he must have habitually sought their company and expressed his solidarity with them in the customary manner, namely, by eating and drinking with them.

The meal-fellowship of Jesus is not just one of the many gracious deeds he performed. In a way, it sums up his entire mission. In it are telescoped many dimensions of meaning, which need unraveling.

Gathering in Human Fragments

Any meal shared expresses as well as creates community; it is a meeting of people in intimacy and friendship, a celebration of the togetherness of living. What distinguishes the meal-fellowship of Jesus from the usual family meals was its new basis. The latter had for its basis kinship; the former, the praxis of love.

"Whoever does the will of God is my brother, my sister, my mother." (Mk 3:35) And doing the will of God meant effectively loving one's neighbour. By laying down love as the unifying principle of the new community, Jesus repudiated every restrictive basis, be it kinship, colour, race, cult, or culture. At the same time, he wished to preserve what was good in earlier forms of communal life, as is clear from his use of kinship terms to describe the new fellowship he created. In the new dispensation, everyone will be brother, sister, and mother to everyone else. In other words, man's relations with his neighbour will retain the intimacy and warmth of family ties while, at the same time, superseding their exclusiveness. Seen in this perspective, Jesus' eating and drinking with the marginalized was radical social praxis, aimed at creating a counter-community and a counter-culture.

Neither Buying nor Selling but Giving

The kind of meals which Jesus initiated represented economic relations essentially different from what obtained in contemporary society. In all social formations resting on the division of labour and private property, the satisfaction of one's material needs is possible only through the exchange of products, through buying and selling. In such a set-up, human beings meet one another not as concrete peoples but as owners of commodities. The relation between peoples assumes the nature of relation between things. The quality of a person is equated with the quantity of commodities he possesses. Consequently, the products of labour tend to divide man from man. Such was, in the main, the economic relations that prevailed in Jesus' time. In contrast, the meals he shared contain the seed of a new economy. Here the products of labour - food and drink - are not commodities but gifts. What is given in freedom mediates the mutual love of the giver and the recipient. As such, it binds the many into one, into one community.

Pertinent here is the episode of the feeding of the multitude. To take the Marcan narrative, when the disciples saw that it was getting late and they were in a lonely place, they asked Jesus to send the people off to the farms and villages around to buy something to eat themselves. Nurtured in the school of private property, they could only think of each one buying provisions out of his own income. But not Jesus, who told them, "Give them something to eat yourselves". Still, they did not get the message. Feeding hungry they were prepared to do. But first, they must buy the required provisions. Jesus asked, "How many loaves have you (to give)?" When they answered "five, and two fishes also", he, "taking the five loaves and the two fishes,... looked up to heaven, said the blessing, broke the loaves and gave them to the disciples to distribute." (Mk 6:35-44)

Thus he dissociated himself from the economy of buying and selling and inaugurated an economy of giving, in which the product of work once again becomes the bond between humans. From the fact that the crowd ate to their hearts' content and yet much food was left over, we may surmise that they too responded to Jesus' call, each one sharing with others what he had. It is in this context that we must interpret the saying: "Take note of what you hear; the measure you give is the measure you receive, with something more besides."(Mk 4:24) Clearly, Jesus intended his meal-fellowship to set the pattern for society as a whole.

Meal-fellowship as Political Contestation

To inaugurate a new social praxis is to come into collision with the ruling classes; all the more so in pre-capitalist societies where religious and political power tended to fuse into one. Jesus' meals with social outcasts posed a serious threat to all who in one way or another wielded power in Judaism. It outraged the lawyers and the Pharisees, who imposed their notions of ritual purity on the masses. The priests too had reason to feel threatened, since by repudiating the distinction between the pure and the impure, the young radical from Nazareth had shaken the very foundations on which their profession and livelihood depended. Besides, the practice of eating with tax-gatherers and sinners could easily have been construed as collaboration with the occupying power. For, the Jews believed that they alone were heirs to God's blessings and that only divine vengeance awaited the gentiles. Then came Jesus on the scene offering intimacy and friendship to tax-gatherers ('Jews who had made themselves as gentiles') and gentiles, and thereby proclaiming that these too came within the orbit of divine love. It was now easy for the Jewish authorities to project him as a Roman sympathizer in order to win popular support for their plan to murder him. Truly, it was under the shadow of the cross that Jesus ate and drank with the outcasts of his day.

A Revolutionary Praxis Betrayed

Jesus saw in his table-fellowship with the disreputable classes an anticipation of the reign of God to come. Significantly, he spoke of that future as a festive gathering of people from east and west (of Jews and gentiles) around the table of God (Mt. 8:11). When he sat down at table with those whom the self-styled saints looked down upon as sinners, he was but putting into practice his hope in the realization of that universal community. This is what marks him out from all sentimental visionaries and impotent Utopians who project a golden age to come in order to escape from the challenges of the not too golden present.

His table-fellowship, therefore, is critical, revolutionary praxis aimed at taking man and society nearer to their absolute future. It is the most tangible, concrete expression of his mission and message. Tragically, however, it was soon eclipsed by what subsequently emerged as the Church. The table-fellowship was in essence universal, that is, inclusive of all who loved one another, of all who hoped for total liberation. In contrast, the Church as a community is exclusive, with its own specific creed, cult, and law. The former had *God-to-come* for its centre; the latter is centred upon the *Christ-of-faith* dwelling in the heaven above. The former looked forward to the future, to the final in-gathering of people from east and west; the latter either looks back to the past with a view to preserving what has been handed down, or reduces its hope in the future to an impotent longing bereft of the power to change the world. The former was subversive-creative praxis; the latter is, on the whole, a provider of legitimation for the status quo. The former was essentially bound up with the prospect of the Cross; the latter has managed to eliminate the Cross or to degrade it to a mere symbol suited to feed morbid piety. The Church, therefore, can become relevant and meaningful only if it becomes once again the table-fellowship of Jesus. For that, it will have to die first. But will it?

Here one is reminded of the famous dialectic of master and slave in the phenomenology of Hegel. What cost the slave his freedom was the fear of death. Had he dared to risk his life, he might have been killed. But his death would have been at the same time the supreme affirmation of freedom. Instead, he chose to live and be unfree. Likewise, it is the fear of death on the Cross that prompted the Church to convert itself into a comprehensive system of life-insurance, and, in the process, become a slave of the powers and principalities of this world. Which means that only such as are prepared to take up the Cross, can continue in history the table-fellowship of Jesus.

(Anawim No. 24; *Jesus and Society*, Chap. 17)

14

Christians and Class Struggle

As disciples of Jesus, we are called upon to continue in history his prophetic 'No' to everything that goes counter to the reign of God in the world, i.e. to everything that dehumanizes man and holds him in bondage. Like him we too are sent "to announce good news to the poor, to proclaim release for prisoners and recovery of sight for the blind, to let the broken victims go free, to proclaim the year of the Lord's favour". (Lk 4: 18-19) An essential prerequisite for this is to read the signs of the times and identify the forces in society that oppress the spirit of man, forces whether of exploitation or domination.

This last distinction calls for some explanation. Exploitation has to do with the expropriation either of the means of production or of the product from the immediate producers. The denial of adequate wages, eviction of tenants from the land they till the imposition of bonded labour, lending money at exorbitant interest — these are manifest instances of exploitation. One might go a step further and say that capitalism based on private property and wage labour is itself institutionalized exploitation. Domination, as distinguished from exploitation, has to do with the exercise of power, power meaning the possibility one has to impose one's goals and purposes on others. Domination may be exercised either by persons or by impersonal social structures. At the risk of simplification, one might say that, while exploitation means depriving people of their food, domination means denying them their freedom. Underlying this distinction, however, there is also a unity. For exploitation is either a form or a consequence of domination. For instance, the cultural and religious domination of the higher castes often manifests itself in the exploitation of the lower castes and outcastes. Similarly, the bourgeoisie, in appropriating the surplus product of the laborers, set limit to the latter's economic and cultural options, and thereby also curtail their freedom. However, not all forms of domination involve exploitation. The individual capitalist, for instance, is bound to follow the dictates of the market; the market dominates him. Yet none would say that he is exploited. This means that, while every exploitation is a form of domination, the converse need not necessarily be true. In this paper, I shall speak in terms only of domination, considering exploitation as but one of its forms. We shall now address ourselves, to the task of identifying the systems of domination in Indian society.

The Systems of Domination

On the economic front, we have to contend with the capitalist and the feudal mode of production; the former with its nerve centres in urban areas, and the latter still surviving in rural areas. That capitalism is exploitative is widely recognized; not so the fact that it is a system of the domination of man by man. It denies the direct producers, the working class, any control over the system of production, distribution, and consumption; it denies them any participation in setting the goals, and in determining the organization, of production. Consequently, also, the working class has no control over the conditions of their own life. Their options are reduced to the sole one of working to satisfy other people's needs. In another way too, capitalism poses a threat to freedom, in so far as it manipulates human needs through advertisements to be able to sell its wares. The domination of the bourgeoisie reached an all-time peak during the emergency when the laboring classes were denied even the freedom to protest and trade union activities were banned. The emergency also saw a spurt in the growth of the multinational enterprises in India. Besides causing a drain of profits outside the country, they, through their control over the economy, pose a threat to our national independence. By propagating the values of western consumer society they also commit cultural aggression against our people. To come to the rural sector, the feudal and landed interests which, during the Congress rule, were made to subserve the interests of the industrial bourgeoisie have started to reassert themselves and to lord it over the Harijans and the backward castes and classes.

Political power had already constituted itself into a machinery of repression even before the emergency. The legislative bodies and the organs of self-government had come under the firm hold of the privileged classes and had long ceased to be truly representative of the people. The bureaucracy had been so centralized as to make civil servants irresponsive and irresponsible to the common man. Justice had been reduced to a commodity, an article of conspicuous consumption which only the rich could afford. The emergency must, therefore, be viewed not as a sudden deviation from a hitherto sound democratic tradition but as an accentuation in the extreme of the already existing evils of the political system. It saw a further concentration of power, this time in the hands of one person who used the entire state apparatus — the bureaucracy, the police, the para-military forces, and even the army — to maintain herself in power. The recent upsurge of the people during the elections did no more than bring down the dictator, leaving the main pillars of the political system intact. The demolition of this machinery of repression is an essential precondition for the creation of a socialist society in which power will be replaced with self-management, regimentation from above with free initiatives from below.

To construct a society in which all will have the freedom to be, to grow, and to create, it is no less necessary to overthrow the systems of cultural domination. By culture here we understand the complex of ideas, values, norms, and goals which determine the patterns of thinking, feeling, and acting of a community. The chief among such systems is organized religion, caste, the educational system, and the mass media.

The God of organized religion is one whom the privileged classes have created in their own image to safeguard their vested interests and legitimize their doings. He is projected as the master of all, before whom man is but a slave. No wonder, if those who have set up God as master try to reproduce the master-slave relationship at the social level by installing themselves as masters and by reducing the common believer to the position of slaves. This they do by putting forth the monopolistic claim to be sole distributors of divine favour. And divine favour or grace is the money of organized religion, the universal equivalent of all commodities. Those who can dispense divine favour are in a position to exchange it for whatever they like, wealth, power, or prestige. Within this set up religious authority naturally tends to become centralized and authoritarian. That is why there is a certain affinity between organized religion and authoritarian States. This was made abundantly clear during the emergency which found religious leaders singing hymns to dictatorship. What we have said about organized religion, in general, applies also to the Christian Churches in India. There are, however, welcome signs among sections of believers of a return to the God of the living before whom every man stands naked, defenseless, and vulnerable.

Caste too continues to hold sway over the Indian masses enabling the few among them to look down upon the many as the untouchable, the unlovable, and the unwanted of the earth. Notions of ritual purity, occupational taboos, and status by birth still poison economic and social relations. What is worse, the introduction of universal suffrage has afforded the numerically stronger castes or sub-castes new opportunities to wield economic and political power over the other castes. Casteism has learned to make itself at home in the world of production for profit, and of politics for power.

The prevailing system of education is meant to serve a double purpose: to instill in the youth the values of capitalism and to train the personnel needed for the expanding political bureaucracy. As such, it represents the interests of the ruling classes. The poorer classes who form the bulk of the population have no say in determining the goals of education. This is true, by and large, even of the educational community of the teachers and the taught. These are merely used by the existing system of production and power to reproduce itself. The same interests are served also by the mass media. What they disseminate are the values of capitalism - competition, private interest, efficiency, aggression, consumerism, and individualism.

The three systems of domination - the economic, the political, and the cultural - do not run on parallel lines. They are closely interlinked and tend to reinforce one another. However, their interrelation is not to be so conceived as though the political and the cultural are mere derivatives of the economic. Within the framework of interaction and mutual conditioning, each enjoys a certain autonomy of its own, the nature and the extent of which must in each case be empirically verified. In a vast country like India, it is natural to find variations in the correlations of power which must be closely studied by all who are called to lead the struggles for liberation.

Christians and Class-struggles

To do away with the existing social system based on the domination of man by man, nothing less than an organized struggle on the part of the masses is needed. But how can the disciples of Jesus reconcile the inclusiveness of the reign of God with the exclusiveness of class struggle, the demands of universal love with class hatred? For an answer, it is necessary to have a clear grasp of what class struggle is. To arrive at it, we shall institute an evaluation of the prevalent forms of struggle in India, and that too in the light of a critical reading of Karl Marx, the main exponent of class struggle.

Marx defined class in terms not only of the role people play in the system of production but also of their organization and consciousness. In the Eighteenth Brumaire of Louis Bonaparte he wrote:

> "In so far as millions of families live under economic conditions of existence that separate their mode of life, their interests, and their culture from those of the other classes, and put them in hostile opposition to the latter, they form a class."

In so far as there is merely a local interconnection among these small-holding peasants, and the identity of their interests begets no community, no national bond, and no political organization among them, they do not form a class. Seen in this light, not even the industrial proletariat in India may be called a class. For they are fragmented based on conflicting political and trade-union loyalties. Nor do they share a common culture different from that of the bourgeoisie. They have been largely integrated into the value system of the latter. For this reason, the strikes and demonstrations carried on by the industrial working class cannot be called class struggle in the strict sense of the term. They are but struggles organized by certain limited sections of the working population to further their own sectional interests, and that too, often to the detriment of the weaker sections. For, compared with the unorganized laborers, the landless poor, and the unemployed, the organized industrial proletariat is a privileged stratum of society. When they demand a bigger share of the cake, it can only be at the expense of those who have less or none at all.

There is yet another reason why the prevalent forms of struggle on the part of workers cannot be called class struggle. What they want is not the abolition of classes, but their reconciliation within the capitalist relations of production. It is not the end of capitalism they seek but rather the end of the conditions which deny them a greater share in the fruits of capitalism.

What characterizes genuine socialist class struggle is that it aims at the abolition of the capitalist relations of production and the construction of a new society based on the socialization of the means of production. For whatever are the felt needs of the working class, their real, objective need is to abolish the system of private property, the root causes of their alienation. But private property dehumanizes not only the proletariat but also the other classes in society. In capitalism, even the bourgeoisie is condemned to an alienated, truncated existence. In the words of Marx,

> "The possessing class and the proletarian class express the same human alienation. But the former is satisfied with its situation, feels itself well established in it, recognizes this self-alienation as its own power, and thus has the appearance of human existence. The latter feels itself crushed by this self-alienation, sees in it its own impotence and the reality of an inhuman situation."(The Holy Family)

What is true of the bourgeoisie is true also of the other sections in society. We have already noted how capitalism uses students and teachers as mere tools for the furtherance of production for profit. The same holds of scientists, technicians, writers, and intellectual labour in general. Also, the psychic structure of man in capitalist society is shaped by the fetishism of commodities, the tendency for all human relations to take on the character of the relation between things. Finally, with the growth of capitalism, the peasants, the tenants, and the traditional artisans are progressively drawn into the alienation characteristic of wage labour. Therefore, the abolition of capitalism is to the advantage of all. That is why Marx could write:

> "From the relation of alienated labour to private property it also follows that the emancipation of society from private property, from servitude, takes the political form of emancipation of workers; not in the sense that only the latter's emancipation is involved, but because this emancipation includes the emancipation of humanity as a whole. For all human servitude is involved in the relation of the worker to production, and all the types of servitude are only modifications or consequences of this relation." (Paris Manuscripts).

It follows then that the final result of the struggle of the working class is the emancipation of all men from all alienation. However, one cannot subscribe, without reservations, to the Marxian view that all human alienation is but a derivative of economic alienation, a view based on inadequate recognition of the autonomy of the spheres of life other than the economic. Besides, in contemporary India where capitalism coexists with feudal relations of production, the industrial proletariat is not in a position to play the historic, messianic role of the universal class whose emancipation will lead to the emancipation of all. The objective situation requires that they join hands with the peasantry, the landless labourers, and the rural artisans.

In any case, if the end-result of the socialist struggle is universal emancipation, that fact must be consciously apprehended by the oppressed classes. In other words, they must have in mind not only their own good but also the good of all, not excluding their Exploiters. Now, to will the good of others is to love them. Hence, the 'hostile opposition' between classes, Marx spoke of earlier, should be understood as a dialectical opposition between the objective need of the proletariat and the felt need of the bourgeoisie and not in a moral term as an opposition involving hatred. More precisely, the opposition of the exploited classes is directed against the capitalist system, not against the persons who constitute the bourgeoisie.

If the goal of the socialist struggle is universal (the emancipation of all from all alienation), so must also be its social base. The society we want to construct is one in which the exploited and the exploiters of today will meet as equals on the common ground of their humanity. This all-inclusiveness must be reflected as far as possible in the struggle itself. There must be continuity between the dynamics of the new society envisaged and that of the struggle aimed at creating it. But how is it possible? Here the distinction we earlier made between exploitation and domination is very much relevant. In capitalism, though not all are exploited, all are in one way or another dominated by the system. To be dominated is to become alienated, dehumanized. This opens out the possibility of creating a broad axis of revolutionary struggle comprising both the exploited classes and enlightened sections from the more privileged classes and groups, like the petty bourgeoisie the students, the intellectuals, and even the capitalists. This possibility must be exploited to the full by all who stand for a socialist revolution. Broad-based revolutionary solidarities of this type must be built up from the village level upwards.

Our discussion thus far shows clearly that the requirements of genuine socialist class struggle and those of commitment to the reign of God converge and even become identical. The conscious commitment of the exploited classes to the emancipation of all including their exploiters is in harmony with the demands of Jesus' message of universal love. Similarly, the universality of the social base of revolutionary struggle as well as of the new social order envisaged dovetails with the all-inclusive character of the New Heaven and the New Earth. Therefore, the disciples of Jesus need to have no inhibitions in joining the struggle for socialism. Rather, they must see in such struggle a historical concretization of their faith in the Kingdom.

Socialism Here and Now

The Marxists in India tend to relegate the realization of the classless society to a distant future. They further project it as the inevitable outcome of the breakdown of international capitalism. As a result, the concept of the classless society has become something like a myth, a new kind of opium for the exploited masses. It is divested of any functional relevance for the struggles of the working class here and now. Since socialism will come into being in its own time with the inexorability of a law of nature, all that the working class can do in the meanwhile is to agitate for higher wages or take part in the politics of power. This enabled the communist parties to combine radicalism of goals with the conservatism of means, theoretical revolutionism with practical reformism. The dichotomy between theory and practice, between ends and means, have rendered these parties incapable of providing any leadership for revolutionary struggle.

If socialism is not to be reduced to a myth, to an alibi for self-seeking and lust for power, it must be capable of being realized, however imperfectly, here and now. This means that the result of each struggle must take the people concerned a step further on the road to socialism in terms of both food and freedom, of overcoming both exploitation and domination. The birth of socialism should not be thought of merely as a once-for-all global event. The macro-revolution we have in mind must be viewed as the point of arrival of countless micro-revolutions at the local level. For this, people will have to organize themselves to bring under their common control factories, estates, Panchayats, Municipalities, the local bureaucracy, schools, colleges, theatres, and other institutions and services.

The realization of structural changes at the local level will give opportunities to the common man to train himself in decision-making and self-management. Such a pedagogy is absolutely necessary for the construction of socialism. Without it, the revolution will inevitably give birth to the dictatorship of a class or party over the rest of the people. The same fate will follow if a merely political revolution takes place without a corresponding social and Cultural Revolution. Those who capture power will necessarily have to ride roughshod over the masses to make them fall in line with the new regime. Therefore, what Marx says of the global revolution is also applicable to the micro-revolutions we have postulated:

> "For the creation on a mass scale of this communist consciousness, as well as for the success of the cause itself, it is necessary for men themselves to be changed a large scale, and this change can only occur in a practical movement, in a revolution. Revolution is necessary not only because the ruling class cannot be overthrown in any other way, but also because only in a revolution can the class which overthrows it rid itself of the accumulated rubbish of the past and become capable of reconstructing society."(German Ideology)

Here too, demands of revolution accord with the logic of the Gospel. Christians who join the struggle of the masses, for the progressive structural transformation of the class society of today into the future will be but translating the original concern of Jesus into the contemporary historical initiative. For, what marked him out from the prophets of old and from the apocalyptic visionaries was his teaching that the future hoped for, the kingdom of God, was already emerging in the present, where man's response met God's challenge. This was reflected in his practice as well. His meals with the outcasts of Jewish society in defiance of all existing taboos was an attempt to realize, though only in miniature, in the here-and-now of his life that meal of the end-time when many will come from east and west to feast with Abraham, Isaac, and Jacob in the kingdom of God. The disciples of Jesus have to do the same, namely, to help the oppressed masses in India bring the present they live in closer and closer to the socialist future they hope for.

(Anawim No. 11, Sept-Nov 1977)

15

Church a People's Movement

The word Church is used in this paper in the broad sense to refer to all those who call themselves Christians to whichever denomination they may belong. As communities, they are variously structured according to their respective beliefs, practices, and institutions. Is the Indian Church, understood in this sense, a people's movement?

One may notice two trends in the Church: one dominant, the other emerging; one bound to the past, the other straining to the future. The answer to the question we have posed will depend on which trend we have in mind. If it is the dominant trend, the answer crystallizes into the following statements:

The Church is not a Movement

All movement is toward a goal. But the Church does not seem to have a goal beyond herself. Or rather, her goal is herself, her own reproduction, whether simple or extended: to preserve and perpetuate her traditions, to grow in numbers, to have more church edifices, more schools, more colleges, more hospitals. She also projects herself as a goal for all men and women, who are to come to her to drink from the fountain of salvation which she is. Everything exists for her, the redeemed community. In this perspective, if there is any movement at all, it is cyclic as evidenced by the ever-repeating cycle of daily, weekly, monthly, and seasonal rituals. By conforming to these rituals and observing the commandments, believers hope to attain to personal salvation in some heaven above of de-sexed angels and disincarnate souls.

There is yet another reason why the Church is not a movement: she is tied down to money, power, and the God of the dead. Through her religious and secular institutions, she is integrated into the capitalist economy. As a significant consumer of commodities, she has close links with the commercial bourgeoisie. She is also subject to the laws of international capitalism, insofar as her main source of income lies abroad. Further, the safeguarding of her economic interests compels her to support whichever political party happens to be in power. Her link with money and power is sanctioned and legitimized by the God of the dead, we call him God of the dead because he is enthroned over much accumulated dead labour (money, property), sanctions a political system that condemns millions to death and, more importantly, presides over dead ossified dogmas. He is God, petrified into an idol, which does not speak or challenge the consciences of men and women. He can only be worshipped, washed, clothed, anointed, and put to bed. He reigns in the heaven above, bestowing his grace equally on the just and the unjust. He is a God spawned up by a faith turned ideology.

Not until the Church has wrenched herself from the stranglehold of money, power, and the God of the dead can she become a self-transcending movement.

The Church is not a People

For the Church to be truly a people, she must have a sense of community, she must be a communion of minds and wills. Such assuredly she is not. She is divided based on caste, language, class, liturgy, and doctrine. There is often more mutual distrust, suspicion, and hostility between Christian denominations than between Christians and non-Christians. Among her members there are exploiters and exploited, rich, and poor, educated and illiterate. The economic and political interests of Christians are conflictual, reflecting the many contradictions in secular society.

There is only a tenuous bond uniting all Christians, that is, the belief in Jesus Christ as the saviour of the world. Even this belief is interpreted differently by different denominations so that it cannot form the basis of any concerted action. Concerted action, however, may be possible for the defense of religious freedom and minority rights, but such action is geared to self-preservation and, for that reason, can never become a movement that takes society forward to a higher level of humanization.

If the Church is neither a people nor a movement, it is idle to talk of her as a people's movement. Nevertheless, the discourse about the Church as a people's movement is not entirely without basis. It is born of a memory and a hope: memory of early Christianity as a prophetic movement of the poorer classes in Palestine and the Roman empire; the hope that the Church will recapture its original prophetic drive and become a historic force capable of renewing the face of the earth. Between memory and hope, there is also the saving realization that the Church is not what she ought to be, that in her belief and practice she is estranged from her source which is the life and message of Jesus, the Nazarene. This statement, however, needs to be qualified. Right from the beginning of her history, there were groups in the Church that fought institutionalization and compromise with the powers and principalities of this world and strove to remain true to Jesus' option for the poor. Though they were often marginalized as heretics by an orthodoxy that had come to terms with the world, their dissenting voice was never fully smothered. Today with the intensification of class struggle in the wake of popular enlightenment especially in developing countries, the prophetic trend within the Church is reasserting itself. In India, it has assumed the form of Christian activist groups committed to the struggle of the poor for bread and freedom and that based on a new understanding of the message of Jesus. Though dispersed and riddled with inner contradictions and ambiguities, in and through them something new is struggling to be born. That something is the prophetic Christianity of the future.

The emerging trend in the Church need not necessarily come to a successful issue. It can be aborted or be tamed and reabsorbed into the Establishment. If, within decades after his death, the prophetic movement Jesus initiated began accommodating itself to wealth and state power, how much more vulnerable to deviation are the emerging trends in the Indian Church which have yet to crystallize into appropriate structures and practices! If such a historical miscarriage is not to take place, a threefold challenge will have to be met by the contemporary disciples of Jesus:

Back to the Living God

Hitherto our discourse about God has had for its point of departure the myths, dogmas, and theo-logos developed in the West in the course of a history we do not share. We have been speaking of a God whom we have known only by proxy, through the mediation of the western mind. In the process, we have ignored the God next door, the God who challenges us through the history of our people. He meets us in the eyes of the hungry, the naked, the homeless, and the unwanted. His message can be read only in the signs of the times. And that message is always something new, something unpredictable, unlike that of the God who presides over the repetitive cycles of rituals. To encounter the living God is to burst the bonds of cyclic time and launch out into the unknown to be shaped in *theandric* dialogue. The living God is the God of our unknown future. He is not a subject of whom we form predicates as we do when we say, God created us, God loves us, God is the defender of the orphan and the widow, God forgives our sins, and so on. Our discourse will have to reverse the order and start with predicates which act as pointers to the Unknown. Thus we would have to say, All new creation is Divine; Loving one's fellowmen is Divine; Forgiving one another is Divine; showing concern for the widow and the orphan is Divine. In other words, the subject is the human caravan on the march of which the Divine becomes a predicate, its unknown point of arrival, which defies all defining. This way of discoursing about the Divine may be called *theolectics* in contradistinction to theology for which God is a subject already known. The theolectic revolution will put an end to the arrogant verbosity of traditional theology and reinstate silence as an authentic language of faith.

A New Ecclesiality

The new ecclesiality will be a community of those who have encountered the self-revelation of the Divine in Jesus. In this sense, Jesus is its focus. But he is by no means the primary focus. For, to encounter the Divine in Jesus is at the same time to encounter the Divine whom Jesus encountered. For, the focus of Jesus' life and teaching was not himself but the Divine yet to come and show his face, that is, the unknown God, not seen but believed in and hoped for. Jesus is no more than a vanishing focus pointing to the God ahead. Therefore, the adequate expression of the new ecclesiality is the scene of the disciples sitting around Jesus but that of their marching with him to Jerusalem and the cross, in response to the Divine call. It finds symbolic condensation not so much in the temple as in the arc of the covenant marching with the Israelites in their desert days. Being with Jesus means walking with him.

But the community of disciples who have encountered the Divine in Jesus and have encountered the Divine whom Jesus encountered is and probably will always be a minority. There are others 'outside' who have not encountered the Divine in Jesus but have encountered the Divine whom Jesus encountered. They may be Hindus, Muslims, Jains, and Buddhists. Jesus' disciples share with them the same primary focus, the Divine yet to come. The latter, therefore, are not against us but with us. More, just as Jesus is a centrifugal focus pointing to God's reign, the community of disciples exists for the wider community of all who believe in the God, Jesus believed in, though they may not have met God in Jesus himself. Let us call this wider community basileic. The new ecclesiality thus proves itself subservient to the basic community. The former is but one among the many ways in which humanity's search for the Absolute finds sociological expression. It does not claim any monopoly of the Divine. On the contrary, it recognizes that others 'outside' may have more of the Divine in them than within its ranks. Whether the ecclesial community is more revelative of the Divine (has greater basileic density) than others is to be tested against the practice of loving one's fellow humans, caring for the poor, and defending the widow and the orphan.

Maieutic, Liberative and Celebrative Praxis

These ecclesial communities will have for their aim bringing the human community at large nearer to its ultimate goal of theandric fullness. This calls for a communitarian praxis which is at the same time:

Maieutic, playing mid-wife to the nascent forces of the new age to come. The disciples of Jesus must individually and collectively foster, the trends and forces in society that are in harmony with the reign of God, in other words, such forces and trends as are instinct with love and concern for one another, contain the promise of freedom, equality, and peace, and are creative of the beautiful. Maieutic praxis is our response to the presence of the Divine already in the here and now of history.

Liberative: That is, aimed at freedom from exploitation, political domination, and ideological repression as well as manipulation. That discipleship calls for liberative praxis is sufficiently recognized at least among radical Christian groups in India. But the strategy adopted is often counterproductive as it rests on the assumption that to liberate the masses it is necessary to exercise political power over them. The correct approach is to initiate struggles that enable people to have power over the economic, political, and cultural systems. This, in turn, is not possible without a reeducation of the masses.

Celebrative: Maieutic and liberative praxis have a dimension of transcendence in so far as their ultimate point of arrival is *theandric* fullness. The depth dimension implicit in all basileic praxis needs to be made explicit. This is possible only through symbols: through music, dance, drama, poetry, and rituals. Celebrative praxis not only expresses people's faith, love, and hope but also reinforces them. Besides it alone can release the creative energies of the collective unconscious and weld the many wills and minds into a single agent of action and passion.

Corresponding to the bipolar character of the new ecclesiality, there will be celebrations specific to the disciples of Jesus whereby they re-enact and recapture his commitment to the reign of God, and other forms of celebration common to Jesus' followers and to all those who seek the true visage of God and man, to whichever community or religion they belong. This means developing new symbols, rites, and services which have Inter-communitarian appeal.

It follows from these reflections that the real subject of all collective praxis - excepting such celebrations are specific to the disciples of Jesus - will be the basileic community. The new ecclesial communities can only act as catalysts in forming broader basileic communities as agents of people's movements.

(*Ingathering*, Chap. 20)

16

Between the Church and the Reign of God

The primal focus of the life and teaching of Jesus was the reign of God, understood as the dawn of a new age of freedom, love, and the peace born of the communion of minds and wills. It was the mainspring of his life, of all that he said and did. With him, this hope was not just a dream. It became the practice of preaching the good news to the poor, proclaiming release to prisoners, letting the broken victims go free, giving sight to the blind, and restoring the earth to the dispossessed.

The new liberating practice he initiated had to be continued in history and extended to the four corners of the world. Hence he gathered around him a group of disciples. Thus was born what we now call the Church. As a fellowship of disciples, the Church had its centre in Jesus. But this statement needs to be qualified. For, Jesus was not his own centre. His being and striving centred upon the living God. He could not be likened to a pool of still waters inviting the passers-by to come and have a dip. He was more like a violent stream that one could not enter without being swept off one's feet and carried away to the fathomless sea. To encounter him was to come under the grip of the Divine that beckoned from beyond, to become, like him, ex-centric, that is, having one's centre outside oneself, in the God of Abraham, Isaac, and Jacob. This means that regarding the community of disciples, Jesus was a vanishing centre. This holds also of his contemporary disciples.

Hence it would be misleading to represent the Church as a group of people forming a circle around Jesus, worshipping and glorifying him, as though their inner quest came to rest in him. The scene that represents more adequately the destiny of the Church is that of the disciples marching with their Master to Jerusalem in response to the call of the Kingdom. Not the circle but the road symbolizes the true nature of the new community that emerged. Significantly Jesus is not presented to us in the Gospels as one permanently settled down. Rather, the picture we get is that of a wandering prophet moving from place shuttling between town and countryside, treading the highways of Palestine and the pagan regions beyond, like, one having nowhere to lay his head. The earliest disciples too were itinerant prophets who went about preaching the good news, ever in the invisible company of their Master.

But, it may be objected: 'Do not the Gospels picture Jesus sitting at table with his disciples and with publicans and sinners?' True enough. But those meals were not cultic services in which he offered himself to be worshipped but prophetic gestures pointing to the new age when people will come from east and west to share the festal meal of a reintegrated humanity. They at once prefigured and anticipated the end of mankind's planetary pilgrimage.

Therefore, whoever encounters Jesus becomes with him a wayfarer on the road to the full revelation of the Kingdom. But the reverse need not be true. To have taken the path that leads to the God ahead, one need not have come under the spell of the prophet from Nazareth. God is no one's monopoly. He has spoken, in many and varied fashions, to many and varied people. All those who hold on to the hope in a future when men and women will be fully human and are striving to make that hope a reality are citizens of the Kingdom. They have encountered the God of Jesus but without having encountered the same God in Jesus.

Among them are Hindus, Muslims, even Marxists. They share with Jesus' disciples the same ultimate hope and concern. Hence the followers of Jesus are bound in virtue of their very faith to join hands with such men and women, thus forming broader communities. These may be called basileic communities; for the centre that holds the members together is hope in the reign (*basileia*) of God. The vitality of a local ecclesial community is to be judged by its ability to form or establish links with, basileic communities. Seen in this light, the traditional parish which devotes itself exclusively to the care of souls and to the secular welfare of those within the fold has no basis in the teaching of Jesus. Every such Christian ghetto is a standing monument to the repudiation of the call to march with Jesus to Jerusalem and the Cross. Nor is it enough that parishes engage in paternalistic projects aimed at improving the lot of the poor who are outside the Church. What is needed is nothing less than a radical change in the concept and structure of Christian communities. These must shed their inbred, ingrown character and merge with the wider community of men and women.

The need for forming basileic communities is all the greater in countries like India where Christians form but a small minority. No closed group of Jesus' disciples can be an effective agent of social change. In order to translate their faith into meaningful practice, Christians must collaborate with like-minded people professing other faiths or ideologies. In fact, this is already happening today in India. Most activist groups that have sprung up on Christian initiatives in recent decades reflect the prevailing religious and ideological pluralism. Such basileic communities constitute an essential mediation between the ecclesial community and the Kingdom of God. For the same reason, the Latin American type of base communities has little relevance in the Asian context. In countries like Latin America, Christians, being the majority, can on their own initiate socially transformative action. Hence, also the centrality of the Church in the liberation theologies emerging in those countries. Quite different is the situation in Asia. Here not ecclesial but basileic communities will have to be the collective agent of liberation. So too the cornerstone of the Asian theology of freedom will have to be not the Church, nor even Jesus, but the Kingdom of God.

Through the mediation of basileic communities, the contemporary disciples of Jesus must continue his mission, which is at the same time *maieutic, liberative,* and *celebrative. Maieutic* practice consists of fostering - literally, playing midwife (*maia*) to - the positive forces in society: forces in harmony with the demands of the Kingdom of God. Not everything around us is evil. There are initiatives aimed at educating the masses, developing their critical and creative powers, establishing harmony between religious communities, and helping the poor and the needy. They must be identified and given all possible support. Liberative practice, on the other hand, seeks to overthrow the forces at work in individuals and society that are opposed to the full flowering of the human and therefore to the birth of the new humanity Jesus envisaged. The goal here is to set human beings free from oppressive ideas, attitudes, structures, and institutions. Of no less importance is celebrative practice which gives symbolic expression (through music, dance, drama, and other cultural forms) both to hope in the Kingdom of God and its justice and to the experience of the fruits of the Kingdom already won.

(Anawim No. 38; *Jesus and Society*, Chap. 19)

17

Church as the Bearer of New Values

The very title of this chapter poses a problem. It may imply that the Church is something complete in itself, and as such, must also be the bearer of new values, as though these were external to her. In that case, what is called for is nothing more than a peripheral change, which would leave her basic structure and dynamics unchanged. But every social institution is essentially an embodiment of values if by value we mean whatever is perceived as capable of promoting the well-being of the community. In fact, it is the attempt on the part of the early believers to render stable and normative the pursuit of certain values that produced the Church. For instance, the value they attached to cult resulted in the organization of priesthood. That is why the obsoleteness of any value will bring about a corresponding structural change. If from tomorrow, Christians were to see no value in cult, all Churches would be empty and priests would be thrown out of their jobs. That would mean the end of the Church as she exists today.

Further, if the Church is already an embodiment of values, how can she be the bearer of new values? If she is to assimilate new values it can only be by discarding old ones. But she cannot discard the latter without dismantling the structures in which they are enfleshed. This is particularly so if the emerging values are radically new. A change over to a radically new set of values will call for a radical restructuring of the Church. Not a restructuring in the sense of a mere rearranging of old elements but the demolition of the old in view of a new creation. In other words, the Church will have to die and rise up again to new life, to a new vision, and to a new praxis. And what emerges out of the ruins of the old will be so new that even the term Church will have to be superseded. Any further discussion on the topic will make sense only if the reader is prepared to accept the fact that the Church will have I die to her past.

Dying to Old Values

The demand that the Church should embody new values implies that the system of values she currently upholds has become obsolete and irrelevant. Is this true? I personally think so. But to substantiate this we need the results of sociological research into the values actually operative in the preaching and the institutions of the Church (hierarchy, priesthood, cult, schools, social service etc.). No such comprehensive study as yet has been made. But, as participant observers, we are entitled to make a general assessment, which is all that is attempted here. Now, the values which determine the behaviour of Christians are either pre-capitalist or capitalist or a combination of both. In pre-capitalist social formations one attached a high value to group solidarity, to the authority of the guru, to kingship, caste status, personal dependence, and patronage. It is this system of values which, by and large shapes the behaviour of the faithful to the hierarchy, of the laity to the clergy, and, to some extent, also of the faithful among themselves. But with the spread of capitalism in India, the Church was drawn into the orbit of bourgeois values, like private interest (including both individual and group interest), competition, efficiency (in quantitative terms), and consumerism. These values are pursued less in strictly religious than in secular institutions such as schools, colleges, and organizations for social service. More often than not, the two sets of values - capitalist and pre-capitalist - coexist and even reinforce each other. This is also true of Indian society as a whole. This means that the Church is of a piece with secular society. But does she not preach justice, equality and the brotherhood of all? True enough. But what she understands by justice is justice under capitalist relations of production based on the expropriation by a few of the means of production and the product of the many. What she means by equality is the equal chance which unequals have to compete with one another. So too the brotherhood she advocates is a brotherhood in Christ which can easily co-exist with oppression in reality. No doubt in recent times she has come out with quite a few radical statements but they are not matched by any corresponding practice. Besides, verbal radicalism on the part of the Church leaders is often a convenient substitute for subversive praxis, a pathetic attempt to delude themselves and the rest of the world into believing that they are true to their mission.

But one might ask, What is wrong with the Church being in harmony with the world?; Is it not her mission to bring peace? Harmony and peace, yes; but not at the cost of true love, justice, and freedom. And it is precisely these that are set at naught by the prevalence of pre-capitalist and capitalist values. For, if in earlier societies the individual was sacrificed to the group, personal option to community decision, individual verification to traditional authority, equality to caste hierarchy; under capitalism, on the contrary, the group is sacrificed to individual interest, social responsibility to competition, quality to quantity, the enjoyment of the beautiful to the consumption of the superfluous, and, above all, man to the machine. Therefore, if the Church is at peace with the world it can only be at the cost of the free and full development of the individual and the community. Instead of trying to change the world she has become assimilated to it and domesticated by it. In other words, she has allied herself with 'the powers and principalities of the world'. This explains her criminal silence and unconcern about the evils of the prevailing social system: the existence of bonded labour, the oppression of Harijans, the exploitation of landless labourers, the eruption of communal violence leading to mass murder, the economic and cultural rape of the country carried on by multinationals, the corruption and the callousness of the bureaucracy and the police, and the perverted politics of power which thrives on blackmailing the people into subservience. Tragic, indeed, is this silence of the Church.

For it means that she has lost all hope in the new humanity of the future and has long since betrayed the mission, Jesus entrusted to his disciples. To grasp the magnitude of this betrayal it is necessary to go back to the life and teachings of Jesus.

The Values of Jesus

The fundamental concern of Jesus was not so much with values as with the Value of all values, with that Universal Value which confers value on everything else, namely, the reign of God understood as man's total reconciliation with nature, with his fellowmen, with God, and with himself. He called it the pearl of great price, the treasure hidden in the field, which rendered everything else of secondary importance. (Mt. 13:44-46) Seen from the perspective of this Universal Value, what looked valuable to his contemporaries appeared to him as of no or little value; what they held in contempt became pregnant with value. The last became the first, and the first the last. Hope in the reign of God required of him that he commits himself to the subversion of all values not consonant with that hope. Through his subversive-constructive practice he put himself in a situation of conflict with the religious and secular authorities of his day: a conflict that was to end in total rejection and finally in death on the Cross.

That this was the case will become apparent to anyone who cares to study the data of the Gospels. Let me cite a few instances.

1. Judaism attached great value to wealth, believing it to be a sign of divine favour. Jesus rejected this view when he taught that it is easier for a camel to pass through the eye of a needle than for a rich man to enter the Kingdom of God (Mk. 10:25), and called wealth the mammon of injustice (Lk. 16:9, 11). More, he held up the poor as the ones who will receive the blessings of the new age (Mt. 5:3; Lk. 6:20).

2. He criticized the Scribes for their pursuit of status and enjoined on his disciples to take the lowest place when invited to dinner (Lk. 14:7-11).

3. He devalued family ties by making them subordinate to loyalty to the new community he envisaged, which would be based on doing the will of God (Mk. 3:34-35). (Here we must keep in mind the great importance given to kinship relations in all pre-capitalist societies.) He knew that in carrying out his mission he would have to 'set a man against his father, and a daughter against her mother, and a daughter-in-law against her mother-in-law' (Mt. 10:35). And we know from the Gospel according to Mark that he was himself estranged from his relatives who took him to be out of his mind (Mk. 3:21).

4. Contrary to the prevalent tradition which accorded an inferior position to women, he affirmed their fundamental equality with men in so far as he measured the worth of all persons by the same standard, namely, obedience to the will of God (Mk. 3:34-35). In a society in which women were considered a source of moral danger and association with whom was frowned upon, he not only befriended them (Lk. 10:38-42) but even had a retinue of them accompanying him wherever he went and ministering to him out of their means (Lk. 8:1-3). Marcion was probably right when he claimed that at Jesus' trial his free association with women was brought up as a charge against him.[1]

5. Jesus also would not accept the inferior position to which children were relegated, and proposed them as models for all who sought entry into the reign of God (Mt. 19:14).

6. No less forthright was his repudiation of the scale of values based on the distinction between the pure and the impure, a distinction on the basis of which the Pharisees, who strictly observed all the details of the laws of purity, considered themselves righteous and despised the common man as being ritually and morally unclean. In his eyes purity and impurity were not qualities inherent in persons, things, and deeds (Mk. 7:15). It was this conviction that made him go out of his way and seek the company of the impure, the publicans and the sinners and invite them to sit at table with him. (Lk. 15:2)

He even went to the extent of declaring that publicans and prostitutes would enter the Kingdom of God before the Scribes and Pharisees (Mt. 21:31).

7. Similarly, he downgraded cult by subordinating it to love (Mt. 9:13); law, by making it subservient to the well-being of man (Mk. 2:27).

8. In his view even the temple in Jerusalem, which all Jews looked upon as the very heart of their religion and the centre of the universe, sank to the level of a disvalue, as may be seen from his prediction of its destruction. (Mt. 24:1-2)

9. He also repudiated the exercise of power as irreconcilable with the requirements of the Kingdom and wanted it to be replaced by service (Mk. 10:42-45).

There is no need to adduce further evidence. It is already clear from this overview that Jesus, believing as he did in the Universal Value of the reign of God, could not identify himself with the prevailing system of values or with the world outlook it presupposed or with the norms of behaviour it prescribed.

By rejecting the dominant values of his day, which were largely the values of the dominant classes, Jesus initiated a counterculture, a prophetic protest movement, embodying a new vision of the world and a new set of values and norms. That this was his intention is clear from the fact that he sent out his disciples to carry on the same mission which he himself came to fulfill, namely, to proclaim the reign of God and to realize it through individual and collective action (Mk. 3:14). He knew well enough that in fulfilling this task his disciples would have to face the same destiny that was his. He forewarned them that they would be denied lodging (Mk. 6:11), driven from place to place (Mt. 10:23), mocked at the maligned (Mt. 10:24), beaten up (Mt. 5:39), that they would face danger to their lives (Mt. 10:28) and meet the fate of the prophets of Old Testament (Mt. 6:26). But such persecutions suffered for the cause of justice would at the same time be the mark of the authenticity of their mission and a guarantee that they would receive the blessings of the new age (Mt. 5:11).

A Movement of the Disinherited

No counterculture can be borne by an individual prophet or by a handful of his disciples, however, committed they may be. It needs a broader social base to strike roots in and to draw nourishment from. And that social base can only be the disinherited classes. Historically this has been the case with all Millenarian movements.[2] That the social constituency of Jesus was the disprivileged classes in Palestine under Roman rule is abundantly clear from the New Testament itself. He himself referred to them as the poor, the sinners (those considered ritually or morally impure), those who labour and are burdened, the little ones, the least, the simple ones (contrasted with the wise and the understanding), the brokenhearted, the captives, the naked, the sick: in short, the common folk despised by the respectable classes of Scribes and Pharisees. It is the mute longings of the downtrodden masses that found articulate expression in his message of liberation.

The same holds true also of early Christianity. Revealing here are the words of Paul to the Corinthians:

> "For consider your call, brethren; not many of you were wise according to worldly standards, not many were powerful, not many were of noble birth, but God chose what is foolish in the world to shame the wise; God chose what is weak in the world to shame the strong..." (1 Cor. 1:26).

In the second century, too, no significant change took place in the class composition of believers. Around the year 150, Minucius Felix wrote to a pagan interlocutor, "That many of us are poor is not our disgrace but our glory"[3] For the same period we have the testimony of the pagan polemicist, Celsus, who characterized Christians as follows:

> "Their injunctions are like this. 'Let no one educated, no one wise, no one sensible draw near. For these abilities are thought by us to be evils'. By the fact they themselves admit that these people are worthy of their God, they show that they want and are able to convince only the foolish, dishonorable, and stupid, and only slaves, women and little children."[4]

Though this last appraisal may contain an element of exaggeration, it cannot be denied that the bulk of Christians in the second century consisted of slaves, freedmen, and free-born citizens of low social status in the Roman empire.

Prophecy Betrayed

The fact that Christianity was originally a movement of the disinherited classes must be borne in mind if we are to understand its subsequent development into a religion of the status quo. The counterculture Jesus initiated could maintain itself only as long as it had for its social base such strata of the population as had hopes and aspirations that ran counter to those of the privileged classes. And it is just this social base that underwent a profound transformation in the third and the fourth century. On the one hand, the decline of eschatological hope among believers and the policy of accommodation to classical culture made Christianity acceptable to the upper classes; on the other, the Roman aristocracy went through a process of democratization and provincialization, which made it open to non-Roman cults. The result was an influx of intellectuals and aristocrats into the Christian fold, who eventually came to control its destiny. The ground was thus prepared for the degeneration of belief into an ideology of legitimation. To quote Gager,

> "Throughout most of the first century, Christian communities had defined themselves by total opposition to the world. By the end of the third century, however, they had created their own world and were ready to assume the role that Constantine would soon impose on them."[5]

However, the decline of prophecy cannot be explained solely in terms of the changes in the class composition of early Christianity. We must also take into consideration the process of rationalization that set-in in the wake of the non-fulfillment of the hope in the imminent coming of the Kingdom. Christians strove to convince themselves that the Kingdom had already come in the person of Jesus and in the reality of the Church. As a result the focus of faith shifted from the future to the past. At the same time the Kingdom came to be interpreted in a purely spiritual sense so that it could be conceived as coexisting with the real world of unlove, misery, and exploitation. These changes at the level of consciousness in their turn contributed to the transformation of Christianity's social base. In short, it is the dialectical interaction of changes at the level of consciousness and class that gave birth to the Church as we know it today.

It is this Church, which had deviated far from the original teaching of Jesus, that was imported from the West and transplanted on our soil. True to her internal logic, she became in course of time deeply entrenched in the value system of the dominant classes in India. Is it possible for her now to recapture the values of the Gospel and once again become a prophetic movement? For that to happen, she must be prepared to dismantle her cultic-legal-hierarchical apparatus, give up her secular institutions, end her dependence on foreign money, and throw overboard her theology of legitimation and spirituality of resignation. It is unrealistic to hope that she will do so in any reasonably near future, for the obvious reason that most clergy and laity have a vested interest in maintaining the status quo. However, the conditions favourable to such a radical conversion may emerge if a cataclysmic social revolution were to overtake the whole of Indian society, which would, more or less violently, dispossess the Church of her property, money, and institutions.

A Sign of Hope

There is, however, one thing that inspires confidence in the future, and that is the emergence of radical Christian groups who have made an option in favour of the dispossessed and the exploited and feel the need to return to the prophetic, subversive teaching and practice of Jesus. They are concerned less with the Church than with the reign of God. The type of community they envisage is modeled after Jesus' table-fellowship with publicans and sinners. Having solely in view the interests of the new humanity of love, justice, and freedom, they have no difficulty in joining hands with people of other religions or even with atheists and Marxists in the common struggle for the creation of a more humane social order. Though few and dispersed, these new communities are better suited to be bearers of the values of Jesus so long as they maintain their solidarity with the masses, and refuse to be integrated into the ideology and values of capitalism.

(Zacharia 1979, pp. 55-64; *Jesus and Society*, Chap. 25)

18

The Asian Search for
a Liberative Theology

Theology and Transformative Praxis

No liberative theology can emerge when the social system is in a state of equilibrium. For what acts as a catalyst to theological reflection is the ongoing transformative action on the part of those who do not accept the status quo. Here transformative action is used in the broad sense to include not only action aimed at overthrowing structures of exploitation and oppression but also all initiatives that promote the positive energies of the new age already embedded in society and extend the areas of freedom already won. Nor is such action to be seen purely in secularistic terms. For, all transformative action is carried on against the horizon of the human search for ultimate meaning. Inherent in it is the awareness of being taken hold of by the Divine. That is why elsewhere I have termed it *theandric* practice, i.e., human practice in response to the Divine.[1]

The purpose of this essay is to describe the modalities of transformative action in the Asian context and to show how they mould the emergent theology. My reflections will be both descriptive and prescriptive. The descriptive part will necessarily be short since liberative theology in Asia is still in the initial stages.

Beyond the Neutral God

Let us first consider the impact of the struggle for justice on Christian theology. There have been during the last half century many peasant struggles against feudal and semi-feudal exploitation. The most successful were the Thebaga movement (1946), the Telangana struggle (1946-8), the Naxalbari movement (1967), and the Andhra Pradesh movement (1969-71)[2]. All of them were spearheaded by Indian Communists. The brunt of the struggle was borne by small peasants, tenant cultivators, sharecroppers, landless labourers, and tribals. Unfortunately, these struggles were either crashed or called off. They did, however, pave the way for more egalitarian land reforms. Since the late fifties, mainstream Communism has taken to parliamentary politics and confined itself to economistic trade-unionism. With their role defined as the completion of the bourgeois-democratic revolution, Indian Communists have postponed the socialist revolution - revolution against capitalism - to a distant future.[3]

Though the struggle for justice had started much earlier, only from the late sixties did Christian theology take notice of it. The reasons are many. In the preceding decades, such Christians as joined the Communist movement severed all links with the Church, which was understandable since they had been taught to look upon Karl Marx as the very anti-Christ. The situation changed with the Second Vatican Council, which, on the one hand, prepared the ground for dialogue with other religions and ideologies and, on the other, projected the pursuit of justice and freedom as an essential concern of faith. Yet another factor that prompted the search for a liberative theology is the emergence of activist groups throughout the country.[4] The constraints of electoral politics and collusion with rich peasants and medium capitalists prevented Communists from taking up people's causes at the grassroots level, particularly outside their stronghold of Kerala and West Bengal. It was to fill this vacuum that action groups came into being. A large number of them were initiated by Christians. It was they who for the first time voiced the need for a reinterpretation of the Gospel to meet the requirements of the struggle for justice. This led to a search for the historical Jesus, a recognition of the centrality of his message of the reign of God, and a critique of the tie-up between the Indian Churches and the powers that be.[5] The new vision has percolated down to sections of the clergy and the laity of all Christian denominations. A radical wing has thus been formed among Indian Christians, which, though only a minority, is articulate and vocal enough to have an impact over the whole country.

The option for the poor has made both activists and the new theologians critically assimilate Marxism. Their approach, however, is not uniform. Some accept the Marxist tools of analysis while rejecting the philosophy of Marx. Others, including the present writer, hold that critical assimilation must extend beyond Marx's method of social analysis to his philosophy as the two cannot be dissociated.[6] On the practical side, many activist groups seek to come under the umbrella of one or the other of the Communist parties, while others, with greater justice, I think, prefer to maintain a critical distance from the same parties. Be that as it may, Marxism has helped theologians sharpen their prophetic criticism of capitalism and bourgeois democracy and thereby concretize Christianity's historical intervention in society. It has also provided Christians with the tools necessary to identify the socio-economic conditions that contributed to the degeneration of the prophetic movement of Jesus into an ideology of the status quo.

Towards an Eco-Theology

If exploitation pertains to the domain of the relations of production, eco-destruction is the result of the development of productive forces. What distinguishes modern society from earlier ones is the fact that science has become the most important productive force. The growth of science, technology, and industrialization has unleashed, and is unleashing, destructive forces that may in course of time make the planet uninhabitable. Though India is only the tenth among industrialized countries, eco-systemic problems will be more acutely felt here than elsewhere because of the persistence among the masses of the traditional attitude to nature. Scientific technocratic modernity came on the scene before tradition had bowed out, causing dislocation in the psycho-structure of people in addition to the ravages wrought on the environment.

The gravity of the problem has not been sufficiently recognized by the political parties. The parties of order tend to minimize eco-problems, seeing in them the unavoidable price we have to pay for progress. The stance of the parties of revolution is, to say the least, ambiguous. They welcome the development of the productive forces of science while blaming its harmful consequences on the existing relations of production. This is the line followed by eco-groups of Marxist inspiration. Others are critical of modern science itself and look for alternative forms of science and technology.[7]

Indian theologians have still to address themselves to the challenge posed by actual and potential eco-destruction. What follows is my own exploratory thinking on the matter. I am inclined to share Heidegger's view that modern science represents an all too partial conception of human beings and their relation to nature.[8] First, modern science introduces a dichotomy between the human being as subject and nature as an object out there. It forgets that the human being is essentially related to nature. Second, contemporary science is cybernetic in essence in so far as it seeks to control and dominate nature. But every attempt to control nature is fraught with consequences that are beyond human control. It is as though nature is thereby vindicating its true being as that which defies all attempts at manipulation from outside. Third, in virtue of its very method, modern science is detotalizing in as much as it reduces everything in nature to the quantifiable. Fourth, what is quantitatively verifiable is projected as the true par excellence and is held up as the model for human and social sciences as well. Fifth, the scientifically true is then identified with the desirable, the good. Finally, the very domain of human activity - economics, politics, culture, arts - is reduced to applied science or technology. The result is the technocratic hegemony of science.

It is vain to think that science and technology can, through its own resources, solve the problems they have created. What is called for is a conversion away from the quantitative, cybernetic view of nature to a more holistic, reverential one. On the agenda is a revolution of consciousness.

For Christian theology, this involves a twofold task: discovering the Divine within nature and restoring to human beings their position as children of nature. Christians are wont to think of God as above and outside nature. Underlying this is the conception of creation as depicted in Genesis. There the creative act is represented either as a struggle between Yahweh and the chaos of primordial waters or after the manner of an artificer producing an artifact.[9] The creative act of shaping chaotic matter is also normative for human beings. They are commanded to fill the earth and subdue it. I suggest that the spirituality of conquest that the command generated is in part responsible for the growth of a science and technology geared to the conquest of nature and for the present ecological impasse.

The eco-systemic crisis is an invitation to theologians to return to the primitive myth of creation as generation. In the symbolic discourse appropriate to this myth, the world of names and forms remain within the Divine and the Divine within the world of names and forms. In this perspective, the Divine is the hidden meaning of that primal discourse spelt out into hills and lakes and rivers and oceans and stars. There is therefore no growing in wisdom and grace without harkening to the telluric vibrations of the Divine. But we should not rest with the 'naturalization' of the Divine. The human, too, needs to be rooted in Nature. For, under the spell of the same creation myth, we are wont to think of the human being as one whose soul comes from the God above and body from the earth below. No wonder, we feel we are aliens on alien soil. It is this feeling that gave birth to the spirituality of exile so prevalent among Christians. The time has come to leave behind all forms of angelism and recognize the fact that the human community is nothing but the earth become conscious of itself. This means recapturing the sense of kinship with the organic and the inorganic universe. The recovery of our umbilical bond with the earth involves also a new understanding of death as the final resting-in-peace of humans on the lap of Mother Earth, the vehicle of grace Divine. Death shall no more be a farewell to the earth, no more a journeying forth into an over world of disembodied beings. The words, "Dust thou art and into dust shalt thou return" shall henceforth convey not a curse but a blessing Divine. Once human beings see in the visible universe the home and symbol of the Divine, their attitude to it will cease to be instrumental and will become reverential. Rediscovering the immanence of the Divine, however, does not mean sacrificing its transcendence. The transcendence of the Divine will henceforth be seen as revealed in the self-transcendence of nature and history.

Theology Confronting Religious Pluralism and Fundamentalism

The fact that Christians form a small minority living with other minority religions in a country that is predominantly Hindu is of great significance for the new theology. All the more so when one considers the change that has come about in the Hindu attitude to Christianity. In colonial days Hindus were on the whole receptive to Christian influence. In evaluating their own religious tradition, they had no hesitation in using Christian standards, which in fact, gave birth to reform movements within Hinduism like the Arya Samaj and the Brahmo Samaj. Hindu scholars took pride in showing that the teachings of Jesus and Christian saints and mystics were already to be found in the Hindu scriptures, though in the process they did justice to the specificity of neither Christianity nor Hinduism.[10] Since Independence, however, there has emerged a militant wing among the Hindu masses which is increasingly hostile to minority religions. How so? The loss of cultural identity resulting from colonialism, the helplessness of Hinduism before the invasion of capitalist culture, its internal divisions, and lack of centralized religious authority - all this has put Hindus on the defensive.[11] Hindu militancy, however, cannot be explained merely as a defensive mechanism in a period of cultural crisis. It is also provoked by the historical version of Christianity existing in India.

What in this version of Christianity is seen as a threat by Hindus is its foreign character, its aggressive proselytism, and its concentration of socio-economic power through secular institutions and projects. What has been theology's role in eliminating this threefold offense?

It is generally recognized that Christianity must become enfleshed in the culture of the soil, and this not merely as a tactic of survival but as a theological imperative rooted in Christian faith. The principle of inculturation is applied not only to liturgy but also to doctrine. There have been attempts to incorporate symbols and rituals from the Hindu tradition in Christian worship. Likewise, Christian thinkers have sought to rethink their faith in the language of either devotional religion (*bhakti*) or of non-dualist Vedanta.[12] Though the effort to give Christianity an indigenous visage is welcome, inculturation as pursued today is riddled with internal contradictions.

Asian countries are in a period of transition when everything is in the melting pot. Under the impact of science and technology, traditional ideas, symbols, and myths are dying out and their place is taken by new ones. Attempts are also going on to revive rituals and practices long since dead and forgotten. Such being the case, there is no ready-made culture wherewith Christianity may clothe itself. The challenge, therefore, is the creation of a new culture that combines the positive values of tradition with those of modernity. Genuine inculturation can only occur in the process of transculturation.[13] And for this, Christians must join the struggle for the restructuring of society as a whole.

Yet another inadequacy of inculturation is that its advocates tend to identify Indian culture with the Brahmanic-Sanskritic tradition. Though this tradition, particularly in its pre-caste stage, contains elements that are valid today, it is, on the whole, the creation of the upper castes and is meant to promote their social dominance. Hence to project the *Upanishads* and the *Bhagavat Gita* as the supreme expression of the Indian spirit is to side with the privileged castes. It is rather with the religious movements of dissent that the Christian theologian must identify himself or herself.

Still more crucial is the question, What are we trying to enflesh in the indigenous culture? It is taken for granted that it is dogma and tradition. One forgets that dogma and tradition are themselves products of a culture. They were shaped first in the mould of Hellenistic culture and subsequently in those of the slave and feudal society in the West. They are the end-result of a long process of the inculturation of Jesus' prophetic message in an alien culture. Therefore the attempt to clothe the Christian dogma and tradition in Indian culture is but second degree inculturation. It does not make Christianity any less foreign to India. More, the development of the prophetic movement initiated by Jesus into a cultic-dogmatic religion is more an estrangement than a spontaneous unfolding of its creative power. Hence by uncritically transplanting dogma and tradition, one cannot develop a liberative Asian theology.

Now we come to the alleged intolerance and aggressive proselytism of Christianity. The theory and practice of conversion followed from the once prevalent axiom, *Extra ecclesiam nulla salus*, (Outside the Church there is no salvation) which, in turn, was based on the explicit or implicit identification of the Church with the Kingdom of God. Luckily, conversionist theology is on the wane. Since Vatican II, it is recognized that other religions too can be a means of salvation. Nevertheless, the language of conciliar and Papal documents continues to smack of ideological imperialism as may be seen from claims such as, "the Church is the sacrament of salvation for the world," "it is her mission to purify and redeem cultures", "she speaks in the name of truth itself", and so on.[14] Such monopolistic claims devalue other religions and constitute a permanent offense to their followers. Besides, they render truly ecumenical action for a humane social order all but impossible. Nor can they be substantiated either by appealing to the actual life of Christians or the history of the Church.

In the Asian context, all this calls for a radical critique of the current ecclesiology. The Church must be seen as existing not for itself but for the Kingdom. And the Kingdom is universal, present in all human communities in the measure in which they respond to the self-unveiling of the Divine in nature and history.

If so, the Christian community cannot claim to be the sole sacrament of salvation. For the rest, whether a community announces the presence of the Divine in history will have to be ascertained from its actual practice and not deduced from any dogmatic claims. This approach will enable Christians to appreciate the positive values of other religions and to shed their accustomed arrogance.

The Asian theologian, however, cannot rest satisfied with a critique of the current ecclesiology but must extend it to the kind of Christology in which it is based. What is at issue is the divinity of Jesus. Once Jesus is equated with God and the Church seen as Jesus' extension in time and space, the way is clear for the hegemony of Christianity over other religions. In the bargain, the continued self-revelation of the Divine is annulled, since, as God, Jesus is its full and definitive manifestation. This already raises the hermeneutical suspicion that the equating of Jesus with God is a post-paschal interpretation. All that the earliest kerygma claimed was that the power of God was with Jesus, that he was once taken hold of by the Divine. The divinity of Jesus meant his having been invaded by the Divine to the point of his radiating it through word and deed. This formulation leaves open the continued revelation of the Divine in history. Nor does it make revelation a monopoly of the Christian community.

If the Kingdom of God is open to all men and women of goodwill, the effort to make human society approximate to the Kingdom cannot be an exclusively Christian task. Seen from this angle, sectarian institutions, whether charitable, educational or developmental, lack theological legitimacy. Hence Christian involvement for the humanization of society must be in collaboration with people of other religions and persuasions. The agent of social transformation in the Asian context will have to be not exclusive ecclesial communities but inclusive basileic communities. This will be the only effective answer to the Hindu attack on the institutional power of the Churches.

From Patriarchal to Androgynous Religiosity

The forms of oppression Asian women are exposed to are many.[15] On the economic front, they suffer from discriminatory wages and unemployment. With the spread of capitalism, female nudity has become a means of production and of competitive marketing. The dowry system condemns many to spinsterhood. Oppressive too are the cultural taboos regarding dress, social intercourse, choice of one's partner in life, and entering certain professions, not to mention the religious devaluation of womanhood as such.

Organized resistance on the part of women to economic exploitation and cultural oppression is a relatively recent phenomenon in India. In the last two decades, innumerable women's groups and associations have sprung up particularly in urban areas.[16] So far their activities have been confined to certain specific issues like the dowry system, prostitution, and the commercial exploitation of sex. They have not yet come out with any comprehensive critique of religion as an ideology of male domination. Nor have they succeeded in elaborating an adequate theory of women's liberation.

Regarding the position of women, the Indian religious tradition is ambivalent. There is consensus among scholars that the earliest civilization that flourished in the Indus Valley in the fourth millennium B.C. was matriarchal. Even after the invasion of the patriarchal Aryans, matriarchy existed in many parts of India from Kashmir to Kanyakumari. Under matriarchy, property, rule, and priesthood vested in women, especially in the tribal mother. And religious life centred upon the worship of the Mother Goddess, of whom the tribal mother was the visible representative. In such societies, women were unfettered in sexual relations.[17] In course of time, with the transition from hoe to plough cultivation and under the impact of Aryan patriarchy, matriarchy passed over either to matriliny or to patriarchy pure and simple.

Parallelly there occurred a change in religious symbolism. The Mother Goddesses (Saraswati, Parvati, Lakshmi) were married to male deities (Brahma, Siva, Vishnu) and thereby subordinated to the latter.[18] In architecture and sculpture, the female deities were made to serve as mere background to their male counterparts. The Epics, Puranas, and the Law Books reinforced the primacy of the male deities over the female and the domination of man over woman. Nevertheless, even today the concept of the Mother Goddess occupies an important place in the religious consciousness of people, particularly among the lower castes, outcastes, and the tribals. Even in orthodox, patriarchal Hinduism, the concept of the Divine remains androgynous, though the female principle is subordinated to the male. This means that despite patriarchalization, the Indian religious tradition can provide ideational tools for the liberation of women. This does not mean restoring matriarchy but recognizing the primordiality of the Mother principle and embodying it in appropriate social relations and religious symbols.

For Christianity to take root in the Indian soil and become a positive force for the liberation of women, it must de-patriarchalize its discourse about the Divine. Yahweh must be seen not as a father figure inhabiting the remote heaven above but as the depth-dimension of the sexual bipolarity constitutive of nature, conscious as well as unconscious. And, as the ultimate ground and unity of the polarity of sexes, the Divine is in a primordial - not biological - sense androgynous. In this perspective, the earth and the waters cease to be quasi-demonic principles but become symbols of the motherhood of the Divine, which, in fact, they are in the Indian religious tradition. In thus reinterpreting the concept of the Divine, we are but completing a process that the prophets and the Psalmists of the Old Testament had already started. Overstepping the limits of patriarchal discourse, they would describe Yahweh's love for Israel after the manner of a mother's love for her child. Similarly, the conception of Israel as the spouse of Jahweh, the elevation of Mary to the status of the Mother of God, and the attribution of motherhood to the Church are to be seen as so many attempts to compensate for the deficiencies of an all too patriarchal religiosity. But these attempts do not go far enough. The religious aspirations underlying them can come to fruition only in an androgynous conception of the Divine. It alone can take us beyond patriarchal and matriarchal religion while preserving the core of truth contained in both.

The conception of the Divine I have proposed involves a revaluation of sexuality understood in the broad sense to include not only genital-procreative sex but also the specificity of the male-female polarity. The relation between sexes will henceforth be seen as the image and the reflection of the androgynous nature of the Divine. This seems to be implied in the biblical account of creation: "God created man in his own image, in the image of God he created him; male and female he created them" (Gen 1:27). If so, the humanization of sexual relations is an essential element of the divinization of the world. The reign of the Divine and the Holy can announce its presence only as a community of persons in which the male and the female can realize each its otherness in the unity of communing (erotic) and self-giving (agapeic) love.

(John, T. K., S.J. ed., *Bread and Breath. Essays in Honour of Samuel Rayan S.J. on the Occasion of his 70th Birth Anniversary,* Gujarat Sahitya Prakash, Anand, 1991, pp. 100-114; *Jesus and Culture,* Chap. 9)

19

A New Approach to Theological Education

This chapter deals with the question: How to teach theology? But the how of teaching depends very much on what one understands by the term theology. Method and content are intimately related. It is the content which to a large extent determines the method. If this is true of all sciences, it is much more so of theology, where the teacher is personally involved in what is taught. This is not the case, at least to the same extent, with the other sciences. For this reason, it is necessary at the very outset to state clearly what I mean by theology.

What is Theology?

Provisionally, theology may be defined as the analytic, critical, articulate, dialogical, and committed reflection on our primordial encounter with God. I shall now proceed to clarify the meaning of each term.

Theology deals with man's encounter with God. It is on purpose that I have used the word, encounter. Encounter is more than a mere coming-to-know. It is rather a coming face to face with the ultimate ground and goal of our existence, an event that takes place not so much at the level of sensation, knowing or loving, as in the inmost depth of our being, where sensation, knowing or loving have their common root. To meet God in this sense is to be taken hold of by him, to be uprooted and swept away in such wise that one is no more one's own master; in such wise, too, that everything other than God is rendered relative. No one can encounter God and remain the same.

The encounter in question has to be *primordial*. I qualify as primordial that encounter with God which is realized in the real, not of cult, or scriptures or religious institutions, but of life, personal and social. In other words, what is envisaged is an encounter in the domain of praxis understood as man's dynamic relationship to his environment in transforming which he transforms himself. Compared with God-encounter at the level of praxis, the religious experiences one may have in prayer, worship, and the reading of scriptures are derivative, poorer in content, and of secondary importance.

To theologize is to reflect on this primordial God-encounter. Reflection does not mean a return to the inwardness of one's soul, as an *Advaitin* would understand the term. Nor is it an escape from the concrete world. It consists rather in an immersion into the depth of our *being-in-the-world*. We may call it a return to the centre, provided the centre of each person is understood as essentially related to the others. For, each person is at the same time *in-centred* and *ex-centred*, centred upon himself and upon others. Therefore the depth into which reflection is to lead is not man as *being-with-himself* but man as *being-with-others*. But our *being-with-others* has its highest density, its point of incandescence, in *being-for-others*, in love. Therefore, the privileged locus where we encounter God is our experience of love, togetherness, and fellowship.

All this applies to theological reflection in general. Now the question arises, what is it that distinguishes our theological reflection as disciples of Jesus? Like anyone else we too meet God in the domain of practical *life-in-love*, in a common commitment to a cause, in the experience of the beautiful, etc. But unlike others, we have also encountered God as revealed in the life and teaching of Jesus. And yet we are not dealing with two disparate encounters. The same God who confronts us in the varied situations of life also meets in the person of Jesus. Besides, the two modes of encounter condition each other and tend to fuse into one unique encounter. It is in the light of the splendour of God reflected in the face of Jesus that we see God on the face of the earth. Conversely, it is in the light of God's self-revelation in our concrete historical situation that we understand Jesus and his message. But, one might ask, is not our encounter with God in Jesus less original than our confronting God in the practical situations of life? Not necessarily. For our life unfolds between memory and hope; between memory that makes the past present and hope that carries past and present into the future. And who is Jesus but our past become present and active in our midst? As part of our history, as a member of the family of man, he is as primordial to us as anyone living today. As disciples of Jesus, therefore, our reflection must dwell also on our *being-in-the-world*. Let us now try further to define the process as such of theological reflection. Reflection must, first of all, take the form of an analysis of the layers of conditioning and the dimensions of meaning inherent in our God-encounter.

We encounter God not in a vacuum but as men and women inserted at a particular point in the flux of history, and therefore as conditioned by a particular social system and culture. Chief among the conditioning factors are class, culture, and institutionalized religion. The place one occupies in the relations of reproduction (as man or woman, husband or wife, parents or children), in the relations of production (as owners of the means of production or as wage labourers), and in the relations of power (as ruler or ruled) exercises a profound influence on one's God-encounter. Important, too, is the impact of culture understood as the system of meanings and values traditionally handed down, in the light of which the community as a whole sees and evaluates things, persons, situations, events, and the world in general. As one's culture, so is one's religious experience. One thing is the religious encounter of a tribal; another, that of the feudal man; and still a third, that of one living in capitalist society. Deeper than that of class or culture is the conditioning by institutionalized religion. We meet the God of today through the glasses of the creed and cult of yesterday.

The analysis must also lay bare the many dimensions of meaning implied in God-encounter. Space forbids any detailed treatment of them. I shall confine myself to enumerating the more important ones. They are existential (Does my encounter with God reveal the ultimate meaning of my life? What answer does it give to the problem of sin, guilt and the ambivalence of freedom?), the ethical (What unconditional demands does it make on me and the community?), the cosmic (What light does it throw on the meaning of my bodily existence and on the earth, the extension of my body? Does it show the way to freedom from the cosmic law of birth, decay and death?), the social (Is there a communitarian encounter with God? Does the community reveal the face of God?), and the historical (Is God also the ultimate meaning of history?).

The next step reflection has to take is a critical evaluation of what analysis has revealed. Criticism has to do mainly with the factors that condition our religious encounter. The conditioning in question may be positive or negative: positive if it renders us perceptive to all the dimensions of meaning; negative, if it obscures or falsifies them. The aim of criticism is to identify the latter so that by eliminating it we can arrive at a more adequate understanding of our original encounter as well as dispose of ourselves to ever new and richer encounters.

Analysis and criticism are not enough. We need to articulate the dimensions of meaning we have discerned. To articulate means to join together. To reflect articulately is to grasp the various dimensions of meaning as forming a unity in tension. In other words, we must try to find out how the existential, cosmic, social, ethical, and historical horizons of meaning are interrelated. Here I can do no more than raising a few leading questions: How, for instance, is the ultimate meaning of the material universe related to the ultimate goal of human history? What is the relationship between the existential and the social dimensions of our dialogue with God? Is individual fulfillment possible without the fulfillment of all men of all ages? By relating thus every dimension of meaning to every other we come to an understanding of the dynamic structure of that primordial experience of *being-taken-hold-of-by-God.* However, the structure of meanings we discover through articulate reflection must not be set up as a dogma valid forever. It must be subjected to constant revision in the light of subsequent encounters, in the light also of subsequent praxis.

Now we come to a point which has to do with the attitude of mind that should govern the entire process we have traced so far. We have already seen that the theologian cannot, and should not, remain neutral to what he is trying to understand. His has to be a committed reflection, i.e. a reflection carried out in the spirit of self-surrender to the God whom he has met. In other words, it is in the spirit of faith that he should analyze, criticize, and articulate. Where theological reflection loses its moorings in faith it becomes an empty game of words; and the theologian, a sounding gong or a clanging cymbal.

The God whom we encounter is nobody's monopoly. He shows his face also to others who share cultural and religious traditions different from ours. Among these others, there may be men and women who have been taken hold of by the Divine much more completely than we have ever been. This could be true even of professed atheists in so far as they are under the grip of ultimate human concern for the sake of which they are prepared to sacrifice everything also. Furthermore, just as our religious encounter has its own poverty and wealth, so has that of others its own. Hence we have much to learn from them as they have to learn from us. Hence also, all genuine theological reflection must take place within the framework of dialogue with others, believers or not.

How to Teach Theology?
The understanding of theology, we have thus gained, must also determine the mode of teaching it.

To teach theology is to help others reflect on their primordial encounter with God. This is possible only if both the teacher and the taught have gone through such an encounter. I wonder how far this is true of those who teach and learn theology in our seminaries. One cannot rid oneself of the impression that for many, teaching theology is no more than just one career among many others. Possibly too, many young men flock to seminaries not because they have any genuine call from God but for reasons of their psychological or social background. Be that as it may, in what follows, it is assumed that the teachers as well as the learners of theology have, in one way or another encountered their God.

Our earlier analysis has shown that there are factors that either obscure or distort the meaning of our religious encounter. One of the primary functions of the teacher is to help students break these mental barriers and achieve the freedom to think and to respond creatively to the challenges of God.

The first barrier to be broken is that of class bias. What one makes of one's God and his call depends very much on where one stands in the social hierarchy of classes. The class position makes one's religious perception selective so that one tends to see only such elements as pose no threat to one's social or economic interests. Consider, for instance, the interpretation of the Gospels. Even today, most biblical exegesis is carried out from the standpoint of the oppressors, not from that of the oppressed. And, for that reason, it ends up by reducing the message of Jesus into an ideology suited to legitimize the interests of the privileged classes. We have yet to see an interpretation of the Gospels coming from those who belong to, or at least have identified themselves with, the oppressed masses of India. This is not so much because those who teach or learn theology are themselves, owners of the means of production, as because their interests and, more important, the interests of the Churches to which they belong, coincide with those of the economically dominant class. Besides, for many students of theology, joining the seminary is itself an accession to a higher social class than the one they were born to, to a class enjoying economic security, social status, and an elitistic culture.

Theological education must seek to pull down the cultural blocks which hamper any true understanding of God. The system of meanings and values, which seminarians are heir to, are partly feudal, partly capitalist. The predominance of one over the other depends on whether they hail from rural or urban areas. Feudal are, for instance, caste hierarchy, personal dependence, the importance attached to tradition and authority, and the primacy of kinship relations; capitalist are private interest, competition, aggression, consumerism, and the like. At first blush, one may wonder what these ideas and values have to do with the teaching or the study of theology. A deeper reflection, however, will show that they affect not only the quality of our encounter with God but also the interpretations we give to it. How, for instance, can anyone, for whom the social inequalities based on caste, sex, race, or kinship are sacrosanct, accept in all its implications Jesus' message of a new humanity whose fundamental principle of unity is a commitment to God's will? Or, how can anyone inured to the idea of man's rule over his fellowmen, as divinely ordained, grasp the divine challenge to fashion a new communion of men and women in which service will replace authority? Or again, how can one wedded to the belief that the values of capitalism are integral to human nature as such, work for a new age, in which private interest will give way to concern for all, competition to cooperation, aggression to love, and consumerism to creativity?

Much more deeply entrenched, and therefore also more difficult to overcome, are the barriers organized religion itself places in the way of authentic theological reflection. I shall deal only with those that derive from the Christian religion. Our existence as Christians is grounded in the belief that God has uniquely revealed his face in Jesus of Nazareth. Unfortunately, Jesus' message has come down to us overlaid with successive layers of interpretations. Even the earliest Gospel, that according to Mark, is both history and interpretation. Over time, the layers of interpretation became thicker and thicker. In the centuries that followed, further interpretations were added by the Fathers of the Church and by the official Church itself until they crystallized into eternal and immutable dogmas. The subsequent history of official teaching and theological reflection is one of the interpretations of interpretations. What is worse, this whole complex of interpretations bears the imprint of earlier world-outlooks and obsolete modes of thinking. It was shaped by the economic and political interests of the Church in slave, feudal, and capitalist society, respectively. It is this gigantic system of rootless beliefs and alienated concepts that was imported to India and imposed on us from outside as normative for an encounter with, and understanding of, God.

Within this system, we have as much freedom to be and to think as has a monkey to play around whom the monkey-player holds tightly by a rope. Woe to us, if we dare cross the bounds set by dogma, and tradition and go out in search of greener pastures. And greener indeed are the pastures outside than those within. The twin matrices of our theology — God's self-disclosure in Jesus and in our contemporary situation — lie outside the walls which dogma and tradition have put up. This being the case, any teaching of theology must begin with a sustained effort to pull down these walls and thus create the necessary conditions in which students can stand naked before their naked God. This does not mean throwing overboard the entire heritage of the past. What is called for is rather a radical criticism of the past in the light of our present encounter with God. Such criticism will weed out much of what we today hold as sacred, and clear the ground for an original Indian theology.

We have thus far explained the negative, critical function of theological education. But that is not all there is to it. The education has to play also a positive, creative role. This does not consist in passing on to the students, in the form of set formulas or a coherent system of thought, the conclusions of one's own search. To do so would be to bypass the original God-encounter of those whom we are called to teach. What we should do is to help them delve into the depths of their own religious encounter and render explicit whatever is implicitly contained in it. The way the educator has himself traversed should not be made in any way normative for his students. It can be no more than a help to provoke thought and elicit questions. Moreover, the teacher and the taught must show reverence towards each other's encounter with God.

This means that theological education can be best carried on within the framework of discipleship. Classroom lectures are of little use here though they may be suited to the teaching of other sciences.

All through we have presupposed that the teachers as well as the students of theology have had, in one way or another, an encounter with God. Where this presupposition is justified, theological education will never become divorced from historical praxis. For, God is the absolute, unconditioned negating of evil and affirming of good. To encounter him is to be so gripped by him that we in our turn become committed to the negation of evil in every form and to the promotion of whatever is true, good, and beautiful; in other words, to creative, world-transforming praxis. As persons who have encountered God, the teacher and the taught will be involved in the struggle for justice, freedom, and equality. They will refuse to be transplanted into a world of sterile, impotent ideas. The teacher, therefore, cannot rest content with being a mere academician. His role is to be also a leader who can speak with the authority born of commitment, and, in the manner of Jesus, tell his disciples: Come and follow me. It is in their joint commitment that faith becomes power, thought becomes energy, and theory becomes a material force that changes the world. And out of that transforming power, energy and force will be born new and creative ideas, visions, and dreams. Understood thus, praxis is not merely a prerequisite for theological education but is itself an authentic form of such education.

Guidelines for the Future

In the light of our discussion thus far, let us see what changes are called for, in theological education in India.

Decolonization

The theology taught in most seminaries is the one imported from abroad. The problem it poses and the solutions it gives savour of a cultural and intellectual tradition that is foreign to us. Foreign too are the books we read and the authorities we quote. Not being part of the tradition they represent, we understand them poorly. All that we can do is to play back to our betters abroad and that too in an impoverished form, the very ideas they have put into our heads. We are thus reduced to being mere relaying stations for ideas and theories fabricated elsewhere. And it mightily suits the interests of the colonizers that we, to speak in economic categories, rely on imported goods instead of exploiting our own raw materials for original theological production. Theology too has become a multi-national enterprise, with its headquarters in the so-called developed countries, with a wide network of production units and markets in the developing countries, and with its agents and salesmen planted in strategic places throughout the world. How true the saying of Marx that those who control the means of material production also control the production of ideas, myths, dreams, and illusions. Theological imperialism of this kind is further reinforced by economic patronage over the Indian Churches which have their financial arteries in the West. Its perpetuation is assured by the fact that in many seminaries key subjects are still taught by missionaries and by the colonial attitude of their Indian counterparts who tend to invest with the halo of superior wisdom any theological fad patented abroad.

As a first step towards creating the conditions necessary for a genuinely Indian approach to theological education, missionaries must step down from the chairs they occupy in seminaries. If at all they continue to teach, it must be only such subjects as they alone are competent to handle, like the history of philosophy and theology in the West. Much as we appreciate the contribution they have made in the past, we are equally convinced that the time has come for them to play a role different from that of theological educators. Their role in the future will have to be one of encouraging and inspiring through the personal witness of their lives. The Indians entrusted with the task of teaching theology must on their part be highly selective in the use of theological literature coming from the West. It would be a good thing if they confine themselves to reading only such literature as contain the results of positive research on the Bible. Even here they must be wary of interpretations conditioned by the concerns of the crisis-ridden, technocratic civilization of the West. Instead, they must return to their moorings in their own personal encounter with God. Only thus will they be able to develop an original theological vision and speak to their counterparts abroad as equals among equals.

Indigenization

By Indigenization, I do not mean any return to the age of the *Vedas*, the *Upanishads*, or the *Puranas*. Nor do I mean donning saffron robes. What is required is rather an immersion in, and identification with, the contemporary life of the Indian masses. The past should be of relevance only in so far as it is alive in the present and is likely to endure in the future. Only a theology that drives roots deep in the soil can bear fruit. An essential step in this direction is the teaching of theology in the language of the people. Language is much more than a mere means to express one's ideas. It is an original mode of social being, and therefore, also the key to the self-understanding of people. To theologize in a foreign language is to remain outside the life-current of the masses. Seen from this angle, the idea mooted in certain circles of teaching theology in the regional languages is truly welcome.

The prevalent method of teaching theology suffers from over-fragmentation. The division of theology into dogmatic, moral, biblical, spiritual, mystical, pastoral, etc. is a product of western rationalism and a consequence of the estrangement of theological reflection from its own birth-place — man's encounter with God in history. So are also the dichotomies that characterize much of the theology that is taught today — those between matter and spirit, sacred and profane, temporal and eternal, this world and the other, philosophy and theology, etc. To make matters worse, the, in itself valid, recognition that theology must enter into dialogue with other religions and with secular sciences, has led to the inclusion of additional courses in the curriculum, such as on Hinduism, Islam, Atheism, Marxism, Religious Sociology, and so on. The student is thus introduced into a world of diverse and even conflicting ideas which he is unable to integrate into a unified whole. In consequence, when he leaves the seminary he has a wealth of information to talk about but no all-absorbing vision to die for.

To obviate this difficulty, some seminaries have introduced a division of courses into two categories: the basic which all have to attend, and the electives out of which one is allowed to choose a specified number. This solution is inadequate, for it ignores the crucial question: the electives?

In my view, the only valid solution is a centrifugal method of education, which is already implied in the very definition of theology I have given. It consists in returning to the centre, namely, to our encounter with God in history, to discover the many dimensions of meaning it contains. The *unity-in-tension* between the dimensions of meaning thus discovered will in its turn become the point of departure for a movement outwards, to other religions and other sciences. In this way, the student will have a centred core of believing knowledge into which he can integrate whatever is true in other faiths and world views. Naturally, this can be achieved best if the same teacher guides the student in the search for the existential, moral, social, historical, and other horizons of meaning contained in his religious encounter. This will render the present division of faculties largely superfluous. I suggest that this method be adopted for the basic course in theology which all students are obliged to follow. For more specialized knowledge one may attend additional courses given by experts in the respective fields.

There is an increasing recognition today that theological education must be so restructured as to make social praxis an integral part of it. More and more seminaries are getting involved in social services and cultural activities outside the seminary. This is a healthy development. However, a few critical remarks are called for. It looks as though learning and praxis are running on parallel lines, instead of one flowing from the other. How else to explain the fact that the current upsurge of activism goes hand in hand with a corresponding neglect of serious study? Does this not point to a realization on the part of students that, what is taught in classrooms is totally irrelevant for practical life? What wonder if, confronted with the meaninglessness of classroom lectures, they look for meaning outside seminary walls! If theology and praxis never meet, the fault is not of praxis but of theology.

The social praxis, which is to be at once the matrix and the testing ground for theological reflection, will necessarily have to be pluriform, varying with personal aptitudes and the specificity of God's call as revealed in each historical situation. While the traditional type of social service continues to be relevant, the time has come for professors and students of theology to commit themselves to a radical and planned transformation of the social system, whether it be through literary activity (writing novels, short stories, poems, dramas, etc.), through participation in local struggles, or even through direct political action in collaboration with like-minded political groups or parties.

Education through discipleship

Now we come to the most crucial question: Is theological education along the lines suggested possible at all within the framework of seminaries? My answer is an emphatic No. And this for the following reasons: If the richness and the depth of human relationships is the focal point where the human and the divine meet, then life in seminaries, characterized as it is by formalism, regimentation, and alienation from the masses, is not the favourable soil for any true encounter with God. Second, the many biases — religious, colonial, cultural, and economic — that are institutionalized in the customs, rules, and the method of education followed in the seminaries render difficult, if not impossible, any adequate grasp of the demands God makes on us today. Third, the requirements of dialogue and diapraxis with other religious and social forces cannot be met within the ghettos that our seminaries are. For these and other reasons, we have to look for alternative ways of theological education.

That seminaries have become irrelevant is gradually, though confusedly, dawning on the mind of both teachers and students, as is clear from the general restlessness among them and the many experiments being tried. The traditional policy of segregation is being relaxed to let outsiders in, though, significantly, those thus privileged belong as a rule to the richer classes. To escape from the evils of collectivized production, students have in some seminaries formed groups based on common language or shared academic interests. Elsewhere some among them are allowed to forgo the regular course and study privately under the guidance of a professor. Others have opted to live outside with the people while continuing to attend the usual lectures. However, all such experiments, being attempts to revolt against the system within the framework of the system itself, are doomed to failure.

To adequately meet all the requirements of theological education as explained in this paper, it is necessary not to uproot students from the real world, while the teachers too should seek insertion in the life-current of the masses. Planted amid the toiling millions, they should, like any other citizen, work to earn their livelihood whether as wage labourers, professionals, writers, or social workers. Within this setup, they will accept discipleship under any theologian living in the area whose competence is widely recognized. There will thus be more than one centre of theological study in the same city or district. Where necessary, cell-study will be supplemented with wider consultations of all the teachers and students in any given area. I suggest that this method be followed for the basic course in theology referred to earlier.

What then of the existing seminaries? They should be converted into specialized institutes of higher study, each devoted to one branch of knowledge, like Exegesis, Hinduism, Islam, Religious Sociology etc. Such students as have completed their basic course and would like to do further studies in any related branch of learning will attend courses in these specialized institutes. Teaching in these centres of higher learning will have to be so organized as to make it possible for teachers and students to live with the people and be engaged in meaningful social praxis.

I wouldn't be surprised if some among you raise the question: If that is the case, who can be educated? And who can educate? My answer is: Everything is possible for those who have faith. (Mk. 9:23).

(A paper published in Amaldoss 1981, pp.57-69; *Jesus and Society*, Chap. 30)

Notes

Chapter 3

1. Here is a list of recent works: 1. Kappen 1977; 2. Kappen 1983; 3. Kappen 1985; 4. Rayan 1982; 5. Amalorpavadass 1981. **2.** The changes taking place in society are often ignored by theologians. See, for instance, Raymond Panikkar's "Philosophy and Revolution: The Text, Context, and the Texture", *The Living Word*, Vol. 81, 1975, pp. 357-399. **3.** This, admittedly, is an anticipatory extrapolation. The common people, by and large, still cling to the traditional conception of the Divine. We leave open the issue whether the cyclic time and the religiosity germane to it can or even should be completely superseded. **4.** Sau 1981, p.77. **5.** For a fuller discussion of the theme, see, Kappen 1984, Chap. 1 **6.** Kappen 2012. Chap. 6 **7.** Gutierrez 1973, p. 13. **8.** Young India, 31 December 1931, pp. 427-428. **9.** Mk 3: 34-5. **10.** Chapter 4 **11.** For a critique of this approach, see, Lancy Lobo, "Towards an Inculturation in the Non-Sanskritic Tradition", Vidyajyoti, Journal of Theological Reflection, Delhi, January 1985, pp. 16-28 **12.** Kappen 1983 is an exploratory study in this direction. See also Aloysius Pieris' important contribution, "Religions in Liberation Theology", Vidyajyoti, April 1982 and May-June 1982. **13.** Kappen 1983; also Ling 1981. **14.** Kosambi 1962, pp. 31-36. **15.** Fuchs 1965. **16.** Desai 1981. **17.** Unnithan 1979, pp. 68-72; 85-112.

Chapter 6

1. Karl Marx, "Theses on Feuerbach" (Abbrev. Theses), in Marx 1970, p. 82. **2.** Marx, "Economic and Philosophical Manuscripts" (Abbrev. Manusceipts) in Marx 1963, p. 161. **3.** lbid, p. 164. **4.** Theses, Marx 1970 p. 82. **5.** Manuscripts, Marx 1963, p. 175. **6.** Marx-Engels, German Ideology, Marx 1970, pp, 79-80. **7.** Lenin, "What is to be done?" in Lenin 1975, Vol.I, pp.152-153. **8.** Marx, Theories of Surplus Value I, Marx 1970, p. 113. **9.** Theses, Marx 1970, p, 82 **10.** Manuscripts, Marx 1963, p. 155. **11.** Marx 1977, Vol. I, p. 174. **12.** Marx, "The Civil War in France", in McLellan 1971, pp. 193-194. **13.** On Stalinist dictatorship, see Elleinstein 1976. **14.** Karl Marx, "The Critique of Hegel's Philosophy of Right" (Critique), Marx 1963, p. 52. **15.** Marx 1973, p. 304. **16.** Manuscripts, Marx 1963, p. 132. **17.** In an article published in 1850, quoted by Avineri 1969, p. 201. **18.** Marx-Engels 1965 pp. 302-303. **19.** Manuscripts, Marx 1963, p. 165. **20.** For a detailed discussion of the theme, see, Kappen 1983.

Chapter 7

1. Marx, Manuscripts, in Marx 1963, p. 166. **2.** Ibid., p. 201. **3.** Ibid., p. 156. **4.** Marx, Capital III, in Marx 1970, pp. 259-260. **5.** Marx, Theses, Marx 1970, pp. 82-83. **6.** Lk 4: 18-20. **7.** Manuscripts, Marx 1963, pp. 206-207. **8.** Ibid., pp. 127-128. **9.** Ibid., p. 157. **10.** Gn 1:28. **11.** Mt 5:5 **12.** Rm 8:18-23. **13.** Marx, Theses, Marx 1970, p. 83. **14.** Manuscripts, Marx 1963, p. 126. **15.** Ibid., pp. 164-165. **16.** Ibid. p. 158. **17.** Karl Marx, "Grundrisse", Marx 1970, p. 110. **18.** Marx-Engels 1962, I, p. 53. **19.** Mk 3:35. **20.** Karl Marx, Preface, Marx 1970, p. 67. **21.** Marx, Theses, Marx 1970, p. 82 **22.** Capital I, Chap. 5, Marx 1970, p. 102. **23.** Manuscripts, Marx 1970, p. 85. **24.** Ibid. **25.** Manuscripts, Marx 1963, p. 165. **26.** Karl Marx, Critique, Marx 1963, pp. 43-44. **27.** Manuscripts, Marx 1963, p. 167. **28.** Marx, German Ideology, Marx 1970, p. 253. **29.** Manuscripts, Marx 1963, p. 155.

Chapter 11

1. In interpreting the Gospel according to Mark, I have been inspired by the recent work of Belo 1975

Chapter 17

1. Jeremias 1971, p. 226 2. Gager 1975 3. Ibid., p. 94 4. Ibid. 5. Ibid.

Chapter 18

1. Kappen 1986, pp.38-54. 2.   Desai 1981 3. For a critical assessment of the Communist movement in India, see, Chandra 1983. Also: Panikkar 1980. 4. Thomas Kocherry, "Action Groups in India and the Struggles for Liberation," in: *Towards an Indian Theology of Liberation*, Indian Theological Association and National Biblical Catechetical Liturgical Centre, Bangalore, 1986, pp.236-65. 5. The following works may be taken as representative of the new trend: (a) Kappen 1977, (b) Kappen 1985, (c) Rayan 1982; also: Chapman 1979, (d) Amalorpavadass 1981, (f) Fabella 1980. 6. See: Kappen 1983; also Kottukapally 1983. 7. On alternative science, see Alvares 1979, Kappen 1994, pp. 60-76. 8. Martin Heidegger, "Die Zeit der Weltbildes," In *Holzwege*, Klostermann, Frankfurt, 1972, pp.69-104. 9. S.H. Hooke, "Genesis," in: *Peake's Commentary on the Bible*, Nelson, 1962, pp.l75ff. 10. An example is Radhakrishnan 1986. 11. S. Kappen, *"Christian Responses"*, in the issue on Revivalism, *Seminar*, No.284, April 1983, p.25-30. 12. Here are a few relevant works: (a) Appasamy 1928, (b) Chakkara 1932, (c) Fakirbhai 1965, (d) Klostermalier 1977. 13. For a fuller discussion : Kappen 2002, chapters 1 to 6. 14. Treated in greater detail in : Kappen 1986, pp.97-102. 15. On the oppression of women in traditional and modern India the following works may be consulted: (a) Altekar 1938 (b) Mukkerjee 1978, (c) Kishwar 1991.(d) Kaushik 1986, (e) Omvedt 1980. 16. See the special issue of *Lokayan* on the Women's Movements, Delhi, 1986. 17. Paul 1982; Meyer 1971. 18. Kosambi 1962, p.28.

Bibliography

Altekar, A. S. (1938), *The Position of Women in Hindu Civilization*, Motilal Banarsidas, Delhi.

Alvares, Claude (1979), *Homo Faber*, Allied Publishers, Bombay.

Amalorpavadass, D. S. (1981), *The Indian Church in the Struggle for a New Society*, NBCLC, Bangalore.

Appasamy, A. J. (1928), *Christianity as Bhakti Marga*, CLS, Madras

Avineri, Shlomo (1969), *The Social and Political Thought of Karl Marx*, Cambridge University Press

Belo, Fernando (1975), *Lecture Materialiste de L'Evangile de Marc*, du Derf, Paris

Chakkara, V. (1932), *Jesus the Avatar*, CLS, Madras.

Chandra, Bipan, ed. (1983), *The Indian Left, Critical Appraisals*, Vikas, Delhi.

Chapman, Geoffrey (1979), *Breath of Life*, London

Desai, A. R. ed. (1981), *Peasant Struggles in India*, Oxford University Press, Delhi.

Elleinstein, Jean (1976), *The Stalin Phenomenon*, Lawrence and Wishart, London.

Fabella, Virginia, ed. (1980), *Asia's Struggle for Full Humanity*, Orbis Books, New York.

Fakirbhai, Dhanjibhai (1965), *Kristopanishad*, CISRS, Bangalore.

Fuchs, Stephen (1965), *The Rebellious Prophets*, Asia Publishing House, Bombay.

Gager, John G. (1975), *Kingdom and Community, the Social World of Early Christianity*, Prentice Hall, New Jersey.

Gutierrez, Gustavo (1973), *A Theology of Liberation*, Orbis Books, New York

Jeremias, Joachim (1971), *New Testament Theology*, New York.

Kishwar, Madhu and Ruth Vanita, eds. (1991), *In Search of Answers, Indian Women's Voices from Manushi*, Horison India Books, Delhi.

Klostermalier, Klaus (1977), *Kristvidya*, A Sketch of an Indian Christology, CLS, Madras.

Kosambi, D. D.(1962), *Myth and Reality*, Popular Prakashan, Bombay

Kottukapally, J. (1983), *The Hope We Share, A New Christian Approach to Marxism,* Dialogue Series, Barrackpore.

Lenin (1975), *Selected Works,* Progress Publishers, Moscow.

Ling, Trevor (1981) *The Buddha's Philosophy of Man, Early Indian Buddhist Dialogues,* Dent, London.

Marx, Karl (1963) *Early Writings* (abbr. EW), ed. T. B. Bottomore, C. A. Watts & Co. Ltd., London.

Marx, Karl (1977), *Capital,* Progress Publishers, Moscow .

Marx, Karl (1970), *Selected Writings in Sociology and Social Philosophy* (SW), ed. T. B. Bottomore and Maximilien Rubel, Pelican Books.

Marx, Karl (1973), *Grundrisse: Foundations of the Critique'of Political Economy,* Penguin Books

Marx, Karl (1977), *A Contribution to the Critique of Political Economy,* Progress Publishers, Moscow

Marx-Engels (1962), *Selected Works,* Moscow

Marx-Engels (1973), *Manifesto of the Communist Party,* Progress Publishers, Moscow

Marx-Engels (1975), *The Holy family,* Progress Publishers, Moscow

Marx-Engels,(1976), *The German Ideology,* Progress Publishers, Moscow

Marx-Engels (1965), Selected Correspondence, Moscow.

McLellan, David (1971), *The Thought of Karl Marx, An Introduction,* Macmillan.

Meyer, J. J. (1971), *Sexual life in Ancient India,* Motilal Banarsidas, Delhi.

Mukkerjee, Prabha (1978), *Hindu Women, Normative Models,* Orient Longman, New Delhi.

Omvedt, Gail (1980), *We Will Smash this Prison,* Orient Longman, New Delhi.

Panikkar, K. N., ed. (1980), *National and Left Movements in India,* Vikas, Delhi.

Paul, Sharad (1982), *Dasa Sudra Slavery,* Allied Publishers, Delhi

Pieris, Aloysius (1988), *An Asian Theology of Liberation,* Orbis, New York.

Radhakrishnan, S. (1986), *The Principal Upanishads,* Allen and Unwin, London.

Rayan, Samuel (1982), *The Anger of God,* Build, Bombay.

Sau, Ranjit (1981), *India's Economic Development - Aspects of Class Relations,* Orient Longman, Delhi

Kaushik, Susheela (1986), *Women's Oppression, Patterns and Perspectives,* Vikas, Delhi.

Unnithan, T. K. (1979), *Gandhi and Social Change,* Rawat Publications, Jaipur.

Sebastian Kappen's Books

- *Jesus and Freedom* (1977), intr. Francois Houtar, Orbis Books, Maryknoll, New York, Edition 2: Notion Press, Chennai, 2019

- *Marxian Atheism* (1983a), self published, Bangalore.

- *Jesus and Cultural Revolution - an Asian Perspective* (1983b), BILD, Bombay

- *Jesus Today* (1985). AICUF, Madras

- *Liberation Theology and Marxism* (1986), Asha Kendra, Punthamba

- *The Future of Socialism and Socialism of the Future* (1992), Visthar, Bangalore.

Posthumous Publications

- *Tradition Modernity Counterculture – an Asian Perspective* (1994), Visthar, Bangalore.

- *Spirituality in the New Age of Recolonisation* (1995), Visthar, Bangalore

- *Hindutva and Indian Religious Traditions* (2000), ed. Sebastian Vattamattam, Edition 2: Notion Press, Chennai, 2019

- *Divine Challenge and Human Response* (2001), ed. Sebastian Vattamattam, CSS, Tiruvalla

- *Jesus and Society* (2002a), ed. S Painadath S. J., ISPCK, Delhi.

- *Jesus and Culture* (2002b), ed. S Painadath S. J., ISPCK, Delhi

- *Towards a Holistic Cultural Paradigm* (2003), ed. Sebastian Vattamattam, CSS, Tiruvalla

- *Marx Beyond Marxism* (2012), ed. Sebastian Vattamattam, Voice Books, Manjeri.

- *Ingathering – Autobiographical Writings and Selected essays* (2013a), ed. Sebastian Vattamattam, Jeevan Books, Bharananganam

- *What the Thunder Says – A poem and selected Essays* (2013b), ed. Sebastian Vattamattam, Jeevan Books, Bharananganam

Books in Malayalam

- *Viswasathil Ninnu Viplavathilekku* (1 9 7 2), e d it i on 3 : Pusthaka Prasadhaka Sangham, Kozhikode, 2019

- *Nalathekku Oru Laingika-sadacharam* (1973), Edition 3: Pusthaka Prasadhaka Sangham, Kozhikode, 2019

- *Paristhithi Samskruthi* (1988), (Co-author: Sebastian Vattamattam), Edition 2: Ascend Books, Kottayam, 2014

- *Marxian Darsanathinu Oramukham* (1989), tr. of Marx Beyond Marxism by Sebastian Vattamattam, Edition 2: NBS, Kottayam, 2012

- *Kalasrushtiyude Uravidam* (1991), tr. of Martin Heidegger: Der Ursprung Des Kunstwerkes, DCB, Kottayam

- *Pravachanam Prathisamskruthi* (1992), Yatra Publications, Kottayam

- *Socialisathinte Bhavi* (1993), Manusham Publications, Ettumanoor

- *Akraistavanaya Yesuvine Thedi* (1999), Current Books, Kottayam, 2005

- *Irupathonnam Noottandinoru Prathisamskruthi* (1991), tr. of Tradition Modernity Counterculture, Yatra Publications, Kottayam

- *Yesuvinte Mochanam Sabhakalil Ninnu* (2012), Dr. Bishop Paulose Mar Paulose Foundation, Thrissur

- *Daivathinte Maranavum Manushyante Jananavum*, (2015), tr. of Marxian Atheism, Media House, Calicut

About the Editor

Sebastian Vattamattam is a retired professor of mathematics and a writer. In Malayalam he has authored the books: *Ecology and Culture* (with Fr. Kappen), *Language and Power, Unconscious Travels of Language – From Freud to Lacan, Ideology and Symbolic Revolution, Sigmund Freud*. His books in English are *Book of Beautiful Curves* (Math) and *What Dreams Tell Us – Lacanian Interpretations*. Vattamattam has compiled, edited, and published many books of Fr. Kappen.

Contents of the Six Volumes

12. A Lesson in Socialism

13. Table-fellowship as Socialist Praxis

14. Christians and Class Struggle

15. Church a People's Movement

16. Between the Church and the Reign of God

17. Church as the Bearer of New Values

18. The Asian Search for a Liberative Theology

19. A New Approach to Theological Education

Volume V

Part 1: Hindutva and Indian Religious Traditions

1. The Materialistic Conception of History and the Indian Religious Tradition

2. Religious Ideologies and Political Change Hindu-Christian Relations in India

3. Whither Religion? Whither Democracy? 1990

4. Religious Pluralism and the Survival of Indian Democracy

5. Hindutva Emergent Fascism?

Part 2: Essays

6. Response to Comments on Chapter 1

7. Towards a Strategy of Socialist Reconstruction

8. Socialism Through Community Action

9. The Dialectic of History

10. The Marxian Concept of Man in the Indian Context

11. Jesus and India's Quest for Identity

12. Jesus in the Indian Context

Part 3: Editorial Extracts from Negations

13. Cultural Conditions for Social Change

15. The Future of Socialism and Socialism of the Future

Part 3: A Poem and Autobiography

16. What the Thunder Says

17. Ingathering